The Complete Guide to Futures Trading

What You Need to Know about the Risks and Rewards

LIND-WALDOCK

WILEY

John Wiley & Sons, Inc.

Contents

The Complete Guide to Futures Trading

Foreword

As its title suggests, this landmark book makes futures trading accessible to mainstream individual investors. The determination of whether futures are right for your portfolio remains with each individual, but *The Complete Guide to Futures Trading* can serve as an expert advisor to help you make informed decisions about how to participate in the exciting derivatives markets.

Written by experienced industry practitioners, the book answers the questions a newcomer to futures and commodities trading might have about what it takes to establish an account and make a commitment to trading.

This is not a book about *trading* futures, however. It does not offer tips about a particular technical or fundamental approach to the markets. Instead, it serves as a bridge between having an interest in futures—yet knowing little about how to go about acting on that interest—and placing a trading order in your futures account. After reading it, you will know what questions to ask yourself and your brokers and other industry professionals when getting ready to establish a futures trading account.

Readers who are new to futures trading will be interested in the range of topics covered, because it will answer questions about how to get started trading commodity futures:

- Which type of account is best for me?
- What should I know about risk, leverage, and margin?
- Is my comfort level with risk in line with what futures trading provides?
- What questions should I ask when looking for a brokerage relationship?
- How are futures taxed?
- What resources do I need as a futures trader?
- What are the different ways to approach making a trading decision?
- What are the various types of orders I can use?
- What markets can I trade?

Clearly written by contributors with a depth of practical understanding that comes from years in the futures industry, *The Complete Guide to Futures Trading* addresses these issues and others in a well-organized, easy-to-follow style. As chief executive officer of the largest financial exchange in the world for trading futures and options, I can wholeheartedly recommend this volume for the reader who wants to learn the fundamentals of investing in futures.

CRAIG S. DONOHUE
Chief Executive Officer
Chicago Mercantile Exchange
May 2005

CME is the largest financial exchange in the world for trading futures and options on futures—serving risk-management needs globally through a diverse range of derivatives products on its CME® Globex® electronic trading platform as well as on its trading floors. Today the company is in 27 countries, with more than 740 direct customer connections, annual sales in excess of $735 million, and 1,300 employees. In 2004, CME handled nearly 800 million contracts with an underlying value of $463 trillion. The first financial exchange in the United States to go public, CME is traded on the New York Stock Exchange and Nasdaq under the symbol "CME" and has a market value of nearly $7 billion.

Preface

Futures are the investment of the twenty-first century.

At the beginning of the twentieth century, investing in stocks was considered a risky proposition for individuals, who were advised to stick to buying bonds. Now, over 50 percent of U.S. households invest in the stock market directly or indirectly through mutual fund holdings—even in retirement accounts. At Lind-Waldock, we believe writers of the twenty-second century looking back on the twenty-first will say the same about investment in futures.

Although U.S. futures markets began in the mid-1800s, they didn't have global significance until the 1980s, when companies and governments worldwide embraced the instruments as financial management tools. Futures markets have always been about price discovery and transfer of risk, so are ideally suited to environments of uncertainty and high volatility—an apt description of the past 30 years.

The collapse of the gold standard in 1972 led to free-floating currency exchange rates—and the first financial futures contracts, foreign exchange, at the Chicago Mercantile Exchange. Inflation throughout the 1970s and early 1980s led to record-high interest rates—and new futures contracts in U.S. Treasuries and Eurodollars. Stock index futures came into their own during the bull market of the 1980s, and were an inextricable part of the institutional investor's playbook within less than five years.

Now, futures are part of a savvy individual investor's playbook, too.

Technological advances—most significantly, the Internet—have transformed the futures trading landscape. Today, individual investors are on a level playing field with professional traders and institutional investors, particularly in electronically traded futures contracts, with online order entry and execution. What's more, "mini" products created specifically to appeal to individual investors are now standard among exchange offerings.

This book reveals the many ways that individuals can use futures for trading and portfolio diversification. Our aim is to remove the mystique about trading futures, clear up common misperceptions, and prepare individuals to begin using futures as a trading or investment tool in a responsible manner. The products are highly leveraged and marked to the market daily. Thus, the industry is well-regulated and has superior financial safeguards in place to ensure trading integrity.

So, if you understand the risks and are able and willing to accept them, there's no reason you shouldn't take advantage of the benefits inherent in futures. As we point out many times throughout this book though, futures trading is not suitable for all investors.

The first few chapters introduce you to the futures markets, explain their history and purpose, and provide an overview of how individuals participate in the markets. Specifically, you'll learn about the choices you have in trading or investing in futures—from working with a broker to investing in a professionally managed product or trading on your own. This will help you decide which path is right for you.

Later on, we introduce you to the myriad of futures products available to trade—from the Dow Jones Industrial Average to gold to soybeans—and provide a brief background on the factors important to price movement in each market. Yet another chapter delves into the way many traders use technical analysis as a decision-making tool. In addition, you'll learn about options on futures and cash foreign exchange trading in two chapters devoted specifically to those topics.

Our book helps you understand the "hows and whats" involved in futures trading—including opening an account, types of orders, margins, tax treatment, and resolution of disputes.

The Complete Guide to Futures Trading is your futures trading handbook. The professionals who have contributed to this effort bring decades of devotion and experience in the futures industry to the subject matter. We challenge you to learn from their experience, and as a result, make an informed decision about whether futures are right for you and your investment portfolio. We sincerely hope that this book convinces you that there may be a place for futures in your investment playbook, and guides you in making appropriate decisions about how you trade.

A twenty-first–century investor needs to know about the investment of the twenty-first century. That investor is you, and that investment is futures.

> Mark B. Sachs
> President
> Lind-Waldock
> *April 2005*

About the Contributors

Carol Dannenhauer is Director of both the Managed Accounts and Auto-Execute divisions at Lind-Waldock. Carol began her industry career in the late 1970s. She spent a number of years working on the floor of the Chicago Mercantile Exchange before beginning her association with Lind-Waldock in 1986, the year she received her futures license. Carol devotes her time to Lind-Waldock's Managed Accounts division, which serves as the liaison between the client and the commodity trading advisor community, and to the Auto-Execute division, which caters to clients who want to trade using platforms or auto-executing systems in their trading.

Phillip Fondren directs retail foreign exchange trading for Man Financial Inc, Lind-Waldock's parent company. Phil began his career as a bullion trader and shifted to foreign exchange in the early 1980s when international money flows spurred a huge demand for investment services in foreign exchange. He received his futures license in 1981. Phil has run foreign exchange trading and sales operations for several firms, having joined Man Financial Inc in 2005.

Susan Abbott Gidel is Director of Marketing at Lind-Waldock. Susan began her career in the futures industry as an editor at *Futures Magazine*, covering the industry's development during its explosive expansion into financial futures, options, and stock indexes worldwide. She is also the author of *Stock Index Futures & Options: The Ins and Outs of Trading Any Index, Anywhere* (John Wiley & Sons, 1999).

Jim Gombas is Director of Lind Plus, Lind-Waldock's Broker-Assisted division. Jim began his career with Lind-Waldock on the floors of the Chicago Board of Trade and the Chicago Mercantile Exchange in 1984. He received his license in 1985 and moved into the Retail Sales division of Lind-Waldock, which he then managed until 1994 when he started the Lind Plus division. Jim's team of market strategists offers a myriad of services to clients who choose to have a futures professional work with them as they trade.

Greg Gulotta is Vice President of Trade Center Operations at Lind-Waldock. Greg received his license in 1983 and began his career with Lind-Waldock in 1985 in the Trade Center. In the ensuing years, Greg assumed positions of increasing operational responsibility and assumed the position of vice president in 2001.

Dave Howe is Director of Sales at Lind-Waldock, a position he assumed in 2005. Dave received his futures license in 1987 and joined Lind-Waldock as an account executive in 1988. He was promoted to Sales Manager in 1999 after moving up through the ranks within the sales department. His staff is the first point of contact for most investors interested in establishing a relationship with Lind-Waldock.

Dan McMullin is the former Director of Business Development at Lind-Waldock. Dan, who is now an independent trader, has more than 16 years of industry experience, having traded futures for his own account both on the exchange floor and from the back office. He received his license in 1988. He was a principal of a small brokerage firm and has worked with and advised hundreds of professional and retail investors. Dan devoted a significant amount of his time to developing and delivering educational programming to investors.

Laura Oatney is Content Manager in the Marketing Department at Lind-Waldock. Laura began her futures industry association at the Chicago Board of Trade in the late 1970s. In 1982, she moved to the then-fledgling National Futures Association, the industrywide self-regulatory organization for the futures industry, where she served ultimately as Director of Communications and Education. She joined Lind-Waldock in 2003 and received her futures license in 2005.

Mark Sachs is President of Lind-Waldock. Mark has spent almost 20 years in the futures industry, 18 of which have involved increasing levels of operational responsibility within Lind-Waldock. He started with Lind-Waldock as an account executive in 1986, the year he received his license. In the early 1990s, he was responsible for opening and managing Lind-Waldock's London and Hong Kong offices. When he returned to the States, he managed both the firm's corporate relationships and its 24-hour global trade operations. In 2002, he was promoted to the position of president. He has served on various committees for the Futures Industry Association and on the Chicago Board of Trade's Futures Commission Merchant Committee.

Nancy Westwick serves as Counsel to Lind-Waldock. After receiving her Juris Doctor degree in 1996, she completed her Master's in Financial Services Law in 2000, the same year she joined the firm. Previously, she had worked for various equity option traders and security brokerage firms for almost two decades. Nancy currently serves as chairperson of the Futures & Derivatives Law Committee of the Chicago Bar Association.

The Complete Guide to Futures Trading

CHAPTER 1

Futures

*The Investment for the
Twenty-First Century*

Investors have many choices today for investing their money. The first one that often comes to mind is the stock market. It has been estimated that more than 50 million U.S. citizens have some stake in the performance of the stock market, either through investments in individual stocks or mutual funds or via participation in 401(k) or other company plans, individual retirement accounts, government pension plans, or some other program that gives Main Street residents a piece of Wall Street action.

Then there are the bank certificates of deposit and numerous types of bonds that have long been familiar investment vehicles—passive instruments that are based on interest rates and don't require much attention.

So you may be wondering why you should be interested in a more active trading style featuring futures, options on futures, or cash foreign exchange markets, traditionally perceived as more risky places to put your money.

Futures markets have benefits that the stock market simply can't provide, and traders are just beginning to discover what brilliant tools they are for participating in a wide variety of markets. Long known, used, and understood by producers and users of commodities such as grain, gold, and crude oil, futures markets today also encompass such financial products as stocks, stock indexes, and interest rates. What's more, futures markets are not just a U.S. phenomenon—they exist the world over, on every continent but Antarctica. Just take a look at Appendix A, "Domestic and International Futures Contract Volume," and you'll see how diverse the product offerings are and how global today's marketplace really is.

When it gets right down to it, futures aren't hard to understand. In fact, they are fairly straightforward. Like stocks, "buy low, sell high" is the basic premise. What's different is that you can trade futures with leverage, and on either a long or a short position. That introduces an additional element of risk not present in the stock market. Another significant difference is that there is no uptick rule in futures. Thus, it is just as easy to sell short as it is to buy, thus easing entry into a position to capture a downward move in prices.

HISTORICAL ROOTS

Some people say that the concept of futures trading began in China nearly 1,400 years ago and that it was also used in the Japanese rice market centuries ago. But futures trading as U.S. traders know it today has its roots in the mid-1800s when it all started in Chicago, the city that works.

Mother Nature blessed Chicago with a location that lent itself to becoming a center of commerce—at the south end of Lake Michigan and at the mouth of a river system that reached all the way to the Gulf of Mexico. From Chicago, distributors and suppliers could reach the East Coast via the Great Lakes and the midsection of the country by river. This location in the middle of the United States also helped Chicago become a railroad hub.

This was good news for producers and users of commodities, such as wheat and corn. Farmers brought their harvest to Chicago to sell it to the companies that would turn it into bread and other foodstuffs. Chicago provided one central location for buying and selling. It was a great idea but still needed improvement.

At harvest time, the supply of grain overwhelmed the demand, so prices were low. Months later, prices would rise as supplies dwindled. Farmers wanted a way to cash in on the higher prices. Users wanted a way to ensure steady supplies as well as smooth out and better predict how much their raw ingredients would cost. So they started making deals that established the price of grain for a delivery date in the future.

But there still was the matter of what we call today "counterparty risk." The Chicago Board of Trade (CBOT), founded in 1848, solved the problem by creating standardized contracts for the future sale of grain. The contracts were interchangeable, so the buyer or seller of a contract could get out of the obligation without any harm to the original counterparty. In the 1920s, the CBOT added a clearinghouse to become the ultimate counterparty to everyone who trades a futures contract. To date, this clearinghouse system has never had a default.

Economic necessity gave birth to futures markets. And good old American ingenuity has kept redefining the futures markets ever since.

WHAT FUTURES ARE

A futures contract is *an obligation to buy or sell an underlying product at a specific price at a specific time in the future*. We'll explain each key phrase in that sentence, so you can understand the elements that define a futures contract.

"Obligation to Buy or Sell"

The key word is *obligation*. Unless you offset your original position before the contract expires—and nearly 100 percent of speculators do just that—you must eventually buy or sell at the agreed-upon price when the contract expires. Here is a brief explanation of how buying and offsetting a position might work with an E-mini Standard & Poor's 500 stock index futures contract. All futures contracts follow this same scenario, differing only in the total contract size and value of the contract.

Long Position Example   You buy a June E-mini S&P 500 index futures contract when it is trading at 1000. The contract size is $50 times the index level, so your position equals a $50,000 ($50 × 1000) stake in the S&P 500 index. If the index goes up 10 points before the futures contract expires, you would receive $500, less commission and fees.

If the index declines 10 points to 990, the value of the contract drops to $49,500. Unless you offset your position by selling a June E-mini futures contract before it expires in the third week of June, you will be obligated to pay the difference in contract value of the price at which you bought versus the final expiration price to fulfill your side of the deal. This cash payment occurs because the E-mini S&P 500 is "cash-settled." In futures contracts that require physical delivery, you would be required to buy the underlying product. (Most futures positions are offset before expiration, however.)

Short Position Example   You sell a June E-mini S&P 500 futures contract when it is trading at 1000. Just as when buying to initiate a position, the contract size is $50 times the index level, so your position equals a $50,000 ($50 × 1000) stake in the S&P 500 index. If the index rises 10 points to 1010 when the futures contract expires, the value of the contract increases to $50,500.

Unlike shorting in stocks, the next part in futures trading is just like the long position example. Unless you offset your position by buying a June E-mini contract before it expires, you will be obligated to pay the difference in contract value of the price at which you sold versus the final expiration price to fulfill your side of the deal. Once again, this cash payment occurs because the E-mini S&P 500 is cash-settled. In futures contracts that require physical delivery, the seller is required to supply the underlying product to a buyer to fulfill the contract obligation if the position is not offset. (But you don't have to worry about that with stock index futures.)

If you sell and the index declines by 10 points, you would receive the $500, less commission and fees.

"Underlying Product"

Futures contracts originally were created for agricultural products such as corn and cotton. In the 1970s and 1980s, futures contracts on financial instruments such as U.S. Treasury bonds and stock indexes became popular. Futures contracts on individual stocks, called "single-stock futures," are the latest innovation in this financial arena.

Each futures contract specifies a certain amount (and sometimes quality) of the underlying product, so that the contract terms are standardized for all participants. For example, one E-mini S&P 500 futures contract represents exposure to all 500 stocks in the S&P 500 index. Contract standardization means that investors don't have to worry about anything but the business at hand—changes in price.

"Specific Price"

Futures contracts are traded in public, government-regulated forums—exchanges where business is conducted either electronically or in traditional open-outcry pits on a trading floor. Prices are determined by the orders that come into the market from buyers and sellers. When an order from a buyer at $100 meets an order from a seller at $100, a trade occurs and a futures price of $100 is broadcast to the world.

"Specific Time in the Future"

Futures contracts expire at a certain time in the future. For example, a December 2005 futures contract will cease to exist sometime during the month of December in 2005 (depending on rules set by the exchange). Specifically, E-mini S&P 500 futures expire on the morning of the third Friday of March, June, September, and December. As with other elements of the contract, a standardized expiration date makes it easier for investors to focus on pricing decisions.

WHAT FUTURES ARE NOT

Now that you have been introduced to what futures contracts are, let's explore how they differ from other financial instruments you may be more familiar with, like stocks, options, and exchange-traded funds.

Futures Are Not Stocks

It may be too obvious to say that futures are not stocks, but it is essential to understand the important differences between these two investment vehicles, summarized in Table 1.1.

Agreements, Not Ownership A futures contract is an obligation to buy or sell at some time in the future, at a price agreed upon today. A futures contract does not convey ownership, as buying a share of stock does; it is only the promise

TABLE 1.1 Comparing Instruments

	Futures	Stocks	Exchange-Traded Funds	Options
Contract terms	Agreement to perform	Conveys ownership	Conveys ownership	Gives buyer a right, not an obligation
Type of contract	Standardized units, no limit on number	Shares in a company, limited to number issued	Standardized, no limit on number	Standardized, no limit on number
Time factor	Contracts expire	Continue perpetually	Continue perpetually	Contracts expire
Margin	Good-faith deposit to ensure contract performance	Down payment on ownership	Down payment on ownership	Buyer pays premium; seller posts margin
Leverage	High with minimum margins required generally only 2%–15% of contract value	Limited with minimum margin at 50% of share price	Limited with current minimum margin at 50% of contract value	Varies with different positions
Short selling	Simple, involving same process with same margin requirements as going long	Complex, requiring uptick in share price and borrowing shares to sell	As easy to sell as to buy	More complex to determine which option to use

that a buyer and seller will agree to exchange ownership in the future. Like stocks, futures contracts are usually traded on an organized and regulated exchange so the buyers and sellers can find each other easily. Because futures contracts are standardized and interchangeable, they can be traded anonymously among people on an exchange, where all that remains to be negotiated is the price.

All futures contracts are settled daily (assigned a final value price). Based on this settlement price, the values of all positions are marked to the market each day after the official close. Your account is then either debited or credited based on how well your positions fared in that day's trading session. In other words, as long as your positions remain open, cash will either come into your account or leave your account based on the change in the settlement price from day to day.

This system gives futures trading a rock-solid reputation for creditworthiness because losses are not allowed to accumulate without some response being required. It is this mechanism that brings integrity to the marketplace. Or, considered another way, every trader can have confidence knowing that the other side of the trade will be made good. In fact, the clearing member firms—and, ultimately, the exchanges themselves—guarantee that each trade will be honored (see Chapter 14). So, as a trader, you never need to give any thought to the reliability of the person on the other side of your trade.

Contracts, Not Shares   The supply of futures contracts is unlimited. A new futures contract is created every time a buyer and seller make a trade. Unlike shares of stock, there is no limit to the supply of futures contracts. Every time a buyer and seller make a trade, a new contract is created.

Because a futures contract is an obligation to buy or sell at a certain price at a certain future date, there's no getting around the fact that the obligation must be fulfilled. In most cases, the obligation is fulfilled by simply making an offsetting trade (sell if you bought; buy if you sold). Of course, you can choose to carry the position all the way to the delivery date, when it is fulfilled either by the exchange of the physical commodity or by a cash settlement to or from your trading account; but again, that is almost never the case for the speculator. That possibility helps to keep futures prices closely aligned to cash prices.

Contract Expirations, Not Perpetual Assets   Because futures contracts expire on a specific date in the future, a settlement between the buyer and the seller means the contract ceases to exist after that date. Shares of stocks, on the other hand, continue to exist (unless a company dissolves or a stock buyback or some other development reduces the number of shares).

Because of these contract expirations, futures traders sometimes will maintain a position by rolling from one contract month to the next, taking into consideration the trading liquidity available. Say you have a long position in the March E-mini S&P 500 contract, and it is the first week of March with just three weeks until the contract expires. If you want to maintain that position, you would roll into the June contract by selling your March contract and simultaneously buying the June contract. Your brokerage firm could assist with that process.

Good-Faith Deposit, Not a Down Payment The word *margin* means something different in futures than it does in stocks. In stocks it means that you're borrowing money and paying interest. In futures it simply refers to the amount of money that you need to have in your account to enter a transaction.

The margin required for a futures contract is better described as a performance bond or good-faith money. The levels are set by the exchanges based on volatility (market conditions) and can be changed at any time. The Federal Reserve sets the margin level for stocks and has maintained a 50 percent minimum required for leveraged stock trades for many years.

Generally, futures margins are much less than the 50 percent required for stocks. The performance bond (margin) requirements for most futures contracts range from 2 percent to 15 percent of the value of the contract with a majority in the 5 percent area. A brokerage firm may establish or change its own performance bond requirements at any time.

Of course, futures margins refer to the exchange's minimum required balances to place a trade. A trader is certainly free to maintain a much higher balance, or even the full contract value (100 percent).

Leveraged, Not Paid For in Full Leverage is what futures markets are all about. As a futures trader, you can access the full value of a futures contract for a relatively small amount of capital, typically 2 percent to 15 percent of the contract's value. For example, for about $3,500 in margin, you can buy or sell an E-mini S&P 500 futures contract covering stocks worth $50,000.

Because futures markets are highly leveraged, the effect of price changes is magnified. With stocks, you typically pay the price in full (i.e., without leverage) or on margin (50 percent leverage). If you speculate in futures and the market moves in your favor, leverage can produce large profits in relation to the amount of your initial margin. However, if the market moves against your position, you also could lose your initial margin and then some.

For example, assume that you've decided to put $10,000 into a futures account. You buy one E-mini S&P 500 index futures contract when the index is trading at 1000. Your initial margin requirement for that one contract is $3,500. Because the value of the futures contract is $50 times the index, each one-point change in the index represents a $50 gain or loss.

If the index increases 5 percent, to 1050 from 1000, you could realize a profit of $2,500 (50 points × $50). Conversely, a 50-point decline would produce a $2,500 loss. The $2,500 increase represents a 25 percent return on your initial investment of $10,000 or a 71 percent return on your initial margin deposit of $3,500. Conversely, a decline would eat up 25 percent of your original $10,000 or 71 percent of your initial margin. In either case, an increase or decrease of only 5 percent in the index could result in a substantial gain or loss in your account. That's the power of leverage.

Leverage can be a beautiful thing. When everything's going your way, it makes your money work harder and produce more in a shorter period of time than if you paid for everything in full, up front. Indeed, leverage is the key, distinctive aspect of futures trading as compared with stock trading.

But there is a dark side to leverage, too. For example, assume you use $5,000 in your account to buy an E-mini S&P 500 contract worth $50,000. Instead of going up, however, prices fall by 10 percent and the contract's value drops to $45,000. Your $5,000 is completely gone. Unless you get out of the position with an offsetting sale when your maintenance margin level is violated, you'll be obligated to put up even more money if the market keeps moving against you. Leverage is the one ingredient that can produce either horror stories or happy endings. To get the happy ending, it is extremely important that you fully understand the power of leverage and how to manage it well.

Futures Are Not Options

You might think that futures and options are similar, if not identical. But, in fact, the only thing that looks similar about the two instruments is that they both have an expiration date. Despite its expiration, a futures contract is not a wasting asset like an options contract.

An options contract conveys the *right*—not the *obligation*, like a futures contract—for a buyer to assume a position in the underlying instrument at a specific (strike) price at any time before the option expires. When you buy (go long) an option, your risk is limited to the amount you pay for this right. The cost of the option is known as a premium and is based on time, volatility, and the relative value of your strike price to the underlying market.

Futures Always Have Intrinsic Value   A futures contract always has value, calculated by multiplying the current price by the contract unit size—unless the price is zero, of course. Meanwhile, an options contract is a wasting asset, and its value could decline to zero on the expiration date (unless it is in-the-money). If you paid for the right to purchase stock at $50 before the third Friday in June and the stock is trading at $45 on that third Friday, you will not benefit from all the money you paid for that call option as it expires worthless.

Futures Are a Straight, Market-Direction Play   You have to ask only one question before making a futures trade: Buy or sell? The futures price is going to go either up or down from today's price (or stay the same) by the time the contract expires. All you have to decide is which way you think it's going to move.

You have more decisions to make with options. Besides having to decide whether to buy or sell, you have to decide whether to buy or sell a put or a call. Then you still have to consider strike price, time to expiration, volatility, and whether the premium is rich or cheap. And that's not even mentioning alpha, beta, delta, gamma, vega, or other factors that determine an option's price.

Futures Always Have Unlimited Risk   The value of a futures contract is ultimately tied to the underlying product or instrument—the S&P 500 index, gold, crude oil, soybeans, T-bonds—via each contract's specifications. You can either buy (go long) or sell (go short) any futures contract, and your risk (or potential profit) is virtually unlimited.

If you purchase a call or put option, you have a clearly defined risk (the premium you paid). However, if you sell (write) uncovered calls or puts, you are exposed to unlimited risk with options, just as you would be with futures.

Futures Are Not Exchange-Traded Funds

Exchange-traded funds (ETFs) were introduced in 1993 and have become popular investment products. ETFs now exist for nearly every major stock index and sector index, allowing you to purchase a piece of an index just like you purchase shares of individual stocks. Among the best-known ETFs are those on the S&P 500 index (SPDRs or SPY), the Dow Jones Industrial Average (DIAmonds), and the Nasdaq-100 index (QQQs).

Futures and ETFs do have some similarities. For example, they are a liquid market, you can use them to hedge a portfolio of stocks or mutual funds, they don't require an uptick to sell short, they can be used for efficient cash management, and they may not have heavy tax burdens if the securities are held long-term. In fact, futures offer even greater tax benefits because they are treated under the 60/40 rule (60 percent of the gain from futures is taxed at long-term favorable rates and 40 percent as ordinary income; see Chapter 13 on taxes).

But because they are traded like stocks, ETFs do have some of the same disadvantages as stocks when compared to stock index futures. The most significant is the 50 percent minimum margin requirement for ETFs instead of the low margins required for stock index futures. In addition, many stock index futures are traded electronically virtually 24 hours a day, whereas ETFs have limited trading hours; and options are available on leading stock index futures but not on ETFs, giving futures traders more flexibility in establishing and managing positions.

WHO TRADES FUTURES?

Futures participants fall into two broad categories: speculators and hedgers. If you trade for your own financial benefit, you're a speculator. If you trade futures because you have some risk associated with the underlying commodity, you're a hedger. A basic understanding of each group—who they are and what roles they play in the marketplace—will better prepare you to participate in futures markets.

Speculators

A speculator's job is easily defined: Buy low, sell high. Or sell high, buy low. Make money. Speculators come in all shapes and sizes with all sorts of motivations. As any futures exchange will tell you, speculators are the grease that keeps the market wheels turning. Even today, all futures markets exist because of the economic necessity of providing commercial entities a way to transfer risk, just as they did in the 1800s when grain producers and users needed to buy and sell in Chicago. But speculators play a vital role in the markets' success. These speculators include:

- Professional traders, whether trading on an exchange floor or off a computer screen.
- Investors like you, who see futures as a way to try to make money.
- Money managers who invest on behalf of their clients.
- Firms that trade with their own money as a business venture.

Big, small, individual, or corporate, all speculators try to capitalize on their opinion of whether the market is going to go up or down. The diversity of opinion among speculators, and their sheer number, provides the liquidity that hedgers need to transfer their commercial risks to others. The more speculators there are, the more likely there will be someone who is willing to buy or sell at any particular moment at any particular price.

For the most part, it's safe to assume that individual speculators trade a smaller number of contracts than hedgers and hold market positions for a shorter time. Exchange rules and federal regulations limit the maximum number of contracts that can be held by any one speculator in any one market. In futures market lingo, this restriction is known as "spec limits."

Hedgers

Hedgers transfer cash market risk to the futures markets. Thus, making a futures trading decision also involves a cash market decision. Like speculators, hedgers can either buy or sell, depending on their situation.

For example, a cereal company that buys corn futures as a hedge has concluded that cash corn prices will be higher when the company has to purchase corn to make cereal at a later date. When that later date arrives, the company offsets its hedge by selling futures and buys corn in the cash market. If cash prices did rise since the company bought the futures contract, then it is likely that the increased value of the futures contract will reduce the actual net cost of corn to the cereal company.

Conversely, a corn producer who sells corn futures as a hedge has decided that cash corn prices could be lower than today's price when it is time to sell the crop. If the producer is right, the hedge likely will have provided a profit that can be added to the revenues generated from selling corn in the cash market.

Although a hedge transfers price risk, it should also be noted that locking in a price does deny the hedger the opportunity to gain from favorable price movements in the cash market.

MAKING YOUR CHOICE

The choice of which vehicle to use is obviously a matter of preference for each investor. The active short-term trader will probably prefer the cheap transaction costs and the efficient executions offered by futures. Some traders will use stocks, ETFs, or futures as complementary products and may also include options, especially those who want to spread or arbitrage products.

When it comes to the bottom line, futures provide the most leverage and a simple, clear-cut view of a market: If prices are going up, buy; if prices are going down, sell.

CHAPTER 2

Becoming a Futures Trader

Knowing about the markets and deciding to invest in them are big steps for an aspiring trader. But then you are faced with an even greater question—one that will help determine whether you meet your investing goals:

How do I make a trading decision?

This chapter presents an overview of some of the many techniques used today to analyze futures markets so you can make sound trading decisions. Of course, most of these techniques have entire volumes written about them, and a detailed discussion of each topic is beyond the scope of this chapter. Still, with this chapter, you will gain a broad introduction to the meat and potatoes of trading.

You may be surprised to find that this chapter will be useful to both the independent trader and the investor who takes the less-involved route of managed futures or an auto-execute trading system. The independent trader who chooses either the self-directed or the broker-assisted trading approach will certainly wish to know how to make trading decisions. Less obvious, though, is the benefit to the managed or auto-execute investor, who can use the same knowledge to help choose a program from among the universe of programs available for investment.

A basic rule for passive investors is: "Know your manager's investment philosophy." A recurring theme throughout this book is that, whichever approach to investing you choose, it should be a good match to your personality and comfort level. This chapter will help you understand your choices from among the different styles and methods of analysis. So, whether your goal is to choose the right program, to select the best broker, or to learn how to trade on your own, this chapter provides a solid foundation for your decision. Other chapters will go into a more thorough discussion about whether you should be trading on your own or with the help of a broker, managed account, or auto-execute program.

Before getting into the nuts and bolts of forecasting prices, we'll review some issues important to making trading decisions.

TRADING DECISION ISSUES

Let's start with the obvious: For each one of the millions of trades placed every day, there are both a buyer and a seller. Or, looked at another way, for every person willing to buy, another person is equally convinced it is time to sell.

Not surprisingly, you'll find many opinions on the best way to make this trading decision. One person's winning formula may go into a losing streak right when someone else's starts a winning period. Does that mean that one person is right and the other is wrong? Not necessarily. The lesson may be that different strategies succeed at different times—and when applied to different investment time horizons.

Perhaps it's best to approach this chapter with the understanding that no single answer about how to make a trading decision is right for everyone. Different traders will have their own answer to the question posed at the beginning of this chapter. This is the very reason you need to explore the topic individually and choose the methods that work best for you. In fact, did you know that many believe the best trading decision is to not make one at all? Hmm, read on.

Random Walk and Efficient Markets Hypothesis

The academic community teaches that changes in price are "serially independent"—in essence, random and unpredictable. According to the efficient markets hypothesis, the typical investor is unable to beat the market trading actively over time and would actually be better off with a buy-and-hold strategy because of the lower transaction costs. The theory holds that, although financial assets have an intrinsic value, the actual price will fluctuate randomly around that value. Further, although the intrinsic value will change over time, the direction and extent are essentially unknowable. The marketplace itself is efficient in reflecting all known facts at any given moment.

Of course, traders dispute this theory. Their very existence is in contradiction to the idea that markets are perfectly efficient. Traders are dedicated to identifying opportunities to profit from forecasts and mispricings, and they challenge the efficient markets hypothesis on nearly every front. First, they point out that the hypothesis is based on unrealistic assumptions about perfect dissemination of news and events. In the real world, news can take hours, days, or weeks to be fully understood and absorbed. Also, events can cause overreactions, and markets can react differently on different time frames to the same event. Finally, traders argue that markets can have extended periods of both directional trends and choppy, sideways action, all of which can be exploited.

The point made here is that buy-and-hold is considered by some to be the best trading decision of all. So you need to be aware of these two opposing viewpoints and decide for yourself whether you believe forecasting prices is worth the effort. You may conclude that being a passive investor is best for you.

This is yet another example of the importance of choosing for yourself the investment style that best fits your personality and comfort level. In fact, some argue that a mismatch between investment style and investor personality is the underlying root of most trading failures. The main thing to remember is that, if you don't believe in the analysis, you won't stick with it during the down times.

Now, academics aside, there is also a category of *traders* who believe that forecasting the market is nonproductive. Is this a contradiction? Let's consider the argument.

Forecasting versus Reacting

Even among traders, some argue it's best to not have an opinion at all about the direction of prices—that it's better instead to simply react to the market action. Such traders may watch for a trend reversal or a breakout and then jump in quickly in hopes of catching the move. Momentum trading, scalping, and swing trading can be such methods.

But, of course, even a reactive trader is forecasting a price move based on the events of the moment. The only difference is that the forecast is based on events happening in a very short time frame.

Regardless, your best method of making a trading decision may be to simply set yourself up for very speedy responses to fast-breaking events and price action. Many trading arcades and software packages are in place to support just such a style.

So the expected time horizon of a trade turns out to be a significant factor in making a trading decision. Let's explore that concept a little further.

Consider Your Time Frame

Floor traders can tell you that both parties to a new trade can wind up losing or winning on that trade; the trade doesn't necessarily have to be a win-lose situation for those two traders. The reason, of course, is because each trader has a different time frame. The market may rally five minutes into the trade, and the trader who bought gets out with a quick profit. An hour later, the market may fall and the trader who sold will have gotten out profitably as well. Likewise, both traders could also lose on the trade.

The lesson is that your market forecast can look quite different for different time periods. Your final analysis should always keep this in mind. Consider two other points about differences in time frames:

1. In general, shorter time frames will tend to have more random movement, often called "noise." Some traders are able to make the noise work to their

advantage, while others would rather focus on the bigger trends. Still others may do well considering both the trees and the forest. As mentioned before, one of your tasks early on should be to determine which time frames you are most comfortable trading.

2. Whichever time frame works best for you, you may find value in keeping an eye on other nearby time frames. A buzz phrase in recent years has been the "three-screen method" of trading. This simply refers to a principle of drilling down the market analysis from broad to specific, looking at weekly, daily, and hourly charts, for instance. Studying multiple time frames can give context to the events in any particular time frame.

Subjective versus Objective

In addition to the time frame, central to the matter of making a trading decision is the issue of art versus science. Different analysts will interpret the same information in different ways.

We've all heard jokes about a roomful of economists not being able to agree on a reading of certain statistics. So it is with traders. Crop reports and Federal Reserve Board actions are subject to a wide range of interpretations. Chart readers may also see and trade the exact same patterns in very different ways. Again, this fact does not necessarily invalidate the usefulness of forecasting; instead, it points out the influence of individual subjectivity in analysis.

Figure 2.1 shows a basic channel pattern on a price chart. How might different trading styles approach that same pattern?

- Momentum traders might buy on strength near each new high and suffer a series of small losses until the final actual breakout to new highs.
- Range traders, on the other hand, will do just the opposite, selling on rallies to the upper band because they expect the channel to remain intact.
- Breakout traders will buy as the market moves above the channel (or above previous highs), betting an upward move is about to begin.
- Others will count waves within the channel in an attempt to predict when the market will switch from channel to breakout.
- Trend followers who bought earlier may remain long the entire time with an exit stop placed below the channel.

Is one method better than another? The most that can be said may be that different methods work best at different times.

You shouldn't be too surprised at the abundance of viewpoints on how to make a trading decision. After all, the wealth of opinions as to the best course of action is what makes a market. To get around this subjectiveness, certain traders, called systems traders, quantify the buy/sell rules and back-test the results. They seek an objective set of rules that profit over time. (See Chapter 5 for more details on systems trading.)

FIGURE 2.1 Price channel. Different traders approach the same data in different ways. (*Source:* eSignal, www.esignal.com)

While the methods for making a trading decision can be labeled in many ways—systems trading, volatility trading, swing trading, range trading—the underlying analysis typically falls into the category of either fundamental analysis or technical analysis.

Fundamental Analysis versus Technical Analysis

The classic description of fundamental analysis is that it examines the supply and demand factors influencing a market's price. But those factors differ wildly from market to market. You know this intuitively: The factors affecting sugar are quite different from those affecting wheat, crude oil, Swiss francs, or gold. So, as a practical matter, the fundamental trader becomes an expert in a particular market. For this reason, fundamental analysis is sometimes considered to be old-school, perhaps because the most learned experts on a given market are those who have studied it the longest.

Weather is considered a fundamental event and plays an important role, even in markets you may not suspect would be influenced by weather. For instance, bad weather can depress consumer spending, and in turn, corporate earnings and stock index prices. Some traders become mini-experts in the severity and timing of weather events affecting their chosen markets.

Like weather, other dominant macro fundamentals can affect multiple markets—for example, economic conditions may dampen overall demand, or the value of the dollar may influence the pricing of unrelated markets. For the most part, however, fundamental analysis is concerned with the news and events unique to each market.

In contrast, technical analysis is the study of price action, with no regard given to the news and events that lead to that movement. The idea is that the best interpretation of underlying news is already reflected in the price. Unlike fundamental analysis, charting techniques can be applied across many different markets and tend to be more widely used by traders. Even fundamental traders will often consider the technicals to determine the timing of their trades.

So don't worry about choosing the right label to assign to your work; you might find you have a knack for interpreting certain macro events (fundamental) and use that skill to provide a context for your chart reading and indicators (technical).

Some traders find themselves drawn to a market because they started with an understanding of the fundamentals for that particular market. For instance, someone who enjoyed tracking the stock indexes on the nightly news can most easily begin investing in those markets. That same trader may not have the same initial comfort level with agricultural markets or even other financial markets such as interest rates or currencies. Although it's true that different markets can exhibit unique sets of characteristics, your decision about which markets to follow is a personal one and will dictate which reports you watch and what style of trading you implement.

The remainder of this chapter introduces you to some of the general concepts of these two categories of analysis and explores a little more deeply the most important elements of each.

FUNDAMENTAL ANALYSIS HIGHLIGHTS

Fundamental analysts examine a variety of reports to evaluate changes in demand for a product or availability of that product to the marketplace. With experience, an analyst can develop strong instincts on how price will respond to various changes in the minutiae of supply and demand.

Although the effects of supply/demand may seem less evident in markets such as financials, they are the foundation of pricing for most physical commodities, especially in the agricultural markets where the supply is renewable each year and where limits exist as to how long the products can be stored.

Supply is rather straightforward, although it can be subject to frequent revisions. It is the quantity of a commodity available calculated by combining the stocks carried over from one season (or one week/month) to the next with new production and, in some cases, imports from overseas.

Demand is generally more difficult to quantify. In fact, the term used to indicate demand really should be *usage* or *consumption*. Demand may be greater or less than actual consumption. To complicate the matter, demand depends on price: How badly do consumers or the marketplace want the available quantity of this product at this price? Demand for some commodities, like in the energy markets, may not respond much to price increases. Demand for other products, like livestock feed grains, may be very sensitive to price increases because they compete against alternative substitutes.

In simple terms, price is determined by a general formula: What is produced this year, plus carryover stocks from last year, is compared against what is needed this year. Plug in the various supply and demand data to solve for the variable of price. The idea is simple in concept, but difficult in real-world practice.

Traders rely on a number of government, corporate, and private events and reports to get a reading on the key factors that influence prices. Some of the reports are considered to be leading indicators, some coincidental indicators, and some lagging indicators, depending on the data inputs necessary to calculate them and how they relate to current conditions. For instance, the U.S. employment report, which includes numbers of new jobs, unemployment rate, wage rates, and so on, is generally considered a lagging indicator; in fact, jobs tend to be one of the last areas of the economy to recover after a recession.

Several important facts need to be remembered about many of the reports:

- The numbers cited typically are estimates based on surveys or other means of gathering data that have been used historically but may not be absolutely correct. However, they are usually the best numbers the market has to work with, so traders have to be aware of them.
- Expectations for what the estimates should be are often as important as the estimates themselves. Markets tend to build in numbers that are widely perceived to be correct, so what may seem to be a bullish figure vis-à-vis a previous time period may already be priced into the market. Only a surprise may move the market to any large degree.
- Futures markets anticipate. Today's prices may have already taken into account tomorrow's conditions. "Buy the rumor, sell the fact" is a market axiom that describes how prices may react to confirmation of data in a report. Or you may be totally correct in your analysis, but premature with your positions because other traders haven't caught up to the "facts" yet.
- Market conditions change. What is bearish today may be bullish tomorrow, so you always have to relate reports to the current investment situation.
- Over the years, especially with economic reports, different events can take center stage for investors. Sometimes it's inflation, while other times it's interest rates, money supply, gross domestic product (GDP), or retail sales.

Recently investors were preoccupied with unemployment, jobless claims, and the price of crude oil. Now it seems the trade deficit and weakening U.S. dollar are of greatest concern.

- Futures traders must always be prepared for events—those social, political, weather, and other surprises that can sabotage the best of conclusions of fundamental analysis.

The following pages provide descriptions of just some of the major news events and reports watched by fundamental traders, categorized by market. These reports deal primarily with U.S. markets, but many countries have equivalent reports for their markets. In addition, the exchanges sometimes offer extensive background resources for their respective products or links to web sites where you can find more detailed information.

Financials

Stock indexes, interest rates, and currencies are most influenced by reports that have to do with aspects of the economy and with each other—for example, what happens to interest rates may have a major effect on the outlook for the U.S. stock market or for the U.S. dollar. A report that is positive for one market may be negative for another. Economic reports also have a bearing on prices of some physical commodities, notably metals and energy. Here are some major reports that financial traders watch.

Consumer Confidence   Markets are really just a reflection of mass psychology, so anything that provides clues about investor sentiment can be a good indicator of price direction. The Conference Board, University of Michigan, and others survey consumers regularly and release reports on their attitudes. These readings may suggest how much money will be spent by consumers, who account for a large share of the economy, or how likely they will be to invest in the stock market or housing.

Retail Sales   Comparison figures tell economists and traders how well consumers are doing and how the current situation relates to previous periods.

Gross Domestic Product   This is the broadest measure of all economic activity in a nation and indicates overall economic growth—or lack of it. How vibrant the economy is will have an effect on almost all markets.

ISM Index   The Institute of Supply Management (ISM) report indicates the status of manufacturing conditions. What happens in manufacturing has a major bearing on employment, demand for raw materials, and the like, so economists analyze this report and some of its components carefully for clues about future growth.

Factory Orders   The amount of orders pending is a good gauge of how active the economy is and how it might fare in the future. Similar reports about durable goods orders, industrial production, capacity utilization, business inventories, and others measure what is happening in the manufacturing sector and, in turn, what may happen to the job market and other areas.

Employment Situation   Nothing provides a better indication of how much consumers might purchase and how strong the economy is than how many people are working or how many people are unemployed. Monthly employment reports have become a significant market mover in recent years as the economy adjusts to trends in outsourcing and downsizing.

Consumer Price Index, Producer Price Index   These indexes measure price levels of various goods and services and generally are considered to be the best gauges of the inflation rate, which often has a bearing on interest rates. Analysts examine components of these reports to see how current levels compare with previous levels.

Housing Starts, Home Sales   Housing is a major factor in the economy, with the level of activity indicating how much money consumers have to spend and how much demand there will be for raw materials such as lumber or copper, appliances, and all the other items needed for building and maintaining a home. Another related report on construction spending provides similar information about building offices, shopping malls, and so forth. All of these statistics reflect how people feel about the economy and its future and may have an influence on interest rates.

Balance of Payments   Reports in this area deal with the level of a nation's imports versus exports, commonly known as a trade deficit in the United States, and cash flows among nations. International trade figures provide a measure of economic conditions, and current account figures show how much money is moving from one country to another for investment purposes.

Federal Open Market Committee Meetings and Fed Actions   Anything the Federal Reserve Board does or even hints at doing is closely monitored by traders because of the effect on short-term interest rates and the U.S. dollar and the possible repercussions on other markets and the economy. The Fed, which meets about every six weeks, attempts to walk a tightrope between stimulating and tightening spending by adjusting short-term interest rates and reserve lending requirements in an effort to maintain a stable economy. Fed meeting days can produce some volatile market movements.

Agricultural Commodities

The U.S. Department of Agriculture (USDA) provides a number of reports on commodities produced in the United States as well as crops grown elsewhere in the world. These reports on grains, soybeans, cotton, orange juice, and meats can have a significant impact on the futures market prices for these commodities.

Many of these reports affect all of these markets in a ripple effect—for example, the amount of grain produced or in storage will have a bearing on feed prices that, in turn, may affect how many animals are raised and prices at the meat counter. Others cover only selected areas. Because of the seasonal nature of production and consumption, a report in one month may have a much bigger impact than the same report in another month.

Most of the major reports are so-called lockup reports—that is, they are compiled in a locked room and released to the whole world at the same instant. That means individual traders can have access to the information at the same time as the largest trader.

For a calendar of when these reports are scheduled to be released, go to the USDA's National Agriculture Statistical Service web site at www.nass.usda.gov/Publications/Reports_By_Date/ or to the sites of other USDA agencies such as the Economic Research Service or the Foreign Agricultural Service. The USDA releases many other statistics and reports, but the following have the most impact on futures markets.

Crop Production   Not all crops are covered in each of these monthly reports, but these updates of production estimates released about the 10th of each month often set the tone of the market for the month ahead. Some reports are only projections, but other reports during the growing and harvesting season provide survey-based estimates of yields and the size of the U.S. crop.

Prospective Plantings, Acreage   These reports on spring-planted crops indicate the acreage that farmers intend to plant (released at the end of March) and what they actually planted (released at the end of June). The June figures may be adjusted as officials get a better idea of the weather's effect on planting, but they often serve as the base from which crop sizes are estimated during the upcoming season.

Supply/Demand Estimates   USDA officials release revised figures based on the latest crop production report and other information each month, not only for U.S. crops but also for all other major crop-producing countries around the world, such as Brazil, Canada, Australia, and Europe. Total supply takes into account carryover from the previous season, new estimated production, and imports. Total demand is actually the expected consumption, either domestically for food, feed, or fuel or for exports. The remainder left over from supply minus usage is the new ending stocks or carryover figure. A key number that traders watch is the ending stocks-to-usage ratio to see how it compares with previous years.

Stocks in All Positions   In addition to the year-end stocks figures, the USDA also announces estimates for the amount of stocks on farms and off farms each quarter. This provides an important measure of usage as the season progresses. Based on its surveys of stocks available, the USDA sometimes revises its production estimates long after the regular monthly reports have been released.

Crop Progress, Crop Summary   These are important weekly reports that update the condition of crops at the end of the previous week. During the planting season, these reports indicate how much of the crop has been planted, how much has emerged, and so on. Similar figures on the amount of the crop harvested are released during the harvesting season. The amount of the crop rated excellent, good, fair, and poor in each area of the major production regions during the growing season helps traders calculate what the outlook for the size of yields and production may be.

Hogs and Pigs   These quarterly reports (end of March, June, September, December) provide estimates of hog numbers by weight category, farrowing intentions, pigs per litter—in short, all the information traders need to calculate the amount and timing of pork production. Because production plans may change as price or weather changes, actual slaughter figures may result in revisions to original numbers that surprise traders and cause volatile price action.

Cattle on Feed   These monthly reports provide estimates of the number of cattle in feedlots by weight category in the major production states. They do not cover all cattle slaughtered, but just those in states that serve as a bellwether for the cattle futures market. Annual and semiannual summaries of all cattle numbers break down the U.S. herd by type (dairy or beef), breeding herd, calf crop, and other categories.

Cold Storage   Monthly cold storage reports indicate how many pounds of the various meats are in freezers. Although most meat moves into consumer hands without going into storage, this report is important for a market such as pork belly futures.

Softs or Exotics

Although still agricultural, commodities such as sugar, cocoa, and coffee are produced primarily in countries with warmer climates, and the United States and Europe are major importers of these commodities. The Foreign Agricultural Service of the USDA at www.fas.usda.gov does compile statistics and releases regular reports on these markets, which are traded at the New York Board of Trade and in London at Euronext.liffe.

   These commodities all have prominent international organizations made up of both producing and consuming nations, and all have headquarters in London. In addition to weather, which is always a key in commodity production, prices of these commodities tend to be more susceptible to social, political, and labor issues that may disrupt the flow of supplies. Traders need to especially monitor these issues in the major producing and exporting countries:

Sugar is produced in many areas from either sugar cane or sugar beets, making for a competitive world market sometimes protected by tariffs or import quotas. Brazil is a major exporter. For more information on sugar, see the International Sugar Organization web site at www.sugaronline.com/iso.

Cocoa production is dominated by Côte d'Ivoire (Ivory Coast), Ghana, and Indonesia. For more information on cocoa, see the International Cocoa Organization web site at www.icco.org.

The world's largest exporters of coffee are Brazil, Vietnam, Indonesia, and Colombia. For more details on coffee, see the web site of the International Coffee Organization at www.ico.org.

Energy

The primary energy markets are crude oil and natural gas; the product markets are heating oil, unleaded gasoline, and propane. Futures contracts for all of these markets are traded at the New York Mercantile Exchange and at the International Petroleum Exchange in London, which both offer a number of information resources. Of the various grades of crude oil produced around the world, the leaders in futures trading are West Texas intermediate, which is traded in New York, and Brent crude, which is traded in London and Dublin.

On the supply side, the dominant force in world energy markets is the Organization of Petroleum Exporting Countries (OPEC). On the demand side, trends in economic growth prospects have a major bearing on how much oil the world needs. OPEC attempts to set quotas for production that are low enough to maintain prices it deems adequate but not so low as to stifle global economies and, therefore, diminish future oil demand.

In trying to maintain this tight supply/demand balance, energy markets are the most sensitive commodity market when it comes to political, labor, social, and economic issues, particularly in key production areas where supply disruptions may be felt almost immediately by importing countries. For this reason, weekly statistics of U.S. stocks of crude oil and products provided by the American Petroleum Institute at www.api.org and the Energy Information Agency of the Department of Energy at www.eia.doe.gov often are market events driving energy prices.

In addition to economic conditions, extreme weather is a major factor for natural gas prices. Because natural gas cannot easily be imported from overseas or stored, most of the supply moves via pipeline from the well to the consumer. If production is disrupted on the Gulf Coast during the hurricane season, or if unusually cold or hot weather increases demand for heating and air-conditioning, natural gas prices are likely to spike higher and then come down almost as fast when the situation passes.

Metals

Prices for precious metals such as gold and platinum have less of a supply/demand impact than most commodities. Instead, prices tend to respond to the value of the U.S. dollar, prospects for inflation or deflation, geopolitical tensions, or other situations where investors turn to metals as a store of value in uncertain times. Gold prices have been affected at times by central bank sales, but the latest political developments may provide a better gauge of prices than any supply/demand issue.

By contrast, copper, palladium, and silver are nonprecious or industrial metals that *do* respond to supply/demand factors—silver has a dual role among the metals for both its industrial and monetary uses. Copper, in fact, has been called the metal with a Ph.D. in world economics because its price is so sensitive to global economic conditions that play a big role in demand. Any report that deals with economic conditions, especially those related to housing, automobiles, appliances, and the like, may have an effect on prices for these metals. Silver is also sensitive to developments in photography.

All of these metals are traded on the COMEX division of the New York Mercantile Exchange and at several other exchanges around the world. Gold and silver contracts were recently listed on electronically traded markets at the Chicago Board of Trade. In addition to the exchanges, you can get information about metals from the International Wrought Copper Council at www.copper council.org, the World Gold Council at www.gold.org, or the Silver Institute at www.silverinstitute.org.

With this introduction to fundamental analysis behind us, let's now consider the other major approach to analyzing markets—technical analysis.

TECHNICAL ANALYSIS HIGHLIGHTS

Some call it voodoo, but it's hard to argue with the widespread acceptance of technical analysis in the investment community. Technical analysis is the study of price action but also includes a number of statistical indicators, as well as data on volume, open interest, and other factors that relate to tracking prices.

Technical analysis is considered to be both an art and a science. This chapter will focus more on the science part of the story and will leave the art side for you to ponder from your own experiences.

Charts of All Types

First and foremost, technical analysis means charts, and traders use several different types of charts, each providing a different view of prices. Which chart type and which technical indicators you use often depends on a look and feel to which you have become accustomed. Whatever you use, your chart should help you get some understanding of the market's price history and how past price action may provide clues about how prices may unfold in the future.

The following charts all cover about a four-month period of gold futures prices. Note the information conveyed by each and see which type of chart is most helpful to you.

Line Charts   We'll start first with the line chart, not because it is the most popular but simply because it provides the easiest explanation of basic chart construction. Figure 2.2 shows a basic line chart constructed by connecting just the closing prices for periods without regard to other values for those periods, such as highs or lows. As with any chart, the periods viewed could be daily, weekly, monthly, or any intraday period such as 60 minutes or 5 minutes.

Media frequently used line charts in past years to present price action, perhaps because of their simple and uncluttered format. Line charts are still used today for presenting single-value data, such as government statistics or supply/demand values. However, with the proliferation of charting software, most traders have come

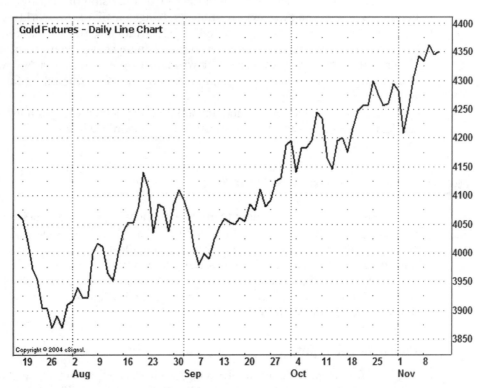

FIGURE 2.2   Line chart. The closing value for each period is connected to the next, without regard to other values for that period, such as the high or low.
(*Source:* eSignal, www.esignal.com)

to expect more sophistication in the charts they view, even in free charts from news and chart vendors. Accordingly, they have moved on to more complex charts readily available from a variety of sources.

Bar Charts Bar charts include quite a bit more information than line charts with only a moderate increase in the complexity or "busyness" of the chart. While a line chart shows only closing prices, bar charts include the high and low prices for the period being viewed as well as the opening price and the closing price.

Figure 2.3 shows a daily bar chart with several sharp spikes up and down at critical turning points and the channels that formed during trending periods. Each bar is drawn between the high and low price for the period, and the open and close are indicated with the small hash marks on the left and right side of the price bar, respectively. Such details were lost on the line chart.

Again, as with any chart type, bar charts are used for many time frames, from weekly and monthly down to intraday 60-minute or 1-minute periods. A bar chart can even be drawn based on a specified number of price ticks, which creates many

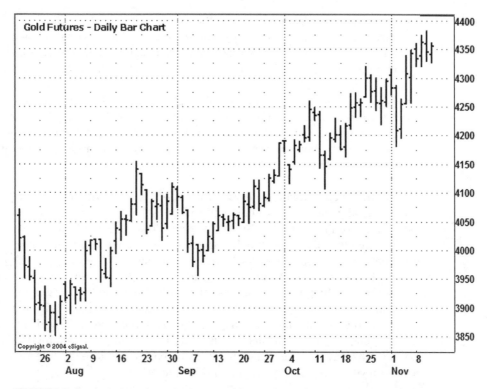

FIGURE 2.3 Daily bar chart. Each vertical bar is drawn between the high and low for the period, and the opening and closing prices are indicated with the small hash marks. (*Source:* eSignal, www.esignal.com)

bars during hectic periods and few bars during quiet times. Which time frame or number of ticks to choose is up to you and will depend on how sensitive you want your charts to be.

Candlestick Charts   Moving beyond the bar chart, some traders like a type of chart with a more visual presentation of price relationships introduced to Western traders in about 1990. These are called candlestick charts because the body, representing the difference between the opening and closing prices, looks like a candle, and the shadows, representing all the price action above and below the body during the time period depicted, look like wicks.

If the closing price is above the opening price, the body is usually clear, white, or green. If the closing price is below the opening price, the body is usually solid, black, or red. Candlestick charts provide a quick visual picture of the relationship between opens and closes and their relative strengths or weaknesses, especially for extended periods.

Figure 2.4 shows a daily candlestick chart with two of the many candlestick patterns labeled.

- A doji is a candlestick in which the opening and closing prices are about the same, resulting in a short body, and the high and low prices for the period extend above and below. It is most useful as a signal when it appears after a run-up in prices and may indicate market uncertainty, which often precedes a turn in the price trend.
- A hammer is a candlestick in which the body is at the upper end of the trading range for the period with little or no upper shadow; another shadow stretching out below the body is at least twice as long as the body. It often occurs at the bottom of a downtrend and indicates a rejection of lows and a reversal higher.

Another well-known candlestick formation (not shown on this chart) is a two-candle signal called an "engulfing pattern." In the bullish version, the first candle is a black, red, or filled candle after a downtrend. The second candle is a white, green, or clear candle with the open below the first candle's close and the close above the first candle's open. In other words, the second candle's body engulfs the first candle's body and suggests the market is ready to change to an upward price direction.

Other colorfully named candlestick patterns include the hanging man, shooting star, harami, and spinning top. What all of these candlestick formations look like, what they mean, and how they can be used in trading is a study in itself that goes beyond the scope of this introductory text. Some patterns involve only one candle; others require several candles. In all cases, much of the interpretation depends on where the pattern occurs on the chart.

Point-and-Figure Charts   A lesser-known charting technique is the point-and-figure chart, which is worth mentioning because of the interesting way it focuses

FIGURE 2.4 Daily candlestick chart. Each vertical bar is drawn between the high and low for the period. The distance between the open and the close is used to form a wider "body" section. (*Source:* eSignal, www.esignal.com)

on price action and eliminates reference to time. Point-and-figure charts appear to have a random series of Xs and Os across a graph instead of a price bar or candle for each time period. They are popular with floor traders, who find them easy to create and update even during hectic trading conditions. Figure 2.5 illustrates the point-and-figure technique, which was more popular in the past than it is today.

A point-and-figure chart has two essential measurements. The first is the price unit for each box on a vertical scale; the second is the number of boxes it takes to reverse a column of *X*s representing an uptrending market to a column of *O*s that represents a downtrend or vice versa.

To keep the illustration simple, this basic point-and-figure chart uses daily gold futures closing prices and assigns a value of $2 to each box and a reversal value of one box. It takes a price change of just one box or $2 to reverse from *X*s to *O*s or *O*s to *X*s. As long as prices continue to make new highs, you place an *X* in a box at each $2 higher increment, building up the *X* column. If the high is not high enough to put another *X* on top of the column, you look at the low, and if it is at least $2 below the value of the top *X* you move one column to the right of the *X*

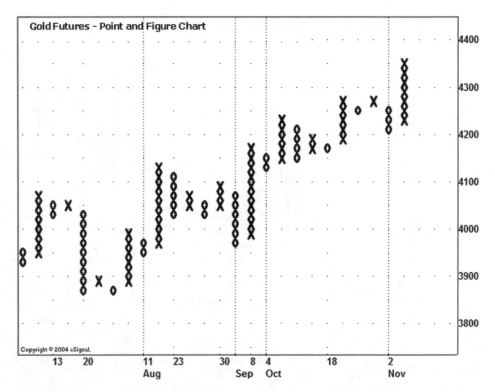

FIGURE 2.5   Point-and-figure chart. *X*s represent upticks and *O*s show downticks. Each new vertical bar begins once the market reverses by a predetermined amount, without fixed references to time. (*Source:* eSignal, www.esignal.com)

column and begin a column of *O*s. Then, every time the price falls by one box or $2, you continue to add *O*s to the bottom of the *O* column.

Because there is no entry on the chart for each time period, as there is for other charts, it may take many periods before the market changes from a column of *X*s to *O*s. Note on the chart that for the whole month of September there was just one column of *O*s and one column of *X*s.

Buy signals occur when a column of *X*s exceeds the previous column of *X*s—or, better yet, several previous columns of *X*s—or when a column of *X*s breaks above a 45-degree-angle downtrend line. Sell signals occur when a column of *O*s drops below the previous column (or several columns) of *O*s or when a column of *O*s breaks below a 45-degree-angle uptrend line.

Point-and-figure charts provide precise price points at which to act—there is less guessing about where a trend line crosses or what some indicator says.

Price-Break Chart   A less established charting format, but one worthy of mention, is the price-break chart. Like a point-and-figure chart, a price-break chart focuses entirely on price action and obscures the reference to time. Technically, time is seen advancing from left to right. Figure 2.6 shows an example of a price-break chart that appears more familiar to traders who have used typical bar or candlestick charts. In this example, a $3 price change produces a new bar.

Reading the Charts

We look only at bar charts in this basic introduction to chart analysis and focus first on chart patterns—those formations on the chart produced by prices themselves.

Identifying the trend is the first goal of the technical analyst, so trend lines are at the heart of analyzing price action. Trend lines are generally drawn across the successively higher bottoms in uptrends or progressively lower tops in the case of downtrends. Figure 2.7 shows examples of each on a mini-sized Dow futures contract. If you can spot points that may lead to a trend early in its development, you have taken a big step forward as an analyst.

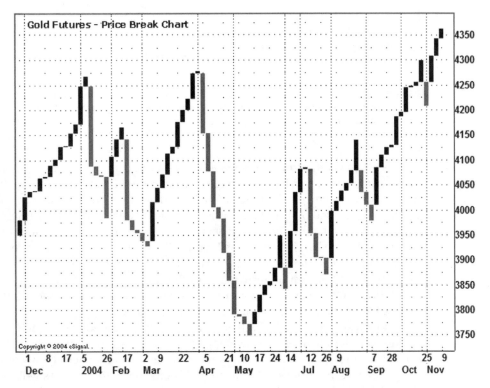

FIGURE 2.6 Price-break chart. In this less-established charting format, fixed references to time are obscured as in a point-and-figure chart. (*Source:* eSignal, www.esignal.com)

FIGURE 2.7 Trend lines. Up trend lines are drawn along bottoms and function as support. Down trend lines are drawn across tops and act as resistance. (*Source:* eSignal, www.esignal.com)

Trend lines tend to be significant areas on the chart, acting as support below or resistance above. Prices crossing the trend line may indicate that a change in direction has occurred. Technicians believe that once violated, support becomes resistance (in a sell-off), and that resistance becomes support (in a rally).

Analysts sometimes like to draw channels using multiple trend lines off a base trend line. Figure 2.8 is the same as Figure 2.7 but adds a parallel line to each trend line to create a channel. Using the uptrend line as the lower channel line, a parallel upper channel line can be drawn across the progressively higher tops of the uptrend. Prices often have a similar range for each bar, so most of the price activity occurs within the boundaries of the two parallel lines.

As with any chart pattern, these channels can be traded in several ways. Some traders use the channel lines as support and resistance, selling when prices approach the upper channel line and buying when they approach the lower channel line, assuming that prices will remain in this channel. Other traders will trade only the breakout of a channel, assuming that when prices drop below the lower channel line of an uptrend, for example, the market is reversing its original direction

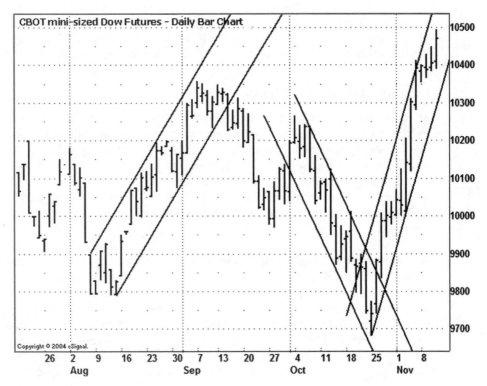

FIGURE 2.8 Channels. Adding a parallel line to a trend line creates a price channel. (*Source:* eSignal, www.esignal.com)

and will continue to move lower. Some traders who see this breakout wait for the market to make a reaction back to the channel, as it often does, and then take a position as prices approach the original trend line. A breakout in the direction of the channel may indicate that prices are becoming overextended, or conversely may wind up being the beginning of an extended runaway market. Evaluate all price action in context with other indicators, studies, and time frames to gain clues about the market's true situation.

How you trade a trend or channel will depend on your own trading style and may vary with your opinion about market conditions. However, being able to identify a channel and the boundaries that may contain price action can be very useful for helping you decide where to place stop or limit orders (see Chapter 7) and helping you see the general flow of price action.

When prices track sideways for an extended period, a trading range pattern forms another type of channel, a sideways channel, which may occur at bottoms or tops until the market makes a decisive move.

So how can you tell whether a trend will continue or it will change? Analysts use a number of chart patterns to make this decision. Broadly considered, chart patterns fall into two categories—continuation patterns and reversal patterns. This chapter looks at only a few of the better-known examples of each, emphasizing that there is much more to chart analysis than what you see presented here.

Continuation Chart Patterns

Many uptrending charts have areas where prices consolidate for a few periods or even make a downward correction. Nearly every trend unfolds in that manner—several steps forward in the direction of the main trend and then a step back where the market appears to be assessing its situation and taking a breather to rest up for the next leg in the direction of the trend.

These congestion areas are a normal part of trend building and channels and often form patterns that look like triangles. Analysts identify several different types.

Symmetrical Triangles or Pennants   The pennant pattern typically shows up in the middle of a trend and is formed when price ranges for each bar become smaller and smaller as highs become lower and lower and lows become higher and higher (see Figure 2.9). As price action tightens as it moves to the apex of the triangle, it tends to spring out with a sharp move, usually in the direction of the original trend. The breakout typically occurs about 75 percent of the way to the apex of the triangle. The breakout that occurs beyond the 80 percent distance to the apex is suspect and may fail to follow through.

Ascending Triangles   These patterns are more likely to appear at market bottoms and feature a series of higher lows while highs form a relatively flat horizontal line marking the top of the triangle. This indicates a strengthening market, and a breakout of the topside of the triangle suggests prices will rally.

Descending Triangles   This pattern reverses the appearance of the ascending triangle and is formed by a series of lower highs while lows make a relatively flat horizontal line that marks the bottom of the triangle. This indicates a weakening situation as traders won't push prices higher, and a breakout through the bottom suggests an ongoing downtrend.

Flags   A flag formation is also a congestion area but instead of prices compressing to an apex as in the triangle, price action is more erratic and appears to be a small countertrend against the main trend (see Figure 2.9 and Figure 2.10). A feature of some flag formations is the flagpole, a sharp move over one or several periods that stands out on the chart, followed by the congestion area that looks like a waving flag.

Analysts use the length of the flagpole as a measuring tool, taking the length of the flagpole from its beginning to the point where the congestion starts to form the flag, and adding it to (or subtracting it from) the point where prices break out of

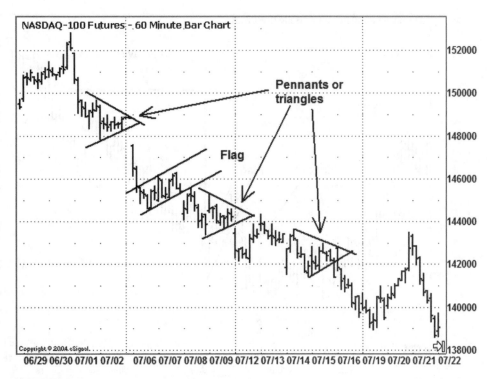

FIGURE 2.9 Pennants and triangles, and a flag. Congestion areas are a normal part of trend building and often form pennants, triangles, and flags. (*Source:* eSignal, www.esignal.com)

the flag congestion area, in order to establish targets for a move after the breakout. The flagpole on the E-mini S&P 500 chart (Figure 2.10) stretches from just below 790 to above 890, a length of a little more than 100 points. Added to the point where prices break out of the flag around 870, the objective is 970, which prices reached about two months after the flagpole after several setbacks marked by smaller flags.

Not shown is a much more conservative forecasting measurement. The vertical distance between the parallel lines of the flag can be added to the breakout point to forecast a minimum price objective. This short-term objective is often so close it remains within the flagpole area.

Analysts also expect triangles and flags to occur about halfway through a longer move, adding another way to arrive at a price target. Of course, all of these patterns and measurements can be rather subjective, depending on the points you choose. However, keeping in mind that some art is involved in chart analysis, they can give you some idea about the potential extent of a price move.

While some patterns suggest the trend in place will persist, other patterns indicate that a trend is ready to give way to a new trend in the opposite direction or

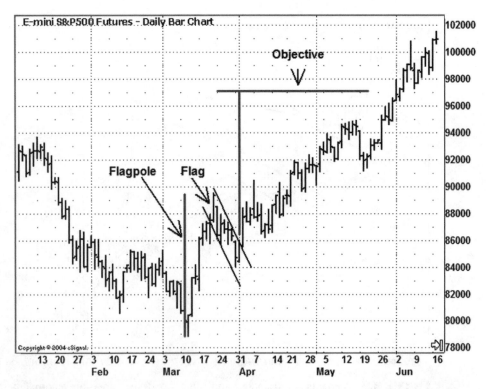

FIGURE 2.10 Flagpole. The length of the flagpole can be added to the breakout point of the flag to forecast an objective for the price move. (*Source:* eSignal, www.esignal.com)

at least a period of sideways price action. Let's review a few of the more common reversal patterns.

Reversal Chart Patterns

Channel Breakouts   The breakout of the channel mentioned earlier is one example of a reversal signal. Some traders may require two closes or three closes below the trend line rather than just an intraday penetration of the trend line or may require the market to move a specific percentage through the trend line to confirm the reversal pattern.

M Tops   In this topping pattern, prices run up to a high, drop back to an interim low, rally again to near the same level as the first high, and then fall back again. When prices fall below the interim low, it's a signal to go short as an M top has been confirmed (see Figure 2.11). The pattern may look like a double top or the second high may be a little below the first high. In any case, breaking through the interim low is the key to this reversal pattern.

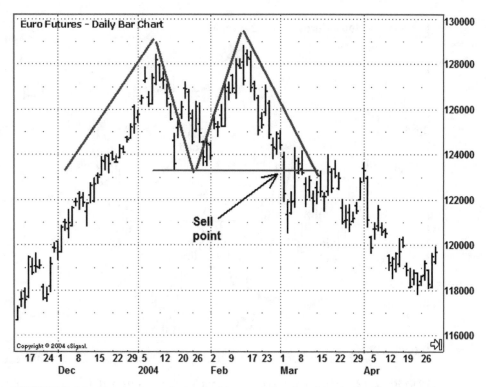

FIGURE 2.11 M top, also called a double top. Prices breaking below the interim low confirm the pattern. (*Source:* eSignal, www.esignal.com)

W Bottoms This bottoming pattern is a mirror of the M top: Prices decline into a low, rally to an interim high, sink back toward the low, and then rally again. Prices moving above the interim high indicate the bottom is in place and it's time to go long (see Figure 2.12). The pattern looks like a double bottom although the second low may be a little higher than the first low. Again, breaking above the interim high is the key to this reversal pattern.

Head-and-Shoulders Top or Bottom This formation is an extension of the M top or W bottom. As a topping pattern, the market makes a high (shoulder), dips to an interim low, rallies again and this time makes a higher high (head), drops again to another interim low at about the same price level as the previous low, stages another rally to about the same price level as the first high (shoulder), and then sinks again (see Figure 2.13). A movement below the neckline, preferably close to a horizontal line, signals the topping pattern is complete and it's time to go short. Typically, however, there will be some pausing action that occurs at the neckline before the market continues lower.

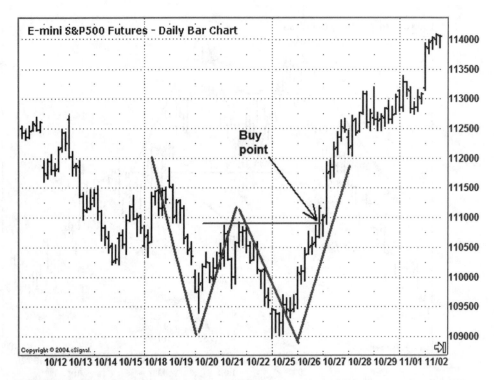

FIGURE 2.12 W bottom, also called a double bottom. This pattern is a mirror of the M top. (*Source:* eSignal, www.esignal.com)

Analysts also use the head-and-shoulders pattern to project price targets. Techniques vary for making this measurement, but one way is to calculate the distance between the top of the head and the neckline and subtract this distance from the breakout area of the neckline to arrive at a price objective.

Rounding Bottoms   These are also reversal types of formations, but the signals aren't as clear as with the other patterns. A rounding bottom looks like a saucer on a chart as prices edge down in a series of lower lows and then begin to creep higher with a series of higher lows (see Figure 2.14). When prices on the right side of the chart move above the lip of the saucer formation, it's a signal to buy. One well-known long-term saucer bottom occurred in gold futures, forming over more than two years and staying within about a $40 range. In some cases, prices reach the lip, then drop lower again before rallying to move above the lip in what some analysts call a cup-and-saucer formation.

V Tops and V Bottoms   These look just like what the letter describes: Prices make a sharp move and spike to a high or a low, then immediately turn around to

FIGURE 2.13 Head-and-shoulders top. In this classic reversal pattern, prices breaking below the neckline suggest a sell-off to the objective. (*Source:* eSignal, www.esignal.com)

move in the opposite direction (see Figure 2.15, page 41). This formation is more evident on a chart in hindsight and doesn't provide good places to establish a position. The sudden reversal of trend has few if any areas of consolidation. Some markets, like meats and currencies, may be more likely than others to form V tops and V bottoms.

Other Chart Patterns

You may have realized by this point that the study of chart patterns can involve quite a bit more complexity and insight than what has been discussed so far. This chapter serves only as an introduction to the subject, but several other important technical analysis topics need to be considered.

Gaps Gaps are price areas on a chart where no trading takes place. For example, the market hits a high of, say, 100 one day and then opens the next day at 105, leaving a five-point gap where no trades occurred. Gaps happen quite often in mar-

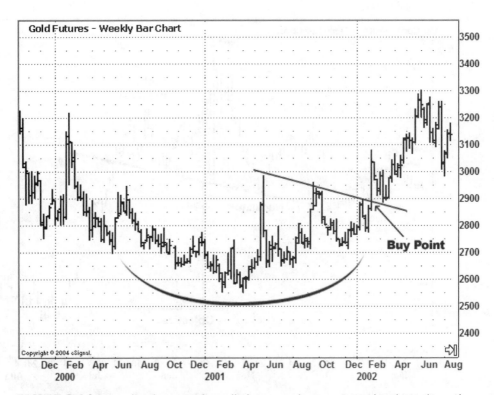

FIGURE 2.14   Rounding bottom, also called a saucer bottom. Prices breaking above the saucer lip suggest the lows may be in place. (*Source:* eSignal, www.esignal.com)

kets that trade for only part of a day because price-moving events and announcements take place during times when markets are closed. However, not all gaps are evident on a chart because follow-up price action covers them up or "fills the gap" in trader talk.

In general, gaps are considered to provide support below or resistance above, although some gaps may have little or no significance, depending on where they appear on the chart. Gap analysis focuses on several categories of gaps:

- *Breakaway gaps.* After an extended move, a market suddenly reverses direction with a strong burst, leaving a gap. A breakaway gap can sometimes indicate the beginning of a significant new trend.
- *Measuring gaps.* This gap occurs about halfway through a move and is a continuation signal. It may not be clear at the time that it is a measuring gap, but as price action leads you to that conclusion, you can measure the distance from the start of the move to the beginning of the gap and then add or subtract that distance to or from the gap to project a price target.

- *Exhaustion gaps.* After an extended move, a market expends one last gasp of energy to continue the move, exhausting all the buying (at a top) or selling (at a bottom) that is left. The exhaustion gap may be a reversal signal, and a drive to new highs or lows is sometimes followed several bars later by a breakaway gap in the other direction. The combination of an exhaustion gap and a break-away gap may leave what is called an "island reversal." On the chart, it looks like isolated price action that is not connected to other price action on either side of the gap area.

Figure 2.16 illustrates all of these types of gaps on a soybean futures chart. You can see what happens to prices after the gaps appear, although prices in this case did not fall as low as the target projected by the measuring gap.

Support, Resistance   Support is a price area that tends to lift the market or prevent prices from going lower. Resistance similarly suppresses prices and acts as a ceiling that prices have difficulty penetrating. Previous lows or highs, trend

FIGURE 2.15 V top. Characterized by a sudden reversal of trend, this pattern has within it few if any consolidation areas. (*Source:* eSignal, www.esignal.com)

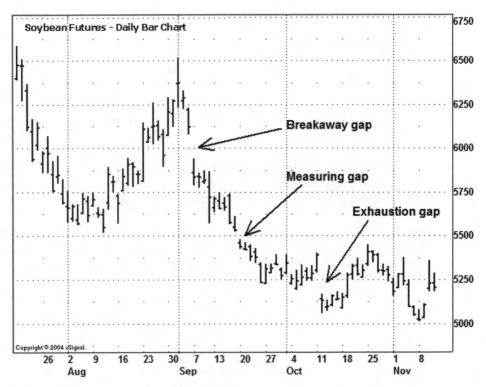

FIGURE 2.16 Gaps. Gaps are often categorized as either breakaway, measuring, or exhaustion. (*Source:* eSignal, www.esignal.com)

lines, moving averages, or other key price points may provide support or resistance to a price move, causing prices to bounce off of them rather than go through them (see Figure 2.17). Often, if a market does get through a resistance area, that resistance turns into support on a decline, or a broken support area becomes resistance.

Retracements A subject closely related to the concept of support and resistance is the matter of retracements. Markets seldom move straight up or straight down but tend to make a move, then a countermove. The countermove may result in one of the congestion patterns mentioned earlier or may go to a point where support or resistance exists from, say, a previous high or low. If traders see a countertrend move developing, they try to forecast how far this correction might take prices.

A popularly identified retracement amount for technical analysts is 50 percent—that is, if prices rally and then decline, analysts might expect the decline to end at the 50 percent mark of the up move. Depending on the extent of the re-

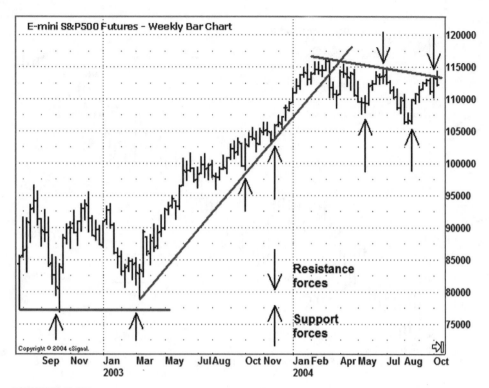

FIGURE 2.17 Support and resistance. Areas of support are found *beneath* chart prices, and resistance is identified as being *above* prices. (*Source:* eSignal, www.esignal.com)

tracement, traders determine the strength of an existing trend. If prices retrace less than 50 percent of a previous move and then continue the trend, the market is considered by some to still be strong; if prices correct more than 50 percent, the market looks weak and may be ready to move in the opposite direction.

If you were trading gold futures in early fall 2004, you watched prices rally from roughly $397 to $426 an ounce and then begin to drop (see Figure 2.18). You might wonder how low prices could go. A 50 percent retracement target of the previous $29 rally would take prices back down to $411.50, one point where you might look for the setback to stop. In this case the gold market did find support at that point and resumed its longer-term rally.

In addition to the 50 percent rule, you have available another, more extensive retracement tool called Fibonacci retracements. This discussion of pullbacks, support and resistance would be incomplete without exploring the topic further.

Fibonacci Numbers and Ratios Leonardo Fibonacci was a thirteenth-century Italian mathematician who discovered the significance and unique properties of a

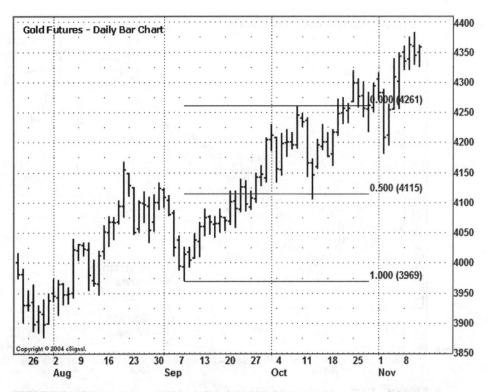

FIGURE 2.18 Retracement. This pullback holds support at 50 percent of the previous rally. The 50 percent retracement level can be the critical turning point for whether a trend remains intact. (*Source:* eSignal, www.esignal.com)

simple number series, now called the Fibonacci series. Fibonacci numbers, and more significantly the ratio of those numbers to each other, can be found in numerous examples throughout nature and cycles (for instance, the structure of pine cones, nautilus shells, sunflower bursts, sprouts along a plant stalk, and even the reproduction of rabbits).

The series, beginning with 0 and 1, simply adds one number in the series to the previous number. Ratios of the numbers to themselves approach certain Fibonacci ratios, like 14.6 percent, 23.6 percent, 38.2 percent and 61.8 percent. Notice in Table 2.1 that each Fibonacci number is about .618 of the one that follows and 1.618 (the so-called golden ratio of mathematics) of the preceding number.

Many believe that markets are simply a reflection of human nature and share traits common in the natural environment. Indeed, certain principles of physics and mathematics—like momentum, rate, acceleration, cycles, fractals, linear regression, and probability—seem to have application in markets.

TABLE 2.1 Fibonacci Numbers and Ratios

Fibonacci Series	Fibonacci Ratios			
0 + 1 = **1**				
	.500			
1 + 1 = **2**		.333		
	.666		.200	
1 + 2 = **3**		.400		.125
	.600		.250	
2 + 3 = **5**		.375		.154
	.625		.231	
3 + 5 = **8**		.384		.143
	.615		.238	
5 + 8 = **13**		.381		.147
	.619		.235	
8 + 13 = **21**		**.382**		.145
	.618		**.236**	
13 + 21 = **34**		**.382**		**.146**
	.618		**.236**	
21 + 34 = **55**		**.382**		**.146**
	.618		**.236**	
34 + 55 = **89**		**.382**		
	.618			
55 + 89 = **144**				
. . . ad infinitum				

Note: Fibonacci numbers and retracement ratios are in bold.

For the Fibonacci analyst, the numbers and ratios in the table indicate important areas on a chart, both in price and, more controversially, in time. The numbers can be used to predict retracement areas during pullbacks, as well as targets, called "extensions," for projected price moves. They can also be used to help determine the strength of a trend. In Figure 2.19, for example, after an extended down move in soybean prices, the market is able to recover only about 38.2 percent of the down move when it bounces in August. A less strong downtrend might have allowed the market to retrace back 61.8 percent or more.

Elliott Wave Elliott Wave analysis is a study in itself, but the basic premise is that markets tend to move in a series of waves within waves—three impulse waves in the direction of a trend separated by two corrective waves. Specific criteria define the numerical sequence of waves, with the middle impulse wave (called "Wave 3") generally the strongest wave, as the weekly chart of Swiss franc futures illustrates (see Figure 2.20, page 47). That's the wave trend followers try to identify and catch early in its development. Corrective waves can unfold in a number of different forms and are more difficult to trade.

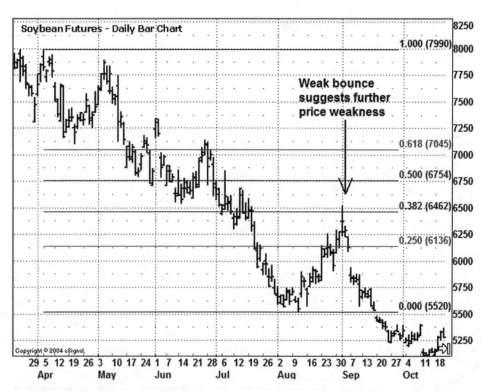

FIGURE 2.19 Fibonacci retracements. In this downtrend the market recovers about 38 percent, an important Fibonacci number. (*Source:* eSignal, www.esignal.com)

The waves essentially reflect the psychology of the marketplace as it makes its normal thrusts and corrections. It takes a trained eye to detect the myriad of Elliott Waves that make up a market, but advocates of this approach point out that Elliott Wave analysis, often in conjunction with Fibonacci ratios, is one of the few methods that attempt to predict future price and time targets rather than waiting for price action to produce indicators that lag the market.

Up to this point, you may be thinking that technical analysis focuses on charts only, but more accurately, it is the study of prices. Accordingly, you have available other means of examining the market price action.

Studies and Indicators

Analysts have developed a number of technical indicators to give them more insight into what is happening inside a market beyond what may be obvious with the price pattern itself. Studies and indicators involve complex computations, but, fortunately, today's analytical trading software programs include many of these indicators. So if it seems like too much of a challenge to calculate and monitor any of

FIGURE 2.20 Elliott Wave. Elliott Wave analysis attempts to predict future action rather than waiting for price action to reveal itself after the fact. Specific criteria define the numerical sequence of waves. (*Source:* eSignal, www.esignal.com)

the indicators mentioned here, remember that the computer will do much of the work for you.

Several other comments should be made about using indicators in general:

- Many indicators are based on *past* price action. Although they can give you a sense of what could happen, they are not always predictive because of this lag effect.
- Indicators should not be used in isolation but should be used in conjunction with other analytical techniques to provide confirmation for trading decisions. No indicator alone is likely to provide a magic clue as to what the market might do.
- Many indicators are based on only one thing, price. Therefore, the corollary to the preceding item is that looking at too many indicators may not be helpful, either, as they all will generate essentially the same signal at the same time.
- Indicators often require some interpretation that can only be gained with experience observing and using them.

- If you don't see what you like in an indicator, it can be tempting to adjust the parameters until you get what you want. In other words, it is easy to curve-fit the indicator to prices. Manipulating an indicator and overoptimizing may give you some misleading results when it comes to actual trading. The indicators on the charts shown here use basic parameters that are intended only to show the concepts of the indicators and not necessarily the parameters you should use. You can spend considerable time researching what works best for you.

Indicators can be divided into two general categories—those that identify trends and the strength/weakness of the trend and those that spot potential market turns. This section provides an introduction to these techniques and how they can be used. Serious traders will want to go beyond this overview to study the many books and other resources available on these subjects to discover what might be most useful in their own trading.

Detecting the Trend   A market is trending either upward, downward, or sideways. And the same market may have different trends in place on different time frames. For example, a 60-minute chart may show sideways action, while a daily chart of the same market is trending higher. You may be able to see a trend in a series of price bars or candlesticks, but the longer-term direction may not be so clear when trading becomes volatile and erratic.

Determining the trend is one of the most important tasks technical analysts have in deciding how to position themselves to profit from price action. Let's consider now a technician's first set of tools for determining the trend.

Moving Averages   This indicator is probably the simplest and most widely used by traders of all sizes. All you need to do is add up the prices for a specific number of periods and then divide the total by the number of periods to get a moving average reading that changes with each new price input. Closing prices are often used, but you can also incorporate the open, high, or low into the calculation.

There are three main types of moving averages—simple moving average (SMA), weighted moving average (WMA), and exponential moving average (EMA). The last two place more emphasis on recent prices. Whichever type you use, you wind up with a single smoothed line that flows across the chart, removing much of the noise from the chart (see Figure 2.21).

Moving averages can be used in a variety of ways:

- Just look at the slope of the moving average line to determine the trend visually, and position yourself accordingly.
- Note where the current price is relative to the moving average. If the price is above the moving average, the trend is up and you should be long; if the price is below the moving average, the trend is down and you should be short.
- Use the moving average line as a point for potential support or resistance.

- Use several moving averages together to refine your analysis. When the shorter moving average (which responds quickly) crosses *above* the longer moving average (which responds less quickly), the trend may be defined as up. When the shorter moving average drops *below* the longer average, the market may be in a downtrend phase (see Figure 2.22).

Analysts use moving averages in a multitude of other ways, but these basic principles should provide you with a strong foundation on the subject. Following is an introduction to a few other common methods for determining the trend. The first is actually a fancy manipulation of moving averages.

Moving Average Convergence/Divergence   Better known as simply MACD, (pronounced "Mac D"), this adaptation of moving averages can also provide several signals, depending on how early you want to get in on a potential move—or take the risk that a move will develop. MACD uses three moving averages, often

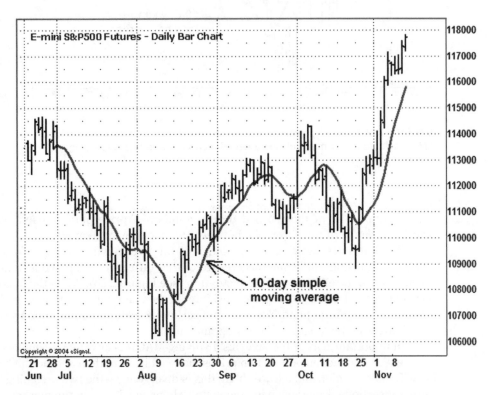

FIGURE 2.21   Simple moving average. This 10-day SMA is calculated by averaging the previous 10 closing prices, plotting each point on the chart, and connecting the points to create the smoothed line. (*Source:* eSignal, www.esignal.com)

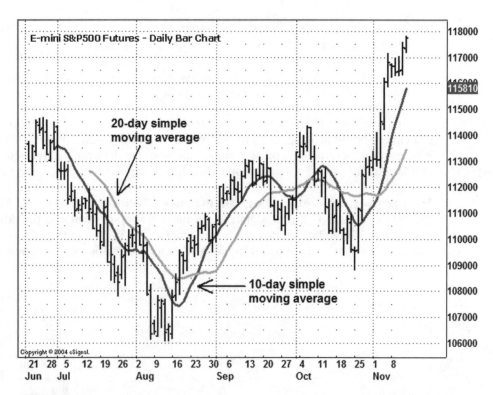

FIGURE 2.22 Moving average crossover. The 10-day SMA moves faster than the 20-day SMA. Each crossover may indicate a new direction in trend. (*Source:* eSignal, www.esignal.com)

exponential—two of them based on the number of price periods used and the third an average of the difference between the two moving averages.

The difference between the readings of the two moving averages is usually shown as a histogram, while the average of that difference is shown as a moving average line plotted on top of the histogram (see Figure 2.23). When the histogram is above zero, the market may be considered to be in an uptrend. Below the line, a downtrend may be at hand. You may find earlier indications of the trend by watching changes in the length of the histogram bars.

An important part of the analysis involving MACD is how its movements compare with price movements. When prices make a high and then another high while MACD makes a high and a lower high, this is divergence—the two are going in different directions. Divergence indicates underlying weakness in the market (in the case of an uptrend) and a potential market turn, and is a technique often used with other studies as well.

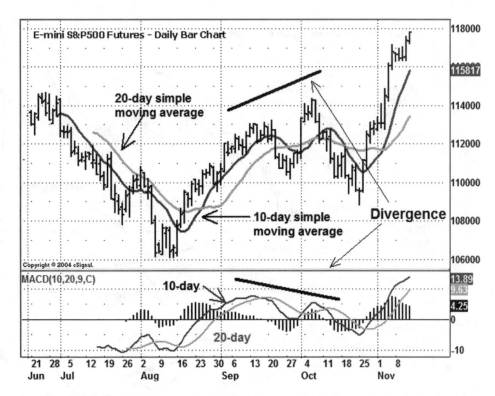

FIGURE 2.23 MACD histogram. The MACD (seen on the bottom portion of the chart) is a plot of the difference between two moving averages. Values above zero suggest an uptrend and below zero suggest a downtrend. Divergence (between market prices and the indicators) can foretell a reversal of trend. (*Source:* eSignal, www.esignal.com)

Directional Movement Index and ADX This indicator has three components, one for upward price movement, one for downward price movement, and a third that measures the difference in these up and down market forces to arrive at an index showing the strength of a trend. Figure 2.24 adds just this third index line, the Average Directional Index (ADX), to the bottom of Figure 2.23. ADX does not indicate the specific *direction* of the trend, just the *strength*. Note that the reading is at 30 during the downtrend at the left side of the chart and during the strong rally on the right side of the chart. As long as a trend is in place, ADX readings will get higher until reaching a point where it is difficult to sustain the angle of ascent. When a market shifts from trending to choppy, ADX readings decline. The main use of ADX is in reinforcing ideas about whether a trend will continue and in gauging the strength of a trend.

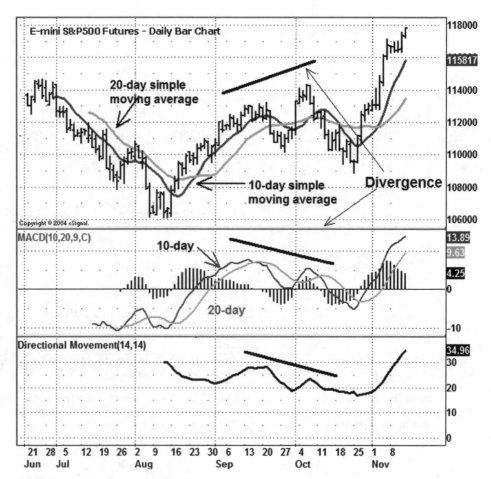

FIGURE 2.24 Directional movement indicator. The bottom of this chart shows only the Average Directional Index (ADX) component of this directional movement indicator. ADX indicates the *strength* of the trend and *not the specific direction*. Notice also divergence in this indicator. (*Source:* eSignal, www.esignal.com)

Detecting the Turn

Markets do not always spend their time trending nicely, but rather will often vacillate back and forth in choppy price action. In many cases, these fluctuations are wide enough to be quite tradable for investors who can discern where the turns will occur.

Analysts use a number of indicators to determine the support and resistance areas that define the trading range within which prices will move. These indicators fit into a general category known as market oscillators, which work best in nontrending trading range situations but can lead to many false signals if a market moves from a trading range into an extended trending condition. Note in the chart examples that some indicators can hang in overbought or oversold territory for some time while a trend continues, making them less useful in these conditions.

These oscillator-type indicators typically are shown at the bottom of a price chart and have a scale of 0 to 100. If the indicator is above a certain level near the top of the scale, say 70 or 80, the market is considered to be overbought and due for a turn lower; if the indicator is near the bottom of the scale, say 20 or 30, the market is considered to be oversold and ripe for a turn higher.

Stochastics   As markets move up, closes tend to be near the high end of the price range for a given period; when closes begin to slip to the lower end of the price range for a given period, a market loses its upward momentum. Stochastics measures the closing price relative to the low of the range for a selected period to indicate rising or falling momentum, providing trading signals when its lines cross into overbought or oversold territory.

To show the relationship among indicators, Figure 2.25 adds the stochastic indicator to the bottom of the previous figure. When %K (the faster, black line) crosses above %D (the slower, gray line) in the oversold area (below 20 level), it's a signal to buy; when the crossover occurs when the lines are in the overbought area (above 80 level), it's a signal to sell. However, the stochastic indicator does not provide specific price signals.

As with the MACD indicator just described, some of the best clues from the stochastic indicator do not come from the crossovers of its two indicator lines but from the convergence or divergence of those lines with prices. Regardless, as an overbought/oversold indicator, the stochastic indicator attempts to forecast turns in market action.

Relative Strength Index   The Relative Strength Index (RSI) compares periods with up closes with periods that have down closes to produce an index reading reflecting the strength of price changes on a scale of 0 to 100 (see Figure 2.26, page 55). Like other indicators, the number of periods can be adjusted to get readings that are more or less sensitive. The index provides overbought and oversold signals, and divergence/convergence with prices again is an important part of the analysis.

%R   This indicator is similar to stochastics except that, instead of comparing closes against the lows of a range, closes are compared with the highs of the range, and the index scale is reversed so that 0 is at the top and 100 at the bottom. (%R is not illustrated within any of the figures of this chapter.)

Rate of Change   There are several variations, but the basic concept is to divide the current close by the close from *N* periods earlier to get a reading on mo-

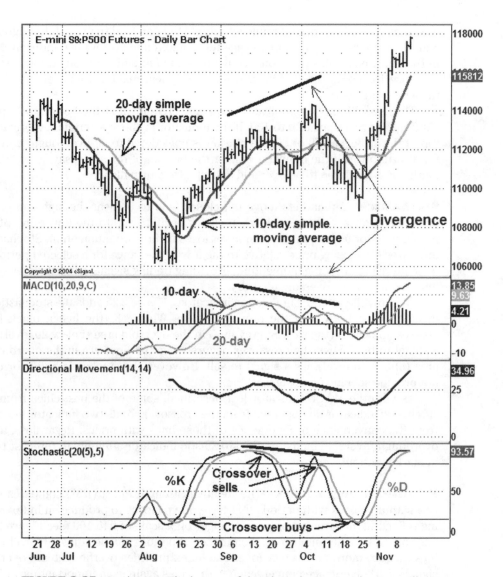

FIGURE 2.25 Stochastics. The bottom of this chart shows a stochastic oscillator. Prices above the 80 percent area are considered to be overbought and below the 20 percent area indicate an oversold condition. Notice again the divergence in this indicator. (*Source:* eSignal, www.esignal.com)

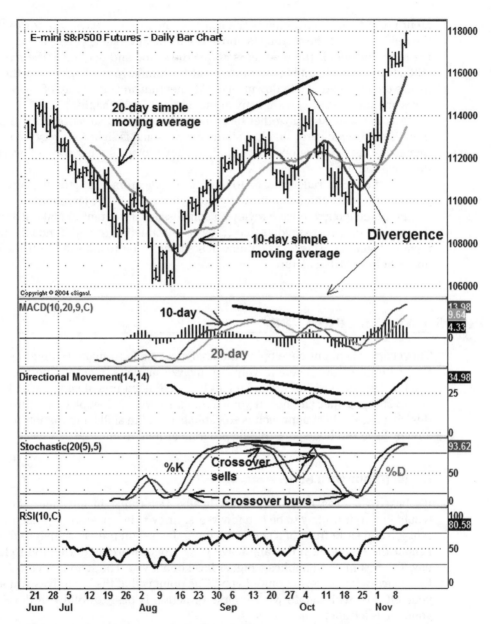

FIGURE 2.26 Relative Strength Index. Similar to the stochastic indicator, the RSI provides overbought and oversold signals, as well as divergence with prices. (*Source:* eSignal, www.esignal.com)

mentum. If the current price is the same as the price 10 days ago, for example, the reading is 0. If the reading is above the 0 line and rising, prices are accelerating to the upside; if the reading is above the 0 line and declining, the market is still advancing but running out of momentum. Similarly, readings below the 0 line assess the momentum of a downtrend. (Momentum and other rate-of-change measures are not illustrated within any of the figures of this chapter.)

Analysts look at many other technical indicators and variations of indicators; there is no one indicator that has all the answers and is right for every trader. Further, many of the indicators are redundant; they provide similar ways of evaluating the price action.

Your task as a trader may be to find those indicators and settings that provide you with the most comfortable method of investing in futures markets.

In this chapter, you have reviewed some issues important to making a trading decision. In the process, you gained a basic introduction to both fundamental and technical analysis. This last section will step back a bit to consider how these elements fit into the big picture.

PUTTING IT ALL TOGETHER

This chapter is about developing the analytical skills to make trading decisions. But, with all of the potential ways to analyze markets, you may be a bit overwhelmed by the possibilities and might have a difficult time deciding which methods to study further and use in your trading. As we have emphasized throughout this chapter, the best approach is to capitalize on the skills and the interests you already have and build your trading program around them.

Develop Your Own Style

It's best to approach trading methodically. Determine in advance where you would like your trading to be in a few years. Are you in a position to quit your current job and sit in front of a screen all day? Maybe you prefer to analyze the markets at the end of each day and leave your orders working during the following day. The first method implies a higher level of activity. The second method would likely have a longer-term point of view. The point is that the objectives you set for yourself now will dictate what course of action is best to follow in developing yourself as a trader.

Once you know your trading goals, establish a trading plan for getting there. Don't try to conquer every type of analysis at once. Instead, focus on mastering one item at a time—maybe concentrating only on chart patterns such as bull and bear flags, for instance. As you become more skilled with that pattern, add other techniques to your studies. You'll discover over time the style of trading that is right for you, and your methods of trading will evolve as you develop and refine your approach.

For instance, fundamental analysts focus on specific markets and become specialists in the news and events that influence those markets. Technical analysts mix and match patterns, indicators, and time frames to create specific methodologies. In the same manner, you may find the best way to achieve your goals is to explore and combine your favorite fundamentals and technicals.

So the answer to the question posed at the beginning of this chapter may represent not just a final goal. Perhaps the answer may also be found in the journey itself—in the process of realizing that answer. Start the process now and build your trading program one step at a time, and you'll be on your way to crafting your trading methods before you even realize it.

CHAPTER 3

Trading with a Broker as a Partner

A re you ready to jump in and start trading? Buy-and-hold, the foundation of stock trading for generations, may not work as well in today's marketplace. Stocks have proven to be vulnerable to tremendous price swings—both up and down. In this environment futures and options on futures can be attractive alternatives for those investors who are seeking speculative opportunities in both bullish and bearish market scenarios as well as for those who are simply trying to protect current exposure via a hedge.

However, you still have a few decisions to make, starting with an honest assessment of your ability and confidence to trade and the amount of help you need to pursue your trading program.

WHAT A BROKER CAN OFFER

Depending on your trading knowledge and experience, one of the most important decisions you might make is what type of brokerage relationship to have. Brokerage firms offer a variety of arrangements, from self-directed where traders make all the decisions independently to professionally managed accounts where traders have no involvement in the trading decision other than providing the money and selecting the money manager.

Many traders prefer a broker-assisted program, which is a hybrid of self-directed and managed accounts offering key aspects of both service levels. Broker-assisted programs can benefit a wide spectrum of traders, whether they are novices seeking guidance at almost every level or seasoned veterans looking for an extra edge on execution or the monitoring of contingency orders. Many traders simply don't have time to watch markets carefully and want the advice and support of a professional who knows what's happening or can serve as a credible sounding board for trading ideas.

Once you have determined that the broker-assisted route makes sense for you, your next big decision is selecting a broker who fits your needs. You might begin by identifying what you consider to be your basic needs for trading. Remember, these needs will change as your experience grows and your strategies and market coverage expand.

Next, you need to identify which of the services that a broker-assisted program offers are relevant to your style and level of trading. Broker-assisted programs offer much more than just trade recommendations, and a careful review of the various services available will ensure that you are optimizing the relationship. The broker's role can be significant or minor, depending on your input when you first interview a potential broker. Allowing the broker to evaluate and analyze your situation will require a two-way dialogue, with you providing as much background information as possible to ensure that appropriate services are rendered.

Following are some added values a broker can offer a trader. Review and consider which of these issues strike a chord with you:

- *Education about the industry.* Especially if you are new to futures, brokers can tell you about exchanges, products, margin requirements, and all the other details traders should know.
- *Education about market analysis.* Brokers may be able to explain charting techniques or the fundamentals of a market, depending on their expertise and what markets they follow. You may be able to get some of this information from the firm's newsletter or online, but the broker can elaborate on important points and keep you up-to-date on the latest developments.
- *Education about the trading process.* Buying or selling may seem simple enough, but you may have several alternatives. A broker can explain the various orders you can use and direct you to the best order to use in different situations to accomplish what you want.
- *Security/comfort.* You may be more at ease if a broker helps you with order placement procedures to make sure you get it right. The broker can advise you about the risks of a trade and suggest where to put stops. Getting help with placing orders may be reason enough to choose a broker-assisted approach.
- *Trading advice and recommendations.* You may not have the time or skill to spot good trading opportunities or the knowledge to best trade them. Brokers are plugged into the market day in and day out and are constantly sifting through data, determining what is relevant and what is simply noise. Armed with this information, they can offer timely, strategic advice about a market to trade and/or a specific strategy to utilize. Equally important, brokers are available to provide feedback about existing trades, given recent market developments.

Many profitable traders attribute their success to guidance they received from a mentor. A broker can be an ideal mentor who can help you learn how to identify trading opportunities, accurately access risk/reward ratios, read and interpret charts, determine appropriate levels to take profits or losses, what kind of order to use, how and when to place stops, how to review your account statement, and much more. The broker's job is ultimately to help you achieve bottom-line results along with trading independence, if that's what you seek, and to make you a more confident trader.

Like traders, brokers have different personalities, different levels of experience, and different areas of expertise. Some brokers specialize in a market area; others may focus on a technical or a fundamental approach. You should find a broker who fits your particular style and trading needs. Whatever you need, you should conduct your broker search just like you would if you were interviewing a potential employee or a partner to handle your money—the broker, in effect, actually is your employee and your partner whom you pay to do a specific job for you.

Just as you evaluate the broker, the broker is going to be interviewing you to ascertain your level of trading knowledge and experience, your trading goals, your tolerance for risk, and other factors that will shape what and how you trade and the relationship with a broker that you will need in order to attain your trading objectives. Following are some examples of issues a broker can help you work through as you develop your own trading program.

Trade What You Know, Know What You Trade

Market participants can be split into two camps:

1. *Hedgers* are the producers and users of commodities who have exposure and vested interest in price movements in certain markets.
2. *Speculators* are the traders who seek to profit from price changes and provide the liquidity that is so vital to a smooth, efficient marketplace.

By listening to your trading goals, a broker can quickly identify which group you fall into, the first step in determining which markets to trade. Of course, if you are a hedger, you obviously know which markets to trade because you deal/invest in the underlying commodity all the time. One of the criteria in your broker search might be finding a broker who specializes in the market you trade, is well-versed in the fundamentals of that market, and understands strategies for hedging.

The vast majority of futures traders, however, are speculators and have no interest in taking or making delivery of any particular commodity. When you get to the point of narrowing down the field of market choices, the broker can guide you to those that best fit your situation. Familiarity should be factored into your decision. Select a market that you know something about when you first begin trading. For example, if you grew up on a farm, consider the agricultural markets; if you are a stock market investor, consider stock index contracts; if you are a salesperson for a mortgage broker, consider the interest rate contracts.

Take advantage of the market knowledge you already have and leverage your prior experience/exposure into a market you know so you can concentrate more of your energy on developing trading strategies and making money. The broker can give you plenty of information to consider when you are evaluating a market and trying to find trading opportunities, and you should use any edge you have. Market familiarity breeds confidence, and confidence begets disciplined, clear thinking.

Initially, you should limit the number of futures markets that you follow so that your focus is not diluted in too many different directions. Ideally, the markets you select to review will have a low correlation to one another. For example, you may want to limit your analysis to only gold, stock indexes, and corn—or some other combination of three or four diverse markets. A broker can help you determine which markets fit you best.

Get as much information as you can about the market(s) you've selected or the trading method you plan to use. The more knowledge you acquire in advance of trading, the less likely an unpleasant surprise will occur while you're in the market. Printed contract specifications and literature are usually available free of charge from the broker or exchanges where the market trades, or you can get most of the information you need on Internet web sites.

You can always explore adding different contracts to your trading account as your experience and comfort level increase, ultimately allowing you to diversify into more areas to take advantage of contracts with low correlation to one another to balance your exposure to any one market segment.

Match Markets to Your Budget

Of necessity, the amount of risk capital you are willing to devote to futures trading will play a big role in determining which markets are more practical than others. Margin requirements for futures contracts must be considered and should weigh heavily in your decision about which contracts to trade. Your broker can explain why the market choices available to the speculator with $5,000 will not be the same as those for the speculator with $50,000 and can outline the consequences of an adverse move in various markets.

Even though you may have adequate funds to cover the margin requirement, you should also pay attention to the average true range or daily trading range of a market. The average true range study takes the moving average of the true range over a specified period.

$$\text{True range} = \text{True high} - \text{True low}$$

where   True high = the greater of the current bar's high or the close of the previous bar

True low = the lesser of the current bar's low or the close of the previous bar

The E-mini S&P 500 index contract may show an average daily range of approximately 10 to 15 points, which equates to $500 to $750 per contract. A one-day move could represent a 10 percent drawdown on a $5,000 account balance and may prove to be too volatile a market, based on your objective and risk tolerance.

Your broker can help you stay away from the rookie mistake of committing all available capital to cover the margin requirements for open positions. You may think you have a sure thing, but surprises and drawdowns are inevitable in trading. Avoid placing yourself in a position where a nominal adverse market move forces you to liquidate prematurely due to a lack of available cash reserves. A good rule of thumb is to maintain at least 25 percent of your initial margin requirement as cash reserves to cover potentially adverse price movements.

Time Constraints

The stock market offers thousands of individual companies from which the investor can choose. Unfortunately for the investor, each company has its own particular dynamics that need to be evaluated and considered, and the research that goes into just the stock selection can take a great deal of time.

A distinct advantage for the futures investor is that there are relatively few (approximately eight) major futures market sectors to monitor. Should you desire, you can track nearly every noteworthy economic area by following fewer than 25 markets.

Also, market information on futures contracts is readily available through regularly scheduled government reports and data releases made accessible to the public. Best of all, futures traders generally do not have to rely on market information produced by boardroom meetings, management turnover, insider information, officer incentives, and personal or corporate agendas.

Even though you have fewer markets to follow in futures, you still need to consider your own personal limitations regarding your time, one of the most precious of all commodities. Most investors have a day job, and they need to make sure that the markets they decide to follow are a good fit with whatever time constraints they have.

That's when having a broker on your side can be invaluable. The broker keeps a close eye on market developments and can monitor your positions for you or call you with timely trading opportunities that may arise while you are busy. With this arrangement, you can still control all of the trading decisions after getting input from your broker, or you can give a broker some discretion to make decisions for you if you and the broker have an understanding about what you want to do.

The volatility in one futures contract may be considerably greater than another and, as such, may require more of your attention and resources to monitor. The broker is in a position to see what is happening and can help you arrive at a trading decision at the time when it may be critical to take some action.

Compare the dollar value of daily range moves in the S&P 500 and corn futures, for example. A 10-point or $500 change that is a normal daily move in the

S&P market will probably require closer attention than a 2-cent or $100 daily change in corn, which may be a longer-term position requiring less monitoring. Of course, the volatility of any contract can change quickly based on new market information, and a contract that once was considered quiet may now be thought of as volatile.

Don't spread yourself too thin by trying to follow too many markets. Most traders have their hands full keeping abreast of a few markets, even with the assistance of a broker. Day-trading on your own is probably not a good idea if you work during market hours.

Identify Trading Goals

Define your objective up front. Be specific and realistic. This is an area where the help of a broker can be most useful as you discuss your objectives and how you are prepared to achieve them. Having a realistic goal and trading plan will help you determine which markets are more conducive than others to attaining your goal.

Start with your initial deposit and quantify what percentage return you're trying to achieve and what percentage negative return would make you stop trading. You should also identify the time period. It's unrealistic to just say that you want to double your money.

Let's say you establish a futures trading account with $10,000 and, after consulting with your broker, set a modest goal of a 25 percent return in one year—in other words, a gain of $2,500. That may not sound like much compared to the flamboyant claims you sometimes hear in marketing literature, but a return of that kind would exceed the return you can get from many other investments. Achieving a monthly average return of a little over $200 over the next 12 months on a $10,000 deposit won't come easily for a beginning trader, keeping in mind that some trades you make will probably lose money.

The amount of money you have to trade and your stated goal may narrow your field of market choices fairly quickly. Even with a conservative goal, you have to evaluate the current market climate to determine what markets fit best with your billfold and your objective. Grain markets may appear to be relatively calm for several months, for example, but could be very volatile markets during the critical planting and growing seasons.

Contracts with high volatility do not necessarily trend strongly up or down. They could simply bounce around within a range-bound band of prices. A broker can tell you about seasonal patterns and other market nuances with which you may not be familiar and give you some idea of what to expect, based on market history. Several markets present seasonal opportunities and risks, which a broker can help you evaluate.

Also important to remember is that, although large price swings (often associated with volatile markets) offer the potential for larger gains, they also come with the potential for greater losses, as a good broker is likely to remind you. Remember, leverage can cut both ways. Like any other newfound power, you should fully comprehend the pros and cons of leverage before wielding this power, and the broker should indicate the extent of risk you may be taking on with a position.

Use a simulated trading account to see if the markets you choose to trade really do match up with your financial objectives. It's better to figure this out while you are using play money. And you could end up saving yourself some real dollars in the future.

Identify Your Risk Tolerance

As important as it is to identify your objective going into a trade, it is equally important to have a bailout plan and to place a protective stop-loss order whenever possible, given exchange order acceptance policies and market liquidity. You may think you can withstand a big loss on a trade and stick with a trading plan you and your broker have worked out, but dealing with the loss of real money in real trading may affect your perspective of how much you are willing to risk.

Ask yourself, "At what point do I absolutely not want this position anymore?" Call that your doomsday stop, and have it working. If such a stop does get hit, then something was probably very wrong with your analysis and trading position. Keep in mind, stops are no guarantee of limited losses—markets can sometimes move quickly through them. Also, remember that stop orders can remain unfilled, such as in limit moves. In this case, a broker might suggest spreading your risk off in a back-month contract. Picking a place to bail out of a trade is a powerful first step toward taking control of your trading. Your broker is your best resource for helping you determine where to place stops.

If you are new to futures trading, be sure to identify two levels of risk before you start trading. The first is the maximum overall account drawdown you'll accept before throwing in the towel. The second is the maximum loss target for each trade. You should refrain from risking more than 20 percent on any one trade.

The same principle used to match markets traded and profit objectives applies to risk tolerance. You need to make sure the markets selected match your risk appetite. Take into consideration the market's average daily range or true range, and make sure the average price swings fit with your risk threshold. The experience of a broker with an objective view of a position can be a big help to any trader.

OPTIONS VERSUS FUTURES

Up to this point, most of the discussion has focused on using futures contracts to hedge or speculate in the markets. You also may want to consider options on futures as an alternative or supplement to futures contracts because options can add flexibility to your trading program.

An option is the right but not the obligation to buy or sell a particular futures contract at a specified price (strike price) at any time during the life of the option.

The main appeal of buying options is that you can speculate on increasing or decreasing futures prices with a defined and limited risk. The most that the buyer of an option can lose is the cost of purchasing the option (premium) plus commission and fees.

Because options on futures offer defined-risk features, you might think that this would be the ideal vehicle for traders new to futures. Although options positions can offer clearly defined risk, they also have more components that need to be considered.

With futures, your trading decisions are pretty straightforward: You buy if you are bullish, and you sell if you are bearish. With options, you not only have to project which way the underlying futures contract is going to move, but you also need to determine which strike price to select and the value of the premium you are willing to pay. Understanding these concepts is not beyond the novice trader but adds some complexity to the decision-making process.

For that reason, you may need to rely on a broker who has a thorough understanding of options, the conditions when they might be most useful, and the strategies for using them. A broker who knows options can provide perspective on volatility, fair value, liquidity, and other factors involved in options pricing that you may not be able to get from any other information source.

Options may be your best trading choice, but you may not know that without getting some professional help. Used in their most basic form, options may provide traders with unlimited profit potential and clearly defined risk, but may require a significant move for the position to break even or be profitable. Futures, on the other hand, offer unlimited profit and a direct correlation to price movement but are coupled with unlimited risk. Options are an effective instrument for situations where you anticipate a large price swing but recognize the potential for price volatility and the resulting risk.

For a more detailed discussion on options, see Chapter 9. Whether you prefer to trade the market directly with futures or indirectly with options on futures depends on your trading style and risk tolerance.

MARKET SHOULD FIT STRATEGY

When you talk with your broker about the markets you want to trade and the approach you want to use, you may find that your ideas won't mesh with the realities of the marketplace. Different markets lend themselves to different styles of trading. Day traders need volume and liquidity in markets in which they participate so that they can readily enter and exit a position without being concerned about the bid/ask spread, for example. Less heavily traded contracts may have a wide bid/ask spread and, therefore, may not be suitable for day traders, even though you may have decided that's your preferred style of trading.

Options on futures have several strike prices for each contract month traded, and trading activity may be scattered over a number of different options positions. Consequently, many of the strike prices may have very little trading activity on any given day. Such a market is not a good candidate for a short-term or day-trading system. Also, generally speaking, even the most active futures contracts will see volume drop off significantly as you look to the further-out contract months. Again, short-term speculating in these contracts is not recommended.

Those markets with larger daily trading ranges are usually more conducive to short-term trading models (assuming there is adequate volume, of course). For mid-term to long-term trading, you still should evaluate a market's volume and open interest to get an idea about liquidity. Rather than purchasing a contract 12 months out, you may find it more cost-effective to purchase a contract a few months out and roll the position over every three or four months to remain in liquid contracts. You will incur an additional commission charge for each roll, but that amount can be considerably less than the additional cost of entering and exiting a far-out contract with a wide bid/ask spread. A broker can help you get that done.

In general, most short-term traders or day traders tend to concentrate on financial markets for the volume and volatility these markets offer on a regular basis.

PAPER TRADING, BACK-TESTING

Exploring new markets can be an exciting as well as unsettling experience. There is no better way to get acclimated to a market than to take it for a test-drive. Use a simulated trading account and test your strategies before implementing them in real markets with real money. A broker can help you discover flaws that you might not have recognized yourself and can help you find remedies to increase your chances of success.

A simulated trading account can also help you determine if the markets you select to trade really do match up with your financial goal and strategies. Tweaking the contracts you trade is much easier when it's only play money that's on the line and may end up saving you real money down the road.

Because broker-assisted programs require more of a firm's resources and services that are personalized, a higher commission rate is generally charged. This, of course, is usually what makes traders hesitate about working with a broker.

For a broker-assisted program to make sense, the commission rate has to be reasonable and justified. A general rule of thumb and widely accepted standard is for the commission rate to be double that of the self-directed rate. The additional cost helps defray the expense of dedicating broker staff and resources to monitoring the markets and reviewing trading strategies on your behalf.

Most important, however, is whether the rate is justified. Consider this: If no additional stipend were charged to work with a broker and the trading results and experience did not improve, then what have you gained? Conversely, if you use the services of a broker-assisted program and find that your bottom line improves and that you grow as a trader because of this broker interaction, the decision to spend a little more on commissions becomes easier to justify.

Remember, the ultimate goal of the broker-assisted program is to improve your bottom-line results. Whether you're a seasoned trader or a novice, this should be your goal as well!

CHAPTER 4

Letting the Pros Trade Your Account

For those who would like to take advantage of the benefits that futures provide but don't want to be involved in trading directly themselves, an alternative is a managed account traded by professional money managers.

Managed futures accounts have been used by high-net-worth individuals for more than 25 years as a way to diversify their portfolios and enhance overall rates of return. The managed futures concept, which has been around since 1970, has grown most dramatically in recent years as the number of financial contracts available to traders increased and the interest in more traditional investments fluctuated. The total assets under management have risen from almost $26 billion at the end of 1994 to almost the $120 billion level by the end of 2004, the Barclay Trading Group[1] estimates—an increase of more than 450 percent in 10 years!

More than 400 managed futures programs are offered by commodity trading advisors (CTAs). The programs are created by individuals or groups of individuals who have designed a method of trading that historically has had higher profits than losses.

Anyone who offers a managed futures program in the United States must be registered as a CTA or a commodity pool operator (CPO) with the National Futures Association (NFA), the direct operational watchdog of all futures firms and futures professionals that is itself governed directly by the Commodity Futures Trading Commission (CFTC), a federal government agency. The CTA must hold a Series 3 license, the futures industry's equivalent to the Series 7 license that stockbrokers must have. The Series 3 requirement applies not only to CTAs but also to all futures brokers; to learn more about registration and requirements for CTAs

---

[1]Barclay Trading Group Ltd., 508 North 2nd Street, Fairfield, IA 52556 (www.barclaygrp.com).

and their status, see the NFA's web site at www.nfa.futures.org. A CTA must also publish a disclosure document, explaining the program and including the risk disclaimers, which must be filed with the NFA.

Holding a managed futures investment in your portfolio is not necessarily meant to take the place of your own trading account. However, if it can increase an investor's potential for success, why aren't managed futures a part of more individual portfolios?

The answer could be as simple as the fact that the majority of individual investors lack knowledge and basic understanding of this very specialized area. If you understand how managed futures operate and become confident about the benefits they can provide, it may be an area you will want to consider adding to your portfolio.

WHY MANAGED FUTURES?

So what can managed futures do for you? Table 4.1 summarizes some of the benefits and drawbacks of managed futures versus trading an individual account. In

TABLE 4.1   Going It Alone versus Managed Futures

A benefit for one person may be a drawback for another, so it's difficult to create a clear pro/con table comparing individual and managed futures accounts. Here are some of the main points distinguishing the two types of accounts. Also, keep in mind that managed account programs have their own differences with each other.

	Individual Trading	**Managed Futures**
Benefits	You are in full control at all times. You can close the account at any time. You can adapt methods to various situations. There are no front-end or administration fees; all profits, if obtained, are yours.	Trading is done by CTA; set rules may govern trading in programs. Less day-to-day monitoring is required. Professional is in charge of your trading. Accounts often are more diversified and, thus, generally less volatile. Trading costs (software, research, etc.) are spread across many people, particularly for pools.
Drawbacks	You must have time to commit to research and trading. No one is to blame for poor results other than yourself. You have to pay for software, data, and so on yourself.	Some types, especially pools, set limits on account withdrawals. Manager takes a percentage of profits, if obtained.

Source: Lind-Waldock.

addition to benefits that futures can provide any investor, following are the major benefits of managed futures specifically.

Opportunity for Reduced Portfolio Risk

Nobel Prize-winning economist Dr. Harry Markowitz, creator of modern portfolio theory, states that more efficient portfolios can be created by adding managed futures. Whether the CTA that you choose trades specialized markets or trades all of the markets, it is far more important to realize that these programs have been good portfolio diversifiers historically because of their low correlation to conventional holdings of stocks and bonds.

The Center for International Securities and Derivatives Markets (CISDM)[2] notes in a 2003 paper, "The Benefits of Managed Futures," that CTA programs have often been regarded as high-risk investments. However, over the period 1990–2002, the averaged annualized standard deviation of individual CTAs in the CISDM alternative investment database is, on average, lower than the averaged annualized standard deviation of the 30 individual firms in the Dow Jones Industrial Average (see Table 4.2).

The CISDM goes on to state that investment theory has shown that the potential benefit of adding an asset to an existing portfolio may be measured by the increase of an existing portfolio's Sharpe ratio (risk-adjusted rate of return) when a managed asset is added to an existing portfolio investment (see Table 4.3).

The Swiss Alternative Investment Strategies (SAIS) Group[3] offers a bigger picture of the attractiveness of managed futures investments in a portfolio in its research paper, "A New Passive Futures Investment Strategy," published in December 2002. This paper presents the new passive investment strategy in futures markets based on important economic functions of the actual makeup of the market players and what they provide to commercial hedgers in terms of risk management.

Potential for Enhanced Portfolio Returns

The potential for overall enhanced portfolio returns has been substantiated by a wealth of data over the years, including a landmark study conducted by Dr. John Lintner of Harvard University and reported in 1983.[4] In his study, Dr. Lintner

---

[2]The Center for International Securities and Derivatives Markets, Isenberg School of Management, University of Massachusetts, Amherst, MA 01003 (www.cisdm.org).

[3]Swiss Alternative Investment Strategies (SAIS) Group AG, Baarerstrasse 12, CH-6300 Zug, Switzerland (www.saisGroup.com).

[4]John Lintner, "The Potential Role of Managed Commodity Financial Futures Accounts in Portfolios of Stocks and Bonds," Annual Conference of Financial Analysts Federation, May 1983.

TABLE 4.2 Benefits of Managed Futures, Performance 1990–2002

	GSCI	EACM 100	S&P 500	Lehman Gov./Corp. Bond	MSCI World	Lehman Global Bond
Annualized Return	5.4%	12.9%	9.7%	8.3%	4.2%	7.7%
Annualized StDev	18.5%	4.3%	15.3%	4.2%	15.1%	5.0%
Sharpe Ratio	0.03	1.89	0.32	0.83	-0.04	0.57
Minimum Monthly Return	-12.2%	-4.4%	-14.5%	-2.5%	-13.4%	-3.0%
Correlation with GSCI		0.16	-0.07	0.02	-0.05	0.08

	Portfolio I S&P 500 & Lehman Bond	Portfolio II S&P 500, Lehman Bond, & GSCI	Portfolio III S&P 500, Lehman Bond, GSCI, & EACM 100	Portfolio IV MSCI World, Lehman Global	Portfolio V MSCI World, Lehman Global, & GSCI	Portfolio VI MSCI World, Lehman Global, GSCI, & EACM 100
Annualized Return	9.3%	8.9%	9.5%	6.2%	6.4%	7.0%
Annualized StDev	8.2%	7.4%	7.0%	8.4%	7.6%	7.1%
Sharpe Ratio	0.55	0.55	0.68	0.17	0.21	0.31
Minimum Monthly Return	-6.3%	-6.2%	-6.0%	-5.6%	-5.7%	-5.5%
Correlation with GSCI	-0.06	0.45	0.22	-0.02	0.47	0.25

Note:
Portfolio I: 50% S&P 500 and 50% Lehman Gov./Corp. Bond.
Portfolio II: 40% S&P 500, 40% Lehman Gov./Corp. Bond, and 20% GSCI.
Portfolio III: 40% S&P 500, 40% Lehman Gov./Corp. Bond, 10% GSCI, and 10% EACM 100.
Portfolio IV: 50% MSCI World and 50% Lehman Global Bond.
Portfolio V: 40% MSCI World, 40% Lehman Global Bond, and 20% GSCI.
Portfolio VI: 40% MSCI World, 40% Lehman Global Bond, 10% GSCI, and 10% EACM 100.
Source: Center for International Securities and Derivatives Markets.

TABLE 4.3 Benefits of Managed Futures, Factor Correlations 1990–2002

	S&P 500	Lehman Bond	Change in Credit Spread (Baa–Aaa)	Change in VIX	Change in Term Spread	Change in Bond Volume	Change in Stock Volume	Unexpected Inflation
GSCI	−0.07	0.02	−0.06	0.00	0.01	−0.02	−0.11	0.29
GSCI Agricultural	0.17	−0.06	0.04	−0.20	−0.03	0.01	−0.01	−0.34
GSCI Energy	−0.10	0.02	−0.06	0.04	0.03	−0.01	−0.07	0.32
GSCI Industrial Metals	0.20	−0.15	−0.22	−0.14	0.11	0.10	−0.11	0.29
GSCI Livestock	0.01	0.07	−0.01	−0.04	−0.01	−0.05	−0.01	−0.01
GSCI Non-Energy	0.19	−0.04	−0.04	−0.22	0.02	−0.01	−0.08	−0.09
GSCI Precious Metals	−0.12	−0.02	0.12	0.01	0.10	−0.03	−0.09	0.29
S&P 500	1.00	0.16	−0.13	−0.66	−0.03	0.01	−0.28	−0.21
Lehman Gov./ Corp. Bond	0.16	1.00	−0.06	−0.04	−0.64	−0.09	−0.04	−0.26
EACM 100	0.41	0.15	−0.21	−0.22	−0.01	−0.17	−0.32	0.42

Note: Monthly charges in inflation beyond one standard deviation of the average are used to proxy for unexpected inflation.
Source: Center for International Securities and Derivatives Markets.

wrote that "the combined portfolios of stocks and/or bonds after including judicious investments . . . in leveraged managed futures accounts show substantially less risk at every possible level of expected return than portfolios of stocks and bonds alone."

The SAIS Group's report cited earlier credits the remarkable growth of total assets committed to managed futures in recent years in large part to investor perception, as investors have grown to understand that their conventional portfolios would probably not continue to produce the same level of returns as in the bullish days of the stock market in the 1990s.

It is worth mentioning here that in bear market years the low correlation of managed futures to traditional portfolios of stocks and bonds can even become negative, thus providing the possibility of even greater enhanced overall portfolio returns.

In addition to being an asset class with a low correlation to most other investments, managed futures bring added value with the CTA's use of investment strategies based on the unique skill of the CTA or the unique properties of the underlying systems available to the CTA. In this respect, investments in managed futures have been described as absolute return strategies because the returns do not depend on the long-term return in underlying traditional stock, bond, or currency markets.

Ability to Profit in Any Economic Environment

CTAs are positioned to take advantage of a myriad of economic situations in the futures markets not only because of the mix of market participants but also because they have the ability to buy futures and/or options on futures when prices are rising and to sell when prices are falling. Many CTA programs have the ability to profit in flat to neutral markets by using various combinations of futures and/or options on futures.

Opportunity to Participate Easily in Global Markets

The establishment of global futures markets and the accompanying increase in trader participation have provided the means for CTAs to diversify their programs even further. The relatively low cost of trading commodity futures and options and the proliferation of mini-contracts in many market sectors have contributed to the enticing ease and potential for profit that these markets have to offer.

WHERE DO YOU START?

The first challenge you face if you decide to put money into a managed futures program is to find a program that fits your own personal risk/reward criteria. With more than 400 CTAs each offering different programs, that task can be daunting. This is where a brokerage firm with a division specializing in managed futures can provide invaluable assistance to a client, not only in matching a managed futures program to a client's investment style but also in helping the client get into and out of the program and with everything else in between.

Even though each CTA has a uniquely different method and style of trading, within the CTA universe there are only two broad categories of programs—systematic or discretionary.

Systematic programs trade with a predetermined systematic trading model that has a rigid set of rules and rarely deviates from those rules. Most systematic programs are trend-following. The system can be geared to long-term, intermediate-term, or short-term trading or any combination of the three.

Discretionary programs may also be based on a predetermined systematic trading model. However, the operational word here is *discretionary*, meaning that the individual CTA has discretion as to how to interpret the data. Discretionary CTAs may also incorporate fundamental data and other information into their trading decisions.

When you review a list of managed futures programs, you will find that several successful programs are closed to new investment or have minimums in the millions of dollars. Several other programs have peak-to-trough drawdowns that are above 50 percent. Even though many of these volatile programs make money in the long run, most participants find that kind of volatility too much to handle. A managed futures broker can help you sort out the trade-offs between potential profits and volatility.

Of course, no matter how profitable the CTAs and their programs are, almost all programs experience volatility. Therefore, in addition to producing profits, another important quality that CTAs must possess is excellent risk-management skills. Some programs automatically set a level of risk per position or per trade. When this level of risk is hit, then the unprofitable trade is closed out, if possible. Of course, having a predetermined guideline for each trade in no way guarantees the trader will or can exit at that point.

The market is not going to cooperate with the trader or system all the time. This is when the sound risk-management skills of the CTAs that you choose come into play. Good risk-management skills will minimize your equity loss until the markets do cooperate.

Risk management is as important as rate of return. Experience has also shown that, to execute sound risk management, a CTA must have a very specific risk-management plan, not just say something like, "My program handles different market situations in different ways; sometimes I use a stop-loss order and sometimes I use a market order." No CTA is likely to fully disclose the actual trading techniques that have made a particular program successful, but that type of response is not specific enough and may indicate that the CTA does not have any solid risk-management plan in place.

Although choosing a program that is at or near its average rate of return might seem like a good idea, that may not be the best choice. It is often much smarter to enter a program that is well off of its average highs. It is also smart to look for programs that have rates of return at least two times the highest peak-to-valley drawdown, discounting any huge drawdowns the program may have had when it began trading. Many CTAs experience high volatility in starting a program and then make adjustments to improve the program's risk/reward parameters over time.

Most CTAs manage their programs and client accounts full-time, so they and their programs are always searching for opportunities that the part-time trader may never see.

EVALUATING TRADING PROGRAMS

When researching managed futures, it is important to become familiar with some key measurements that allow you to compare money managers. The best way to do this is to look at a typical performance report and interpret the data published for each CTA (see Figure 4.1).

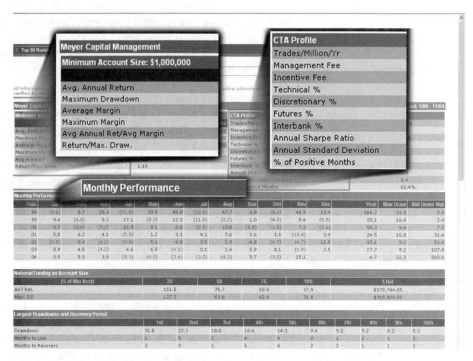

FIGURE 4.1 Meyer Capital Management performance report. The CTA Rankings Site contains performance information provided by Daniel B. Stark & Company, a third-party provider of CTA performance data. (*Source:* Lind-Waldock. Reprinted with permission of Daniel B. Stark & Company, 619–702–1230.)

Average Annual Return

The return on investment using the minimum account size of $1,000,000. Results are shown in both percentage and dollar returns, net of fees and commissions.

Maximum Drawdown

The maximum peak-to-trough decline during a specific period of the stated managed futures program, given in percent and in dollars. In this example, the figure is shown on a monthly basis, using only a month-end quote. Larger drawdowns might have been experienced within the month.

Average Margin

The average amount of money used as margin on positions at any given time during the period of the track record, shown in both percent and dollars.

Maximum Margin

The maximum margin amount in dollar terms that this trader has used historically, quoted as a percentage of the minimum account size.

Avg Annual Ret/Avg Margin

A ratio that compares the average annual return to the average margin figures.

Return/Max Draw

A ratio that compares the rate of return to the maximum loss, calculated in the same way as the preceding ratio of annual return to margin. Investors use this as one means of comparing a CTA with other CTAs.

Trades/Million/Yr

Approximate number of round-turn trades in a managed futures program based on a $1,000,000 account. For example, if the number of round-turn trades per million were 1,000 per year and your account size were $100,000, then the average number of round-turn trades based on historical data would be 100 per year.

Management Fee

A fixed fee that a CTA charges investors for its services. This percentage is based on the assets of the account. If your assets are $100,000 and the management fee is

2 percent, then you will pay $2,000 a year to the trader for handling your account. This fee is usually charged in quarterly installments.

Incentive Fee

A type of fee expressed in percentage terms rewarding CTAs for profitable performance. This fee is based on new profits only for gains above the last high-water mark for the life of the account. Again, it is usually charged on a quarterly basis.

Technical %

Percentage of trades on average conducted in a managed futures program based on preset parameters. The system generates the trades and, therefore, eliminates any emotion from the trading.

Discretionary %

Percentage of trades conducted in a managed futures program based on the CTA's discretionary analysis.

Futures %

Average percentage of managed futures account traded in futures, which are financial instruments or physical commodities for future delivery on a futures exchange.

Interbank %

Percentage of managed account traded in the interbank cash currency markets and not on an exchange.

Annual Sharpe Ratio

A ratio that represents a rate of return adjusted for risk. It also considers standard deviation, which is the distance of observations from the mean or average. This measure is often expressed as a percentage on an annualized basis.

$$\frac{\text{Annual rate of return} - \text{Risk-free rate of return}}{\text{Annualized standard deviation}}$$

It is important when investing to take the CTA's Sharpe ratio and compare it to other relevant investment benchmarks such as cash. The Sharpe ratio gives the expected added return per unit of added risk. It is a convenient summary of two important aspects of any strategy involving the difference between the return of an investment and that of a relevant benchmark (usually cash).

Although the Sharpe ratio is a common measure often used to compare CTA performance, it does not take into consideration correlation. It would be prudent to also do some correlation analysis relative to your other investments and to other managed futures accounts you may have.

Annual Standard Deviation

A measure of the distribution of a set of data from its average and/or mean on an annual basis. The more spread apart the data is, the higher the deviation.

% of Positive Months

Percentage of months where the value of the managed futures account was greater in market value than the previous month's value. This is not as important as many of the other statistics because a CTA may have a very acceptable annual rate of return, yet be profitable in very few months.

Monthly Performance

A series of percentage figures that reflect how much the value of the CTA's managed futures accounts changed from their previous month-end balance. This is based on a composite of all accounts traded by the CTA, so any one particular account may be slightly different than the composite.

Notional Funding on Account Size

Many clients notionally fund their managed accounts to some degree. The grid on the Meyer Capital Management profile illustrates the annual return and maximum drawdown based on the percentage of the minimum account size that is deposited in cash. Notionally funding the account can increase the probability of receiving a margin call for additional funds. However, for clients with a higher risk tolerance, this allows them a more efficient use of their investment capital.

Largest Drawdowns and Recovery Period

This series shows the largest percentage drawdowns the CTA has suffered during the period of analysis, how many months it took to go from peak to trough, and how many months it took the account to accumulate profits to recover from the trough back to the previous peak. These figures provide a test of your willingness to stick with the CTA's program—how many down months in a row could you handle, especially at the beginning of your trading program? This gives you an idea of what you might have to endure, based on historical data.

INVESTING IN MANAGED FUTURES

Investing in managed futures is done in one of two ways:

1. Opening an individual managed futures account, where the power of attorney is given to the CTA to trade the money.

2. Participating in a pooled account, which is very similar in concept to a mutual fund in that money from a number of investors is placed into one account managed by the CTA. Some funds require the investor to meet certain established financial criteria in order to invest in the fund.

Either account can be opened through a futures commission merchant (FCM). CTAs do not hold money for individual accounts, and funds are placed with an FCM for each account.

Table 4.4 compares some features of the two ways clients can be involved in a managed futures program. Comparing the two investment options, individual accounts are much more liquid than pools, giving investors the ability to cancel their account at any point and have their money returned within a few days. One disadvantage with pooled accounts is that investors are generally required to stay in the fund a certain minimum amount of time and after that period can liquidate only monthly.

If you open a managed account, you have full transparency of what is happening in the account. Each investor is notified of every trade. A monthly statement from the FCM is also sent to investors, and many offer the ability to view the accounts online in real-time format. Pools do not offer this transparency of trading.

TABLE 4.4   Managed Accounts versus Pools

Both types of accounts offer some of the same benefits compared to trading an individual account on your own, such as having a professional trade and manage your money. Here are a few distinguishing characteristics of these two types of accounts.

	Managed Account	Pooled Account
Benefits	You can close the account at any time.	Smaller initial investments are available.
	There is full transparency in trading; you are notified about every trade.	Risk is clearly defined by the amount of capital invested.
	Current statements are available, often real-time online.	Diversification is obtained if funds are allocated to a number of CTAs.
Drawbacks	Usually a sizable amount of money is required to open an account.	Often there are limitations on account withdrawals.
	You may be at risk for more than the amount of the initial account.	There is no transparency in trading; you get only one figure every month.

Source: Lind-Waldock.

Investors receive a monthly statement giving a summary of trading and the net asset value of each share purchased. You will not be able to view the trading of the CTA (or CTAs) involved in the fund.

When investors place their money in a pooled account, the money is commingled with other investors' money and managed by the CTA. The first major advantage of this type of account is that the investor can enter the pool with a significantly lower amount of money than most CTAs' minimum account size. A second advantage of a fund is that the risk is defined by the amount of overall capital invested. Third, many funds allocate the money to various CTAs so that you are, in effect, not only getting diversified into a number of markets but also are getting a portfolio of CTAs for a relatively small investment.

Managed Futures Account Costs

A CTA is compensated in one of two ways. The first is a small management fee, typically 1 to 2 percent of total assets under management. The second way is a performance-based fee that rewards CTAs if they achieve positive returns on the overall performance of the managed futures program. An FCM is compensated by a specified commission on each trade executed by the CTA for every client account. Also, an FCM may share fees with CTAs. If this is the case, it is disclosed in the CTA's disclosure document.

CHAPTER 5

Using an Auto-Executing Trading System

You may have heard the expression, "a nice place to visit but I wouldn't want to live there." You might have a similar impression of futures at this point—a great idea but you wouldn't want to trade them yourself.

After reading the previous chapters and recognizing that trading successfully requires considerable effort, you may be about to conclude that you don't have the time . . . or the knowledge . . . or the trading skills . . . or the personality . . . or you have some other shortcoming that might keep you from venturing into futures. But you can still participate in the futures markets and reap the potential benefits by tapping the expertise of experienced traders who have already worked through all those issues and have developed methods that can help you.

One of the emphases in the previous chapters has been having a trading plan before you enter a trade. This plan should be a well-thought-out approach that takes into account not only when and how to get into or out of a position but also the amount of risk you'll accept, the size of the position you should be trading, when to increase or diminish your position, and every other detail of every trade you make.

However, you may not have a trading plan or the time and resources to do the research to develop one, much less trade it. A solution could be purchasing or leasing a trading system that already has a record of actual trading and can provide you with the trading signals that you don't have time to discover yourself. However, as you continue reading, you must remember that a trading system does not eliminate the risk of loss from futures trading.

WHY AN AUTO-EXECUTING TRADING SYSTEM?

A turnkey trading system lets you skip many of the steps it would probably take to develop your own trading method. Having a broker automatically execute a trading program puts you into the market quickly with a tested approach to trading and may be a good addition to your portfolio, even if you already have a futures trading account. Here are some reasons why you might want to consider buying or leasing a trading system.

Developed by Professional Traders

Successful systems usually are offered by traders who have years of experience with the market. Although you can learn the basics of futures trading rather quickly, it might take you years of trading to discover all of the parameters and the details that go into building a successful system. By the time you finally find one that does work—if you ever reach that point—you may have devoted not only hours of research but also thousands of dollars to systems that didn't perform well.

May Save on Costs of Trading

You usually do have to pay a one-time charge up front or an ongoing fee for trading system software, so there is some additional expense to use someone else's system. But, depending on the type of system you get, you may not have to pay for a data feed, analytical software, programming fees, or some of the other costly items that most traders need in order to develop their own trading method. You also may not have to pay management fees or incentive fees associated with a managed account arrangement. And, theoretically at least, the added benefits you receive from trading a program, over and above what you could do on your own, should help pay for the system.

May Reduce Errors

A broker usually has multiple, redundant data feeds that can catch errors in price quotes and prevent a system trading on your behalf from taking a position on a faulty signal. As an individual trader trading your own account, you more than likely will have only one data feed. If your vendor transmits an erroneous price quote, it could trigger an entry signal that gets you into an unwanted position or an exit signal that takes you out of a favorable position before a correction is made.

Eliminates Emotion

One of the main reasons traders lose money is not because they don't know how to trade or don't have a sound trading method but because they let emotions take control of their trading. A mechanical trading system completely takes away the emotional aspect of trading and eliminates those decisions that may be inspired by fear or greed. It follows precise trading rules without second-guessing itself or deciding that a price move is impossible. When it gets a signal, it makes the trade. This style of trading may take some of the excitement out of trading, but your goal should be making money and not producing excitement, anyway.

Consistency

By taking all trading signals, a trading system provides a consistent approach to trading rather than an erratic trade selection process where you try to pick and choose which signals you'll take—or not take.

Risk Management

By definition, a trading system usually includes some stringent limits about how much risk to accept and what should happen when the risk parameters are reached. This should be part of everyone's trading plan, but traders without a system sometimes let a bad trade go because they "know a market will come back." A system employing rigid risk-management provisions won't let one big losing trade jeopardize an account.

Supplements Your Own Trading Decisions

Even if you already know how to trade futures and have an active account, buying or leasing a trading system can be a smart move. The most convincing evidence is that even some professional traders place some of their money with other systems or with other money managers. Whatever type of system you get, you now have a second opinion about a potential trade you want to make. Someone else's system may give you more confidence to make the trades that your own system is signaling when you know the other system has performed well in the past with similar signals.

Diversification

As suggested in the previous item, a trading system you purchase may even be the basis for a separate account that provides diversification to your portfolio—different markets, different methods, different time frames. The system may provide you with something you might never be able to do on your own.

LOOK AT YOURSELF FIRST

Many of the issues related to selecting a trading system come back to who you are and what your goals as a trader are. Dozens of trading systems and advisory services are being offered today. If you decide to use a system, your challenge is to find one that fits what you want to accomplish. Here are some questions you might ask yourself:

- Will you be able to evaluate the various trading systems yourself, or will you need assistance to help you make the right choice for you?
- How much risk tolerance do you have? Are you a nervous Nellie or a laid-back Larry? Can you live with the size of drawdowns the trading system has experienced in the past?
- Do you want to be aggressive or conservative as an investor? It's not unlike choosing a mutual fund for growth or income or for some other goal. You have to go with a style you like.
- How much money will you be trading with the system? It won't do much good to look at systems that trade a broad array of markets or a large number of contracts per trade if you have only a small amount of money to trade, because you won't be able to take advantage of the benefits of diversification or size in those kinds of systems.
- What time frame are you comfortable trading—short-term, intermediate-term, or long-term? The shorter the term, the more trades and the smaller return per trade you will usually have. You need to realize how many trades you might expect to see in your account in a given time period so you aren't surprised by the amount of trading activity.

WHAT TO LOOK FOR IN A TRADING SYSTEM

Once you have an idea what you will bring to a trading system, it's time to begin scrutinizing the systems themselves. Many of the things you should evaluate in a system are the same things you would look for if you were selecting a managed futures account, as you will note by comparing the performance report for the Trendchannel system in Figure 5.1 with the report on managed futures accounts explained in Chapter 4. Rather than duplicating explanations of all the details on a performance report, we'll refer you to the managed futures account chapter for much of that information.

However, there are some definite differences between selecting a managed futures account and a trading system. With a managed account, a professional money manager trades your money, and you pay a management fee based on assets under management, an incentive fee based on the amount of profits, if any, that the manager produces, and commissions. With a trading system, you pay for the system, either outright or on a monthly lease basis, and then pay the broker commissions for making the trades automatically based on the system's signals. The net profits, if any, from the trading system you select are all yours.

You won't get a disclosure document with a trading system, as you generally get if you choose a registered commodity trading advisor to manage your futures

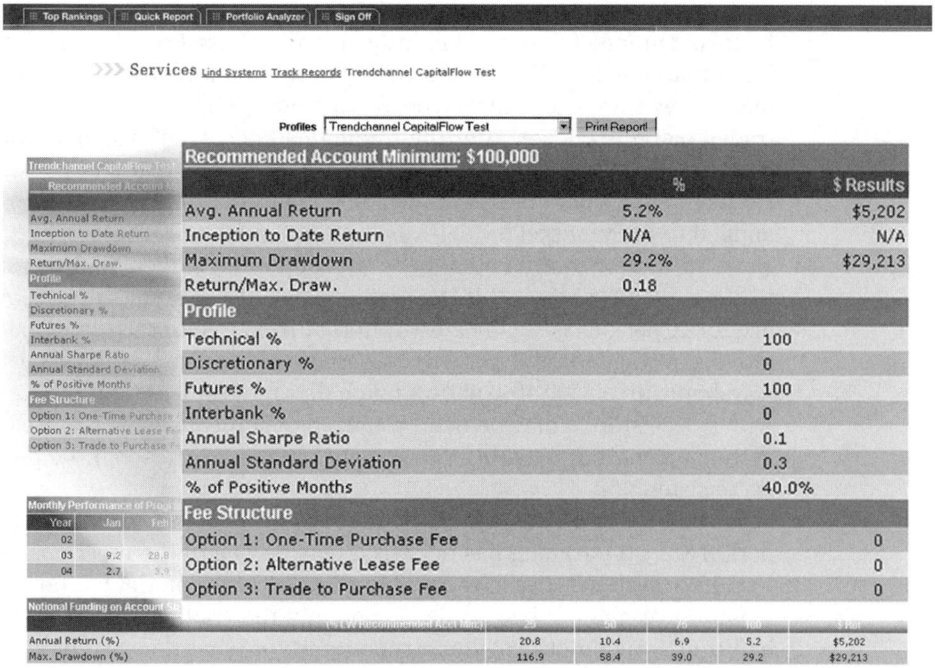

Top Rankings | Quick Report | Portfolio Analyzer | Sign Off

>>> Services Lind Systems Track Records Trendchannel CapitalFlow Test

Profiles Trendchannel CapitalFlow Test | Print Report!

Recommended Account Minimum: $100,000	%	$ Results
Avg. Annual Return	5.2%	$5,202
Inception to Date Return	N/A	N/A
Maximum Drawdown	29.2%	$29,213
Return/Max. Draw.	0.18	
Profile		
Technical %	100	
Discretionary %	0	
Futures %	100	
Interbank %	0	
Annual Sharpe Ratio	0.1	
Annual Standard Deviation	0.3	
% of Positive Months	40.0%	
Fee Structure		
Option 1: One-Time Purchase Fee		0
Option 2: Alternative Lease Fee		0
Option 3: Trade to Purchase Fee		0

Notional Funding on Account

	25	50	75	100	$
Annual Return (%)	20.8	10.4	6.9	5.2	$5,202
Max. Drawdown (%)	116.9	58.4	39.0	29.2	$29,213

FIGURE 5.1 Trendchannel CapitalFlow track record demonstrates this system's performance as of a particular point in time. (*Source:* John Tolan, Trendchannel developer; reprinted with permission of Trendchannel.)

account. However, just as in selecting a commodity trading advisor, you should ask to see key numbers such as net return, drawdowns, number of trades, percentage of winning trades, Sharpe ratios, and so on when picking a trading system. You should study the system's trade-by-trade track record carefully and ask some of these questions:

- Is the performance based on hypothetical results or actual trading results? There may be quite a difference between the two, just as there can be between paper trading and real trading.
- What data was used to produce the trading results? Was a separate set of out-of-sample data used to produce the system's results after the system was developed on another set of data?
- How volatile are the system's results? Is the equity curve a relatively smooth line moving ever higher, or is it a choppy path higher with sharp gains and losses from one month to the next?
- How large are the drawdowns from peak to valley, not only in dollars but also in time? A system should have guidelines about what to do in the event

of dollar losses, but what about time? Can you live with a system that may be losing money for several months in a row, based on its historical record?

- What markets does the system trade? Is the track record based on the same markets you want to trade, or does it include results from big moves in thinly traded markets chosen after the trading had occurred? You may want a well-diversified portfolio but not one that includes illiquid markets.

- Do the system's parameters do well in all markets, or are different parameters applied to each market?

- Have the system's parameters been overoptimized and curve-fitted in an effort to show the best results? If the performance of a system with a moving average for 10 periods is significantly different from that of the same system with a moving average for nine periods, you may have an overoptimized system. Or if a system with a $500 stop shows much different returns than the same system with a $600 stop, it may be overoptimized. Ask the developer for results of the system's signals applied over a range of parameters to see if the performance is consistent.

- What time period does the track record cover? Selectively choosing a time period after the trading has occurred may be one of the most misleading factors in a system's track record. Starting at a point right after the system would have made a bad trade—or ending the trading period right before a bad trade—may not provide a true picture of what the system will do in actual trading in the future. A track record based on the bullish trends of the stock market of the late 1990s may look much different than the track record during the sideways market a couple of years later. Look carefully at the time period of the track record.

- How far back does the system's track record go, both in terms of time and in number of trades? Is that enough statistically to give a good feel for what could happen in the future?

- Does the track record include all trades for a period? Or does it overlook a selected bad trade or two that might skew the results? Ask for a system's trade-by-trade listing and then compare the list with a price chart. If it seems that a trade should have been on the list based on the system's rules but is not, find out why the developer excluded it.

- Is much of the system's profit for a given period based on one or two big winning trades? If one trade accounts for most of the system's gains, think about how the system would have performed if you had missed that one trade.

WHY "SUCCESSFUL" SYSTEMS MAY FAIL

A system that performs admirably on past data may not do so well in the future. It may not have anything to do with the system's design, although much of the blame can probably be placed on overoptimization or on presenting the results for only those periods when the system did well. And, as you might expect, some trading system performance results may sound appealing but may be misrepresented to entice traders to buy the system.

Still, even the best systems may fail over the longer run. Here are some reasons why:

- The current market environment may be different than when the system was developed or when the track record was compiled. However well the system's parameters may have done in the past, the current price action may not be a good fit for those parameters.
- Some of the most profitable systems may also produce the most volatile results. Traders may not be able to take the drawdowns, either in dollars or in length of time, and they give up—more than likely, when system performance is at a low point and just before it turns upward.
- Where traders have control over the system's trades, they may cherry-pick the signals they want, sometimes leading to disastrous trades, while ignoring signals that turn out to be the biggest winning trades. Letting a broker automatically execute the system's signals takes you out of the emotional decision-making loop and increases your odds for success—assuming, of course, you have sufficient funds to trade the system as it was designed to be traded.

SUMMING UP SYSTEMS

The system-assisted approach to trading is a viable and cost-effective way to participate in trading futures. Programs have been created for a wide variety of markets and time frames. Whether you are a seasoned trader or a green newcomer to futures, there is a trading program that will complement your existing strategy or help you get started trading.

CHAPTER 6

Resources for the Self-Directed Trader

If you decide to be a self-directed trader making your own trading decisions and entering your own orders, you undoubtedly will need to rely on some resources to help you in that process.

What you need and where you will get it depends to a great extent on the type of trader you want to be, the trading style you believe will be most suited to your personality, and the amount of money and time you have to devote to trading.

Do you want to be a day trader, moving in and out of positions intraday and winding up with no positions overnight? Or would you prefer to be a longer-term trader, taking positions that you might hold for days or weeks in an attempt to catch bigger price moves? Would you be most comfortable trading spreads? Or would you be better off in the options on futures market?

Whatever type of trader you choose to be will have some bearing on the resources you need. Years ago all you might have needed to trade was a phone and an idea, but the resources you almost certainly need in today's trading include a personal computer and an Internet connection to link you to the marketplace—plus the plain old telephone service of the past as a backup. Beyond that, you may be able to get everything you need from a brokerage firm. Or you may want to supplement what a brokerage firm offers by subscribing to some of the many specialized services available, especially if you are looking for a particular type of analysis offered by a software program or an advisory service.

BROKERAGE FIRM CHOICE

Even if you plan to handle all of your trading details yourself, you still have to go through a brokerage firm to execute your trades. Selecting a broker is covered in

Chapter 3 of this book, but because the brokerage firm is such an important re-source for your trading, there are several overall matters you should consider be-fore making this choice.

Operations Support

Trading online is great, but sometimes you do need to speak with someone when placing an order or checking a balance or just trying to find an answer to a ques-tion. The resources a firm offers may be great, but they won't do you much good if you can't access them when you need them the most.

Find out how much staff a firm employs in its client call center operations. Will you always be speaking with the same dedicated team of people or will you be shuffled around to someone new each time you call? Also, ask if the call center is open 24 hours a day during the trading week and what type of assistance you can expect from the center's professionals.

Does the firm have redundant facilities in place in case there is some dis-ruption in its connections to exchanges or in its ability to communicate with you?

Product Offering

Many people come to realize that an investment in futures can form an important part of their overall investment portfolio. However, some just don't have the time, experience, or inclination to trade the markets on their own. Many also realize that they like both the hands-on *and* hands-off approach to investing in futures and opt for multiple accounts.

Your firm should offer a full range of services in case you decide to shift or add to your style of trading. It should include a managed accounts division, which deals with professional futures managers; an auto-execute division, which can ac-cess systems where trading signals can be executed automatically; and a broker-assisted division that can match you with a broker who helps you when you have your own ideas but wish to work with a professional to assist in implementing your trading plan.

In trading, nothing beats experience, and these divisions can put that experi-ence to work on your behalf.

Accurate Accounting

You may be focused on trading, but you should also expect all of your trading re-sults to be recorded quickly and accurately and reported to you in a timely man-ner. You will want to monitor the status of your account daily, and your statements are your scorecard that reflects how you are doing.

TRADING PLATFORM

Selecting the firm and a trading platform is an important decision because you may find that the broker's trading platform includes most of the features you need—not only to enter your orders but also to do your analysis. There are several aspects of a platform to consider.

Type of Platform

Does the firm offer a downloadable version that highlights speed and accuracy? Does the firm have a browser-based platform as well? The Internet is still a rather fragile network and may not be the most reliable means of conveying your orders, especially when it comes to critical periods when timing is most important or when you must be able to count on your orders being transmitted and executed.

If there is some disruption in your online connection to the brokerage firm, is technical support readily available to assist you with any questions? If you cannot use the trading platform for some reason, is a trading desk available by phone to take care of your orders 24 hours a day during the trading week?

Can the trading platform handle wireless trading? Finally, are there any charges for using the platform or some of its features?

Ease of Use

The platform should be simple to understand and operate to facilitate the transmission of orders quickly. For the active trader, the firm's platform should offer market depth, which is the listing of a market's most recent bids and offers. Check to see if you can place an order from the market depth screen. Customization is another important feature. What data do you want to see when you're trading? Figure 6.1 illustrates the flexibility that Lind Xpress, a downloadable platform, offers you as a trader.

If you are looking at a chart or price quote, a platform may formulate the order for you so all you have to do is click "Buy" or "Sell." Procedures to enter an order should be clear and easy, yet should have enough safeguards to reduce your chances of making mistakes as you make your trades.

Market Access

To which markets do the platforms provide access? Some platforms trade only selected electronic markets such as stock index futures or offer trading on only a limited number of exchanges. They may not take trades for open-outcry markets or may not have the capability to trade options on futures.

You want a trading platform that has the most flexibility to trade any market you want. You never know which markets you may want to trade next week, so

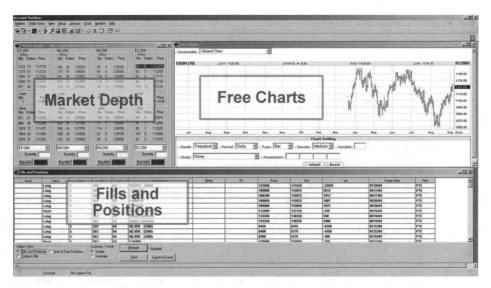

FIGURE 6.1   Lind Xpress lets you customize screens to meet your unique trading needs.
(*Source:* Lind-Waldock)

find out to which global exchanges the firm is connected. New, attractive contracts are being established all the time all around the world. If you see a trading opportunity on an overseas exchange, your broker should be able to accommodate you and be there 24 hours a day during the trading week to facilitate trading in those markets.

Simulated Trading

One of the most useful training tools to learn how to trade, how to use a trading platform, or how to test a trading system is simulated trading. Everything about the trading is real except that you use so-called virtual money instead of real money.

Although it cannot match the emotional involvement that characterizes real trading, simulated trading helps you learn the mechanics of trading and become familiar with the trading platform before you have to deal with the pressure of trading real money in real trading situations. Depending on your knowledge of trading and your skill level, it is like using a simulator to learn how to fly an airplane or drive a car before being placed in real—and possibly dangerous—situations. You enter trades, get fills, receive account statements, and so on just as an active trader does and can learn from your mistakes without having to pay real money to gain the experience. Bear in mind, however, that when you first start trading your knowledge level isn't where it will be after a few years of experience.

So don't let a few successes or failures on the simulator be the sole determinant as to how you proceed. You may want to seek help or advice from the team of professional market strategists Lind-Waldock has on staff.

TRADING SUPPORT TOOLS

You might expect that a brokerage firm's trading platform would have to be able to handle your orders and provide you with a report of what you have done. That might be all you get from some limited-service firms. But when you pay brokerage commissions, you should expect more than just a trade execution and an accurate statement. Here are some other resources the brokerage firm should provide.

Price Quotes

To keep up with the current status of the market, self-directed traders will probably need some type of price quotes updated on a regular basis. How much data you need and how often you get it will depend on the type of trader you are and the amount of money you are willing to spend.

Real-time streaming quotes are up-to-the-second prices updated continuously as prices change. Quote services usually report the last trade price, but some services also report bids and offers. Based on your level of trading activity, these quotes usually involve exchange fees of $30 to $65 per month per exchange. If you want to be an active intraday trader, you will probably need real-time quotes for those markets you trade. In some cases, exchanges offer real-time quotes at no charge to encourage trading in a market, typically for a new contract or for an area that the exchange is promoting.

Real-time delayed quotes provide the same information as real-time quotes but are delayed by 10 to 30 minutes. Obviously, this time lag will not be suitable for the active day trader. However, for the trader whose approach is not so close to the market, delayed quotes may be sufficient, and currently they do not have exchange fees as the real-time quotes do.

Snapshot quotes are live quotes but are available on a refresh basis; they do not stream. Like delayed quotes, snapshot quotes may be all you need.

End-of-day quotes provide the open, high, low, and close prices for each day, a function that used to be much simpler when markets only had regular trading hours during a day session and did not trade almost around the clock as many markets do now. This is a basic quote service used for some trading systems that provide only one signal based on a day's trading activity.

A brokerage service should offer current price quotes for a trade you are contemplating or for a market in which you have a position. In some cases, you receive a specific number of free quotes during a month and then pay on a per-quote basis after that. Active traders may receive quotes on a sliding fee basis, depending on their level of activity. Check with your broker for details on quote availability and pricing.

A broker may provide all of the futures price quotes you need, but some traders prefer to subscribe to services from data vendors because they can get equities quotes as well as futures quotes or because the vendor package includes more sophisticated or specialized charting or analytical capabilities. These data packages may be quite expensive, and you need to weigh their cost versus their potential benefit to you in your trading.

Charts

Many traders use charts of some type to show them the price history of a market, whether on a short-term basis for the day trader or on a long-term basis for the position trader. Traders need charts to study what the market has done in the past in similar situations so they can attempt to discover trading signals and projected targets based on what their analysis of the past suggests for the future.

In the past, weekly printed charts were sufficient, but in today's fast-moving markets, most charting services are offered online in a variety of formats. They may allow the user to produce monthly, weekly, daily, or intraday charts of different types for many different time frames with a click or two on a computer. Your firm should be able to offer you various levels of charting that will fit your needs.

Analytical Software

Analytical software provides a wide array of charts as well as a number of studies and technical indicators and perhaps even some means to test the performance of a trading method you develop. The studies generally range from simple moving averages to a series of momentum indicators such as stochastics or relative strength. Many are based on the same input—price—so there is a danger of putting too much weight on signals that are similar.

The system-testing capability, like simulated trading, gives you an opportunity to try out ideas in market situations without having to use real money to test a theory. You can test a variety of parameters to arrive at the best set for your risk/reward profile, but you have to be wary about overoptimizing, which can result in excellent performance on past data but then may not hold up in forward trading.

News, Reports, Statistics

Although prices respond to technical signals on charts, the underlying driving force for any significant market movement comes from fundamentals such as supply and demand. Often, these are revealed in government reports and statistics that have scheduled release dates. You need to be aware of these key dates and the numbers that traders expect to see in the reports, so you should have a source for a calendar of reports, last trading days, contract expirations, and the like.

In addition, an unexpected event can also cause extreme price fluctuations, especially in the short term, and you need to have a news source that can keep you apprised of these events in a timely manner so you can analyze how you might want to position yourself—or perhaps more important, *not* position yourself—in a market in a volatile environment. By the time you read about a market-moving event in the newspaper, it may be too late, and television news reports may be too brief and shallow to help you as a trader, assuming the event has caught the news department's attention to even be mentioned.

News services that can provide all of this information are available online and may be provided by a broker or as an add-on service for a fee. Like price quotes, the cost usually depends on whether you receive the news reports real-time or delayed and whether you need a specialized service that covers a particular market in depth.

Research Reports, Background Information

Brokerage firms offer research information of all types, from one-paragraph market summaries to white paper types of reports that include more details than most traders will ever want. If you are making your own trading decisions, you will want to have access to a variety of research sources, ranging from the end-of-day reports to the institutional-quality research that can give you insights into a market that may not be widely known.

A brokerage firm should give you reports not only on current market situations but also on trading strategies, how to analyze a market, how to trade, and other educational topics that will be helpful to traders of all skill levels.

Trading Recommendations

As a self-directed trader, you may not need anyone else's advice on what or how to trade. Even if you don't plan to use the recommendations, it can be helpful to listen to what a broker or analyst is suggesting for several reasons:

- Understand what other traders are thinking and how they might be reacting to the same type of market developments you are watching.
- Compare someone else's trading decisions with your own.
- Maybe even take a recommended trade because the analyst who presented it has probably done more research and considered more inputs than you have and has formed a good case for making the recommendation.

MATCH RESOURCES TO YOUR NEEDS

An essential resource for one trader may be impractical for another. As the opening statements in this chapter stress, the key point is not to accumulate resources but to find those that can help you most as a trader. That will depend on your trading style.

In most cases, the first place you should check for resources is your brokerage firm. If the firm doesn't have what you need or if your trading needs grow as you gain experience, then you may want to take a look at some of the many other resources now available.

CHAPTER 7

Knowing Your Margins and Marching Orders

Self-directed traders obviously should know the market they are trading and how to develop their own trading approach to analyze it to make a trading decision. But that's not the complete picture. They also should have a thorough understanding of two important concepts related to the mechanics of trading: margin requirements and order terminology.

TRADING ON MARGIN

Trading on margin in stocks is considered to be somewhat risky, especially for beginning traders. But every trader in the futures market is trading on margin. The difference is that the term *margin* has a different meaning in these two investment arenas, as the previous chapters suggest.

In stocks, you make a down payment to own shares of stock and must put up at least 50 percent of the value of the shares, a minimum margin requirement established by the Federal Reserve years ago.

In futures, you do not own anything—whether you buy or sell—but are only speculating on the price movement of the market, unless you are hedging your risk. For this right to speculate on how prices might change from your entry point, you must have a sufficient amount of money in your account to assure the marketplace that you will perform your side of the transaction when the time period for the contract expires. This amount of money is typically called margin. It actually should be called a good-faith deposit or a performance bond because that is how it functions, but because *margin* is the conventional term commonly used by traders, we'll use it in this discussion.

Exchanges set the minimum margin requirements for each contract, continually adjusting the amount to account for the value of the contract, volatility, and other market conditions. At the most basic level, suffice it to say that margins are designed to cover a normal or average move in the market without incurring a debit at the account level over a reasonable period of time.

Exchanges adjust minimum margins regularly, and clearing member firms are at liberty to require higher amounts. Therefore, you need to check with your broker to see what the current requirements are.

There are two types of margin:

1. *Initial margin* is the sum required to establish a futures position for the purpose of holding it overnight.
2. *Maintenance margin* is the minimum balance required to maintain a futures position.

Beginners often think they have to add the two numbers together to arrive at the margin requirement for what they are trading, but that is not correct. Maintenance margin is really a subset of initial margin. *Margin calls*, a term that sometimes creates anxiety, happen when your account balance falls below maintenance margin levels.

Maintenance margin is usually a smaller number than initial margin and doesn't come into play unless the account balance shrinks due to losses. If the value of the account balance falls below the maintenance level, then you are required to get the account back into compliance (a margin call). You can do this either by sending more money (raising the balance back up to the initial margin) or by lightening up your positions (lowering the initial margin back down to the balance).

For example, if the initial margin requirement is $4,000 per contract, you will need to have at least that much money available in your account to buy or sell a single contract that you hold overnight. If the maintenance margin requirement is $2,800 and the value of your account balance falls below that amount, you will get a margin call requiring you to bring your balance back to at least $4,000. However, if your position generates a gain, you can withdraw any excess funds (those funds above the required initial margin) or use them to fund additional market positions.

Minimum initial margins on futures typically run 4 percent to 10 percent of contract value with a few exceptions, most notably single-stock futures, which have a minimum initial margin of 20 percent of the contract's value. To determine the actual percentage rate at any time, find out the current margin requirement from your broker and divide that number by the full contract value. For example, if the initial margin on E-mini S&P futures is $4,000 and the full contract value is $55,000 (1100 × $50), your initial margin is about 7.3 percent of the contract's value compared to the 50 percent you are required to have to purchase stocks.

The fact that margin requirements are such a small portion of contract value underlies the most important feature of futures trading: leverage. Assume that with the $4,000 initial margin on one E-mini S&P contract, you decide to buy December E-mini S&P futures at 1070 and the market then rises to 1080. The 10-point move is not uncommon on any given day. Whether you offset or stay in the market, your account has appreciated by $500, which is 12.5 percent of the margin or performance bond.

Of course, the opposite holds true for a move 10 points lower; if you are long, you could lose 12.5 percent of your money with a 10-point decline. Leverage is a powerful tool, but it is a double-edged sword. Traders should understand the impact that low margins and leverage can have before getting into a futures position.

ORDER TYPES

Everything you know about trading will not be very useful if you do not know how to tell the market what you want to do. Your wish is conveyed to the market in a variety of orders that specify the contract, quantity, price, conditions, and time frame to buy or sell. The type of order you choose and the manner in which you use it play a big role in how you enter or exit a position.

Exchanges and brokerage firms offer a large number of acceptable order types for all active markets. The most common and those you will probably find the most useful are market, limit, stop, and market on close (MOC) orders. All open-outcry markets accept those orders as well as many others. However, not all electronic exchanges accept all of these orders all of the time. For instance, e-cbot, the Chicago Board of Trade's electronic platform, does not accept a market order before the open, but a market order is accepted during trading hours. In addition, some electronic exchanges do not accept open orders or require stop orders to be made as stop limit or stop with limit orders.

When placing orders, it is important to be aware of proper price increments and trading conventions for markets that you are trading. Unlike securities, individual futures markets vary greatly in terms of contract size, price increments, and valid order types. For instance, grain futures trade in $1/4$-cent increments, bond futures in 1/32nds, and gold futures in 10-cent ticks. Correct prices stated in the correct way are essential to create a valid order that will be accepted by an online trading platform or by the trading floor.

An open order is good until canceled or filled or until the product goes off the board—that is, the contract has expired and is no longer available for trading. Open orders are also referred to as good till canceled (GTC). A day order is good only for the regular trading session during which it is placed or for the next session if placed in between sessions. All orders are assumed to be day orders unless otherwise specified.

Entry/Exit Orders

Here are brief descriptions of the most used orders and when and how they are employed. The online abbreviations often used on trading platforms are shown in parentheses.

Market Order (MKT)   A market order is filled at the first available opportunity. Buy orders are filled at the first available offer, and sell orders are filled at the first available bid. A market order is the fastest and surest way to get a fill. In most situations, you cannot cancel a market order if the market is open.

When placing orders over the telephone, you say "at the market" instead of stipulating a price. If you are trading online, trading platforms usually have you select "MKT" from a drop-down menu under "Order Type," and you leave the price field blank.

Use this order when you definitely want a fill and are not concerned about possible slippage. Some traders are unable to watch real-time market prices, so only market orders will suffice.

Stop Order (STOP)   Commonly referred to as a stop-loss, stops are often used as loss limiting orders, indicating that you want to get out of the market at a specified target level if the market trades at or through your stop price. Buy stops are placed above the market and become market orders if the market trades or is bid at or above your stop price. Sell stops are placed below the market and become market orders if the market trades or is offered at or below your stop price. Generally, bids and offers affect stops only in open outcry markets.

Although stops are most commonly used to exit a losing position, they can also be used to protect profits or to enter positions as markets move into territory considered to be a favorable entry point. Keep in mind that, although stops become market orders when elected, they are subject to slippage. Slippage occurs in fast-moving markets when stops are filled at prices worse than the stop price. In addition, in markets with limits, stops may be "unable"—that is, not able to be filled because no trades are allowed beyond the established limit moves. A stop placed as an open order, or GTC, may be "unable" for several successive sessions if the market is in a limit up or limit down situation but will be filled at the first available opportunity.

When placing a stop order on the telephone, it is important to use the word *stop* for the order type at the end of your order placement instructions. Stops on electronic-only markets usually have to be placed daily.

This order is mainly used to exit markets, hence the term *stop-loss*, but it can be used to enter positions on a favorable price signal or to protect profits and liquidate positions as markets start to rise or retreat.

Limit Order (LMT)   A limit order specifies that you only want to be filled at the limit price or better. A limit buy order is placed below the market, while a limit sell order is placed above the current market price. Although a limit order implies "or better," it is useful to say "or lower" for buy orders and "or higher" for sell orders.

A limit order provides protection against slippage and is advisable in thin markets. However, a limit order does not guarantee you will get into a position even if the price you specify is hit. If you absolutely must be sure to get into or out of a position, you should probably use a market or stop order.

Use a limit order when you want a position at a specific price or better and in thin markets to enter positions and possibly also to exit positions. However, you must be prepared to watch markets if you believe you have to trade with limits.

Or Better (OB) The use of this term is helpful when placing limit orders when the market is trading at or through your limit price. The "OB" designation indicates that your order is indeed a limit order. For example, you may use an "OB" order type such as, "For account 12345, buy 5 March yen at 9345 OB" when the last price in the market is 9344. That indicates you are willing to pay 9345 or less, but you do not want to buy if the market rises to 9346 or higher. "OB" isn't needed in fully electronic markets, and can be counterproductive in open-outcry markets. You may want to check with your broker before using "OB."

Stop Limit (STL) A buy stop limit order becomes a limit order at the stop price when the market trades or is bid at or above the stop price. A sell stop limit becomes a limit order at the stop price when the market trades or is offered at or below the stop price. The stop and limit are the same price. These orders are designed to eliminate slippage on stops. However, they may come back "unable," which simply means they are not able to be filled, and cannot be considered as protection in fast-moving markets.

This is not a common order type in open-outcry markets but may be almost a necessity on some electronic markets due to lack of liquidity. However, many other electronic markets are now very deep, and the use of such orders is generally unnecessary. In addition, the possibility of an "unable" renders these order types useless in terms of protection.

Stop with Limit (STWL) This order type is similar to a stop limit in that a limit price is established. However, the limit on a stop with limit is different from the stop price and provides some allowance for slippage on the stop. Once the stop is elected, the order works as a limit order and, as is the case with the stop limit order, may come back "unable" so it cannot be considered as protection in fast-moving markets. Although created for use in open-outcry trading, these orders are most functional on electronic platforms that accept them, such as Globex.

This order is useful when you want to place limit orders slightly above the market on buys and slightly below the market on sells. The additional room to fill the order may eliminate missed market opportunities. However, check with your broker before using this order type actively.

Market on Close (MOC)   Use this order if you want to be filled during the closing price range. An MOC is a market order that is executable only during the closing range and can be filled at any price in the closing range. The closing range is a defined period of time that varies by market, usually the last 30 seconds or one minute of trading.

Use this order when you do not want to carry a position overnight. Many day traders use MOCs to close out positions on the close.

Market if Touched (MIT)   An MIT is similar to a stop but is positioned on the opposite side of the market. A buy MIT is placed below the market while a sell MIT is placed above the market. An MIT becomes a market order when elected. For example, with the market in April live cattle trading at 8420, you may place an order such as, "Buy 4 April live cattle at 8390 MIT." If the market trades at or below the trigger price, your order becomes a market order and can be filled at the first available opportunity.

As with a stop, this order type is also subject to slippage because you may not be filled at your MIT price. Using the same example, an appropriate sell MIT would be placed at any price above 8420, such as 8435. Some traders use this type of order to enter markets that trade to price levels that appear to be good entry points.

Unlike a limit order, which can be "unable" if the market trades only at but not through a price, an MIT becomes a market order if elected and will almost certainly be filled. In most cases, you will not miss the market if you correctly determine the bottom or top for the session.

This type of order is great when you are able to pick a peak or valley and want to enter a position. It avoids the frustration of limit orders when the market trades at the specified price but the order is not filled.

Stop Close Only (SCO)   This is a stop order that will be executable if the day's closing range is at or through your stop price. There is no reference point to determine if this is a good order and, as such, it can be placed at any price within the day's allowable range. If the market has no limit, there are no such restrictions within reason.

Use an SCO when you do not want a stop order to be activated during the session but do want it to be activated if the market trades at your stop order level during the closing price range. This order helps you avoid being taken out of a position on a stop that might be hit during intraday price fluctuations.

Order Cancels Order (OCO)   This order type actually gives the broker two instructions at once. Execution of one order automatically cancels the other. Buy and/or sell instructions cannot be combined. For option orders, the order can only include one strike price and can be for either calls or puts but not both. An OCO is not allowed on many markets, so be sure to check with your broker.

The most common use of an OCO is to take profits if the market trades to a certain level but to get out if it goes too far against you. For example, if March

S&P 500 index futures are trading at 1142 and you are long one contract, you may place an order such as, "Sell 1 March S&P at 1155, OCO, 1132 stop." If the market trades to 1156, you can expect to be filled on the limit order, and the stop will be canceled by the executing broker. If the market trades to 1132 first, you will be filled on the stop, and the limit will be canceled. The broker will execute whichever comes first.

Cancellation Orders

In some cases, you may just want to cancel an order or replace the original order with another order. As long as the original order is not a market order and has not been executed, there are specific orders to accomplish this goal.

Straight Cancel (CXL)   If you have an order working that you no longer want working, you may attempt to straight cancel. These instructions are clear that you do not want a fill on the order. If the order has already been filled or the cancel instructions do not reach the broker in time to stop the order from being filled, you will receive a "too late to cancel" (TLTC) notification. Depending on market conditions, the TLTC response may not be immediate.

Electronic-only markets generally provide an immediate "confirm out" (discussed later) once an order is canceled, sometimes denoted by an asterisk next to the order number. A confirm out on an order placed for open-outcry trading may require a response from the floor through your broker.

When placing a straight cancel over the telephone, inform your broker or order desk that you wish to straight cancel an order and follow the same procedure as you would to place a new order. For example, you could say: "For account 12345, access code 6789, straight cancel order number 481 to sell 4 March E-mini S&P at 113850."

Because the E-mini S&P is a strictly electronic market, a confirm out would be nearly instantaneous and could be provided by the broker if asked.

Canceling an order while trading online merely involves selecting the working order and submitting the cancel instruction. Bear in mind that an order submitted for cancel is not the same as a "cancel confirmed" or "confirm out." Never assume an order is out unless actually confirmed out by your broker.

Cancel Replace (CXL REP)   These instructions are used to modify an existing order. A cancel replace must be for the same contract and delivery month. Buy/sell instructions cannot be changed, but you are allowed to change quantity, price, and order type. In addition, you can change open/day order designation.

Placing a CXL REP over the telephone is basically the same as cancel order instructions. You inform your broker or order desk that you wish to cancel and replace a working order and provide the details on the working order. Once the working order has been found, you can proceed with the instructions to modify. For example: "This is Smith, account number 12345, access code 6789. I want to cancel replace order number 481, which is selling 4 March E-mini S&P at 113850. The new order is to sell 4 March E-mini S&P at 113600."

If you are trading online, you select the order you wish to modify and choose "Replace." The screen will pull up the existing order and allow you to make modifications within the stated parameters. It may be too late to cancel the order, at which point the new order would be out and you would receive a fill on the original order. In some open-outcry cases, you may receive notification that you are TLTC and prices follow later.

Confirm Out   An order is confirmed out when it is verified as not working or filled. As mentioned earlier, orders for electronic markets are usually confirmed out instantaneously and are noted as such through various means, depending on the trading platform.

However, a number of U.S. markets trade in open-outcry pits or rings, as they are referred to in New York. Open outcry presents a variety of circumstances with which traders must deal, and a market's trading platform is the most important determinant in the time it takes to receive information about orders. Regardless of order-routing technology, a confirm out on an order sent to open outcry must be obtained by your broker or order desk.

Options Orders

Options on futures orders are placed in the same fashion as futures orders, with the addition of two other pieces of information: strike price and whether the position is a call or put. Insert that information between the commodity name and the price, if any. For example, with the March bond 112 calls trading at 1-35:

Limit order: "Buy 2 March bond 112 calls at 1-26."

Stop order: "Sell 2 March bond 112 calls at 1-25 stop."

Your broker or electronic platform will also ask if the trade is to open or offset a position. This information is obtained for purposes of placing the order but does not confirm your position in the market.

One other important note about options orders: Option price increments may differ from the underlying futures contract increments. In the preceding orders, for example, note that Treasury bond options are priced in 64ths while futures are priced in 32nds. Be sure to check the contract specifications or ask your broker.

Futures Spread Orders

A futures spread order involves the simultaneous purchase and sale of the same or related contracts. Most spreads involve two legs—a purchase of one contract month and the sale of another, usually at a simple differential.

Spread orders are used by traders who trade changes in price relationships between two markets as well as those who are simply rolling positions from month to month as they get close to first notice days or last trading days. The spread order ensures that both sides of the trade are filled, so there is no worry of legging out and missing the market on one side. A broker cannot return the order with a fill on one side only. The spread order is either filled on all sides or not filled.

Spreads are quoted with one contract at a premium to the other. A premium is the difference in prices between the months or contracts being spread. When placing an order, the premium nearly always goes on the higher-priced contract of the spread.

For example, with April cattle futures quoted at 7475 and June cattle futures at 7075, the premium "on the board" is 400 to the April side. "On the board" refers to the spread price based on quotes, which may not accurately reflect where the spread is trading in the pit. In open-outcry markets, it may be necessary to get a spread bid/offer from the pit to determine the true market, especially if one or both sides of the spread are at the daily limit. For the cattle example, a sample telephone order would be: "For account 12345, access code 6789, spread order, buy 3 June cattle, sell 3 April cattle at 400 to the April side."

This order may be used by a trader who is long 3 April cattle and is looking to roll the position to the June contract. If the order is filled, April would have to be priced at least 410 points over the June contract, and one of the sides of the spread price would have to be within the day's possible trading range. The actual prices on each leg would be determined in the pit.

A few important points to note about spreads:

- Although outright prices can indicate where a spread may be trading, only an actual bid/offer will provide true spread premiums.
- Some markets, most notably interest rates and currencies, have pricing conventions that do not necessarily equate to the norm of premium to the higher side. As a result, some markets may utilize negative spread premiums. Consult your broker if you are unsure as to the correct pricing convention.
- Although traditional markets generally adhere to premium to the higher side, markets can invert. For instance, referring to the cattle example, suppose April cattle trade at 7230 and June at 7170, with a premium on the board at 60 to the April side. It is acceptable to place an order that reads: "Buy 2 April cattle and sell 2 June cattle, with the premium at 30 to the June side." This order means that the market would have to invert, and June would have to trade at a premium to April by at least 30 points. Because the prices are relatively close to begin with, this order is not unusual.
- Spreads can be traded at even, meaning the same price on both legs and also implying "or any premium to the sell side."
- Spread premiums on listed electronic spreads are readily available.

Option Spread Orders

Option spread orders work essentially the same as futures spread orders, with a few notable exceptions. Premiums are derived using the same premises as discussed under futures spreads. However, a greater variety of spreads is accessible with options. We will mention only the most actively traded scenarios, using these prices:

> April gold 420 calls trading at 700
>
> April gold 440 calls trading at 300
>
> April gold 410 calls trading at 1000
>
> April gold 410 puts trading at 1210

A typical spread order might be: "Account 12345, access code 6789, place an option spread order. Buy 2 April gold 420 calls, sell 2 April gold 440 calls, premium 380 to the buy side."

Note the premium is 400 "on the board"; you do not double the premium to do a two-lot spread. Always use the lowest common denominator when calculating an option spread.

Conversely, an account may be long the 420 calls and may wish to roll to the 440 calls. This could be accomplished by placing this spread order: "Buy 2 April gold 440 calls and sell 2 April gold 420 calls, premium 410 to the sell side."

An account may wish to place an order to buy both the calls and puts, expecting a big move in the market but not sure which way. To accomplish this, you could place this order: "Account 12345, access code 6789, option spread order. Buy 3 April gold 410 calls and buy 3 April gold 410 puts at 2200." Again, the premium is calculated at 1:1 and is not multiplied by 3.

These examples are just a few of the almost unlimited ways that option spreads can be placed to accomplish your objectives. Keep in mind that many options are not very liquid, they may not trade frequently, and last prices may not be relevant although theoretical values revealed by an option calculator may be a pretty good indicator of where these spreads may trade.

PLACING ORDERS

If you place orders online, the trading platform will pretty much direct you through the order process—although it won't prevent you from making a mistake such as entering "Buy" when you meant "Sell." If you telephone your orders, setting up a similar procedure not only will help you organize your paperwork but also will greatly reduce the possibility of an error due to miscommunication.

When using the phone, place orders in a clear and concise fashion by following the same pattern for every order. For example, with March bonds trading at 110-28, you might say: "Buy 10 March bonds at 110-21." Add GTC if applicable. The word *limit* is not necessary on a telephone order; it is assumed.

State other order types such as a stop at the end of the order to avoid confusion. Saying "I would like to place a stop" and then reading the order without saying "stop" for the order type may result in an error. For example, say: "Buy 10 March bonds at 111-05 stop."

A market order implies no specific price, so the price field is blank when entered online. The resulting order would read: "Buy 10 March bonds at the market."

In addition, day orders are assumed, and it is not necessary to specify that.

Hints for Placing Orders

Here are some other important points to remember in placing orders:

- Phone clerks are instructed to listen carefully to the order you want to place and will read the order back to you for your okay. Make sure they have read the exact order you intended.
- Day orders with prices on markets that have daily limits must be placed within the day's trading range.
- Limit moves or circuit breakers may preclude orders from being filled. In addition, market and stop orders may be filled at prices that you may not expect.
- Fast market conditions on open-outcry markets may lengthen the time it takes to get an order filled or canceled or to obtain a response from the floor. Government report releases and extraordinary news items are the most common causes of fast markets, but they can occur at any time as determined by the exchange.
- Use discretion in placing orders. In markets with no limit, do not place day orders way off the market. Be especially diligent when canceling and replacing orders. Open-outcry markets are sensitive to the amount of paper going into the pits, and every new order instruction adds to the total. It is not necessary to chase markets by changing an order every tick or two or moving your stop every time the market moves another two ticks.
- If you are using OCOs, do not place the limit and stop orders too close together because that can cause problems for the filling brokers.
- Cancel the opposite side if working both stop and limit orders. Be sure to check working orders constantly.
- Be sure to cancel an open order stop if you decide to exit a position before the stop is elected. Stops are not canceled automatically; you must place the cancel instructions.
- It is imperative to specify "open order" if, in fact, you do want a GTC order. All orders are assumed to be day orders unless otherwise specified.

- If products trade on more than one exchange, it is important to specify which product it is that you would like to trade. In cases where there is a clear dominant product, your broker will often assume that you are trading the highly liquid, dominant product unless you specify otherwise.
- Many products now trade side by side on both the floor and the computer, as is the case with currencies at the Chicago Mercantile Exchange and financials at the Chicago Board of Trade. If you are not getting input from your broker, it is important to specify where you would like the order to work. To trade single-stock futures, you must stipulate the exchange, or your broker will ask.
- The names of some months sound alike—September and December, for example. To avoid errors, many firms use "September Labor Day" and "December Christmas" when reading back orders.
- Numbers such as 15 and 50 or 16 and 60 also sound alike and should be read as "Fifteen, that's one five" or "Sixty, that's six zero" on quantities and prices.

Trading online can eliminate much of the confusion that may occur with telephone order placement. All you have to do is familiarize yourself with the trading platform, especially the symbols. Electronic trading depends totally on choosing the right symbol for the product you are interested in trading.

For instance, if you wish to trade the yen on Globex, you must use a different symbol than you would if you want to trade the yen open-outcry market. If you place a market order in the yen on Friday afternoon at 3 P.M. Central time, the order will go in a queue for Monday's open if you use the open-outcry symbol. However, it will be filled on Friday afternoon if you use the Globex symbol! That could make quite a difference in the trade's outcome. Make sure you receive an order number as confirmation.

Learning and becoming comfortable with the trading platform can streamline the order placement process and make the whole experience more enjoyable.

TIPS ABOUT TRADING MECHANICS

Here are a few issues to consider before placing futures or options orders.

Margin Calls

In general, if you get a margin call, it means that the market has moved against your position. Many professional traders and money managers advise against ever meeting a margin call. Meeting the call means wiring the amount of money necessary to bring the account back to full initial margin. Other options include offsetting positions or a combination of both wiring money and offsetting some contracts. In any event, your broker will insist that you take some action to reduce the overall exposure and risk, or the position will be closed for you.

If you decide to offset, your broker may want you to place stops to protect the account from going debit while you are still holding positions. Do not be offended by this. The broker is merely following the firm's fiduciary responsibility to both the clearing member to maintain the integrity of the market and, most important, to you the client.

Some strategies to reduce risk include adding positions by spreading with both futures and options. However, these strategies are not recommended when you are on margin call.

Another strategy to deal with adverse market movement is to simply avoid incurring a margin call by reducing the size of your positions gradually as needed. Some traders employ a strategy whereby they wire funds to hit the account before a call is incurred. The additional funds can buy some time, and if the amount sent puts the account above the minimum maintenance margin requirement, it may be less than you would have had to send to get back to full initial margin in the event of a margin call. Sending additional funds is okay, but it defeats the principle of not meeting a margin call.

Deliveries

Taking physical delivery of a commodity (where that provision applies) is not intended for individual investors, and you should avoid the delivery process. It is relatively easy to take delivery of some products such as grains and precious metals and retender because they simply involve exchanging receipts and money. However, for other products such as livestock and coffee, the process is not easy and can involve significant expenses. Delivery expenses can include additional commissions, surcharges for processing the delivery, storage, interest, insurance, and replacement of product that fails inspection. Rule of thumb: If you want to maintain a position, roll into the next active month and do so while open interest remains high.

First Notice Day and Last Trading Day

Contract specifications vary dramatically from product to product. Deliverable products may have a first notice day (FND) before the last trading day (LTD), giving traders who take delivery the option to redeliver the product and offset the position. When the FND is before the LTD, most contracts allow an offset up to the business day before FND to avoid a possible delivery notice.

Other deliverable products may have LTD before FND, which usually means that, if you are holding a position through the close on LTD, you are obligated to make or take delivery. In this case, FND is handled by the exchange as a means of matching buyers and sellers, as is the case with energy contracts.

Individual investors should avoid last trading days in futures. Clients should exit positions at least one day before the LTD, the sooner the better. Some products will have active liquid markets almost up to expiration, but the deeper into the LTD session, the more volatile the price swings can be as liquidity dries up. Products with difficult deliveries are especially dangerous and should be avoided on LTDs. This point cannot be stressed enough.

Cash Settlement

Final contract settlement in cash on expiration day has gained in popularity over the past few years as more contracts adopt that provision. Although primarily the domain of indexes, other products are cash-settled, including some physical commodities. Cash-settled contracts can be held through expiration and do not have to be offset. At expiration, an offsetting trade is added to your account at the final contract settlement price. This book entry closes out the trade, puts the money right in the account or takes it out, and completes the round turn for commission purposes.

Keep in mind that the cash-settlement algorithm will vary by market and may not be what you expect. Consult your broker for details. If you are in doubt and you do not want to take on any perceived cash-settlement exposure, offset your position before it expires.

Option Expirations

Long options on futures positions may be exercised. Short options on futures positions may be assigned. Most U.S. options are exercised automatically if they are in the money by a tick, meaning that the holder of a long call becomes long the underlying futures at the strike price and the holder of a long put becomes short the underlying futures at the strike price. Having a futures position may come as a surprise to those who gave up on a long option as it expired. Long options can be abandoned on the option's last trading day, meaning that no action is taken.

Short option holders in the money by a tick or more as of expiration may be assigned—a short call may become a short position in the underlying futures at the strike price and a short put may become long the underlying futures at the strike price. You can never assume that an in-the-money short option will be assigned or expire worthless. Out-of-the-money short options can be assigned, so if you hold a short option through the close on LTD for the option, you will not know for certain exactly what your position will be when the next session opens. In practice, however, far out-of-the-money options are often assumed to be worthless and rarely have any repercussions.

Short option holders must also consider "pin risk"—that is, when the underlying futures contract settles exactly at the strike price. In this scenario, they have to wait until shortly before the next regular trading session to determine their position. Some traders will offset short options on LTD and spend a small premium to do so, just to ensure they know their position.

If a long option holder is expecting to take an automatic exercise, the account should have enough funds to cover the resulting margin for the underlying futures position acquired. The account can use the open trade profit on the new futures position when making the calculation. A broker may liquidate options in accounts that are not funded properly to hold the resulting futures positions.

Early exercise is another possibility if the option is illiquid. Many options are thinly traded. Some traders may execute futures trades that can offset an option position if exercised and give exercise instructions to their broker. This process will cost the trader a round-turn futures commission but may more than compensate for a poor bid/offer on the option. The exercise on American options can be done at any time up to and including the option's last trading day.

With the exception of serial options, cash-settled futures also means cash-settled options. The cash settlement on the option is based on the final settlement price for the underlying futures contract, which can be confusing, especially in regard to S&P options. A quarterly cycle S&P option (March, June, September, December) is cash-settled to the futures settlement. The futures settlement is calculated the morning after the last trading day and can vary significantly from the last traded futures price.

Serial options on cash-settled futures are not cash-settled options. This is a very important point. A serial option refers to an option month that is not part of the regular cycle but is based on a futures month that is part of the normal cycle. For instance, a February S&P option is a serial option based on the March futures contract. The March futures and options are cash-settled, but the February option is not. If a February S&P option is exercised or assigned, the resulting futures position will be for the March contract.

CONNECTIVITY ISSUES AND QUESTIONS

In the age of technology, glitches can and still do occur. For a trader who has become accustomed to trading online, a computer crash or a power outage at either the trader's end or the brokerage or exchange end can be a traumatic situation, especially for the trader who has a sizable position in an actively trading market. For that reason, some active traders maintain redundant data feeds and brokerage connections to give them alternatives if there is any disruption to their normal trading setup.

In the event of technological difficulties or questions about orders, you should not hesitate to call the brokerage firm's trade desk. Situations may arise that you are unsure how to handle. For instance, e-cbot, the Chicago Board of Trade's electronic platform, does not allow a market order before the open on any of its products. If you place a market order on e-cbot in bonds, for example, you may receive an error message that indicates that your order is not working. Every electronic platform has its own nuances, and the messages you receive may not always be clear.

When in doubt, place a call. Many brokerage firms have trade centers staffed 24 hours a day from Sunday afternoon through Friday afternoon and may be able to deal with your trading questions and concerns before an issue gets out of hand.

CHAPTER 8

Futures

Diverse Markets
You Can Trade

Investors have thousands of stocks from which to choose—in fact, one of the biggest challenges that stock market investors have is that there are many more stocks than most traders can ever hope to analyze or trade. They can spend far more time finding good candidates to trade than they do deciding how to trade them.

In contrast, futures traders focus on relatively few markets and can put more effort into their trading methods. But don't think futures traders are lacking in markets to trade. From futures on individual stocks or stock indexes to futures on government Treasury issues to futures on commodities, traders have hundreds of contracts from which to choose in the United States and around the world.

Although most American traders stick to trading products on U.S. exchanges, the advent of online trading access to electronically traded markets has expanded the horizon. Indeed, a U.S. futures trader could make a trade somewhere in the world anytime from Sunday afternoon, when the markets open in Australia, until Friday afternoon, when the U.S. markets close for the week. That's nearly 120 continuous hours of market availability.

This chapter explains what types of futures contracts are listed, so you understand some of the more popular products. Broadly, all futures markets fall into one of three categories: equity-based, financial instruments, or commodities. Until currency futures began trading in 1972, futures markets were clearly designated as commodity markets because the products traded were mainly agricultural. However, trading in futures on financial products has boomed since the mid-1970s and now accounts for about 75 percent of all derivatives trading volume in the world, with commodities and natural resources accounting for just 25 percent of today's volume (see Figure 8.1, Table 8.1, and Table 8.2).

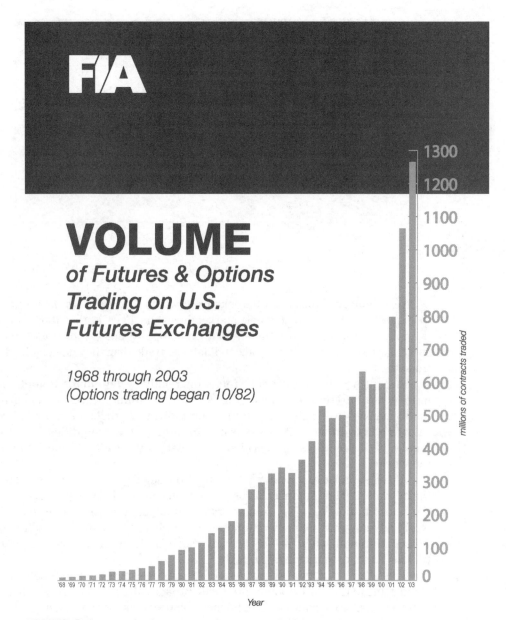

FIGURE 8.1   Growth of Futures Trading on U.S. Exchanges. (*Source:* Futures Industry Association)

TABLE 8.1 Top 20 Exchanges Worldwide by Exchange Contract Volume in 2004

Exchange	2003	2004
Eurex	1,014,932,312	1,065,639,010
Chicago Mercantile Exchange	640,209,634	805,341,681
Euronext.liffe	694,970,981	790,381,989
Chicago Board of Trade	454,190,749	599,994,386
Chicago Board Options Exchange	283,946,495	361,086,774
International Securities Exchange	244,968,190	360,852,519
Bovespa	177,223,140	235,349,514
Mexican Derivatives Exchange	173,820,944	210,395,264
American Stock Exchange	180,074,778	202,680,929
BM&F	120,785,602	183,427,938
New York Mercantile Exchange	137,225,439	161,103,746
Philadelphia Stock Exchange	112,705,597	133,401,278
Pacific Exchange	86,152,637	103,262,458
OMX Exchanges	74,105,690	94,382,633
Dalian Commodity Exchange	74,973,493	88,034,153
National Stock Exchange of India	43,081,968	75,093,629
Tokyo Commodity Exchange	87,252,219	74,511,734
London Metal Exchange	72,308,327	71,906,901
Taiwan Futures Exchange	31,874,934	64,973,429
Korea Futures Exchange*	2,912,894,034	2,586,818,602

*Korea Futures Exchange ranks number one in terms of volume because of the large size of its KOSPI 200 futures and options contracts.
Source: Futures Industry Association.

EQUITY-BASED FUTURES

It's not surprising that some of the most popular futures contracts are related to the equity markets, the most prevalent form of investment. Most major economies with a vibrant stock market also have a futures contract on a stock index that represents that particular economy. For example, in the United States, futures contracts are available on the Dow Jones Industrial Average as well as the broader Standard & Poor's (S&P) 500 Index and the technology-oriented Nasdaq-100 index. Other countries have similar futures contracts, such as the FTSE-100 for the United Kingdom, the Hang Seng in Hong Kong, and the CAC 40 in France; the Dow Jones Euro STOXX 50 covers selected stocks in the euro economy.

All stock markets are influenced by news about the domestic economy, inflation, currency values, politics, interest rates, and the like, because those are the factors that affect companies' earning potential. Technical factors such as tick volume and breadth also come into play.

TABLE 8.2 Top 20 Contracts Traded Worldwide (in millions—net of individual equities)

Contracts Traded	2003	2004
3-Month Eurodollar Futures, CME	208.77	297.58
Euro-Bund Futures, Eurex	244.41	239.79
TIIE 28 Futures, MexDer	162.08	206.03
10-Year T-Note Futures, CBOT	146.45	196.12
E-mini S&P 500 Index Futures, CME	161.18	167.20
Euro-Bobl Futures, Eurex	150.09	159.17
3-Month Euribor Futures, Euronext.liffe	137.69	157.75
3-Month Eurodollar Options, CME	100.82	130.60
Euro-Schatz Futures, Eurex	117.37	122.93
DJ Euro Stoxx 50 Futures, Eurex	116.04	121.66
5-Year T-Note Futures, CBOT	73.75	105.47
Interest Rate Futures, BM&F	57.64	100.29
E-mini Nasdaq 100 Futures, CME	67.89	77.17
30-Year T-Bond Futures, CBOT	63.52	72.95
DJ Euro Stoxx 50 Options, Eurex	61.79	71.41
CAC 40 Index Options, Euronext.liffe	73.67	63.15
No. 1 Soybeans Futures, DCE	60.00	57.34
10-Year T-Note Options, CBOT	41.17	56.88
Kospi 200 Futures, Kofex	62.20	55.61
Kospi 200 Options, Kofex*	2,837.72	2,521.56

*Kospi 200 options trading on the Korea Futures Exchange rank number one in terms of volume, but their rank is based on their comparatively large contract size of KRW100,000 × the index.
Source: Futures Industry Association.

Stock Indexes

Stock index futures contracts were introduced in the United States in 1982, nine years after listed equity options began trading at the Chicago Board Options Exchange (CBOE), the equity options offshoot of the Chicago Board of Trade (CBOT). Interestingly, the CBOT had come up with the idea of futures on stocks in the mid-1960s as a way to diversify its product line.

The Kansas City Board of Trade launched the first stock index futures contract on the Value Line Index in February 1982, followed a few months later by the S&P 500 Index futures contract on the Chicago Mercantile Exchange (CME), which quickly became the leader and continues to dominate U.S. stock index futures trading more than 20 years later. A number of stock index futures and options contracts are now available to traders, covering all areas of the stock market. Here are the major indexes that you are most likely to trade.

S&P 500 Index The Standard & Poor's 500 stock index is a market value-weighted index of 500 large-capitalized stocks traded on the New York Stock

Exchange, American Stock Exchange, and the Nasdaq National Market Execution system. Because the S&P 500 Index is capitalization-weighted, those stocks with the most shares outstanding at the highest prices will have the most influence on the index movement. The S&P 500 Index, introduced in 1957, is currently the investment industry's standard for measuring portfolio performance.

The original S&P 500 Index futures contract was valued at $500 times the index. As the stock market began to surge higher, the index more than doubled in three years. With the index approaching the 1000 level, the value of the contract neared $500,000, and a 10-point change in the index was worth $5,000. The margin requirement for that size contract priced many traders out of the market as the risk became too large.

So the CME took two significant steps:

1. Introduced an S&P 500 Index futures contract that was one-tenth the size of the original S&P 500 contract in September 1997. At $50 times the S&P 500 Index, the value of this new E-mini contract brought the initial margin down to around $4,000.

2. Took a page out of the book of stock splits, cutting the value of the big S&P 500 Index futures contract in half to $250 times the index beginning in mid-November 1997.

Even with a margin requirement of only about 6 percent of the contract's value, the rising stock market put the initial margin at $15,000 with this $250,000 contract, keeping the S&P futures contract out of the reach of many individual speculators. The E-mini put the S&P 500 Index within the capabilities of many individual accounts.

But the real innovation was letting small orders of this new E-mini market trade entirely on an electronic platform and not in the traditional open-outcry pits. CME officials decided that trading orders could take place entirely on a trade-matching computer with no human intervention, giving traders direct access to the market without going through an order handler. Electronic trading would no longer be limited to after-hours trading or to supplement the primary pit contract, but it became the mainstream market for the E-mini contracts as the allowable number of contracts was increased over time. And, as long as trading was all computer-based, the CME also decided it might as well keep the market open almost 24 hours a day.

The radical move caught the wave of online trading and day trading that was revolutionizing the stock market at the same time. Opening-day volume for the E-mini S&P 500 on September 9, 1997, totaled 7,987 contracts. That doesn't sound like much compared to today's volume, which sometimes tops one million contracts a day. But it was the best first day for any CME product, including the big S&P 500 contract. In only a little over a year, the E-mini S&P was the third most active stock index contract in the country, trailing only the big S&P 500 futures contract and options on S&P 500 futures.

The term *E-mini* has come to denote any futures contract (particularly stock indexes) on any exchange whose contract value is appealing to individual investors and trades on an electronic platform. However, "E-mini" is actually a trademark of the CME and has been applied to a variety of CME markets, from stock index to foreign exchange to livestock.

Nasdaq-100 Index   The Nasdaq-100 index is a modified market capitalization index and includes the top 100 nonfinancial stocks (both domestic and foreign) listed on the Nasdaq Stock Market. Dominated by stocks such as Microsoft, Intel, Cisco, and Dell, the index is frequently associated with the historically notorious high-flying technology sector of the stock market.

Futures on the Nasdaq-100 Index began trading in 1996 with a value of $100 times the index. Like the S&P 500 index, the value of the Nasdaq-100 zoomed in the late 1990s, pushing initial margins higher and higher. So the CME followed the same pattern as it did with the E-mini S&P 500 and launched electronically traded E-mini Nasdaq-100 index futures in 1999 with a value of $20 times the index.

Russell 1000 and 2000 Indexes   Futures contracts trade actively on two subsets of the Russell 3000 index developed by the Frank Russell Company as a benchmark for institutional investors. The Russell 1000 tracks the largest 1,000 stocks, and is considered a benchmark for large-capitalization stocks among institutions. The Russell 2000 includes the smallest 2,000 stocks of the Russell 3000 and is considered a small-capitalization benchmark.

The New York Board of Trade (NYBOT) was the first to list Russell 1000 futures in March 1999. Although the CME began trading Russell 2000 futures in 1993, the E-mini version, launched in October 2001, has attracted the most attention. In 2005, two more exchanges listed Russell 1000 and Russell 2000 index futures, creating a very competitive situation, particularly among electronically traded contracts. Russell index futures contracts trade on four U.S. exchanges; the CME, CBOE Futures Exchange, NYBOT, and Eurex US.

S&P MidCap 400   The S&P MidCap 400 index is a capitalization-weighted index of 400 stocks on the New York Stock Exchange, American Stock Exchange, and Nasdaq Stock Market with medium capitalization. Developed in 1991, the S&P MidCap 400 is considered the benchmark for mid-cap market performance. No stocks in the MidCap 400 are included in the S&P 500.

Futures on the MidCap 400 index began trading at the CME in 1992 with a value of $500 times the index. Like the other stock indexes, an E-mini electronic version of the contract was launched by the CME with a value of $100 times the index on January 28, 2002. Volume has not reached the level of the other E-mini stock index contracts.

Dow Jones Industrial Average   The Dow Jones Industrial Average (DJIA) is an index of 30 large-capitalization, blue-chip stocks traded on the New York Stock Exchange, accounting for about 20 percent of the market value of all U.S. equities. The index, first published in 1896, is the most widely quoted market indicator in newspapers, radio, television, and electronic media around the world. Movement in the DJIA is sensitive to the news surrounding the 30 companies represented in the index, particularly those with the highest prices, as the Dow is a price-weighted index.

Futures on the Dow began trading at the CBOT in 1997 after heated competition between the Chicago exchanges for the rights to trade futures and options on products owned by Dow Jones & Company, which had remained reluctant to allow its name to be used in any kind of futures trading for 15 years after the first stock index futures contracts began trading.

The CBOT began trading a mini-sized Dow contract valued at $5 times the average on its electronic platform in April 2002, and although the mini-sized Dow hasn't matched the volume of the CME E-mini stock index contracts, it has grown quickly in popularity.

Single-Stock Futures

Single-stock futures (SSFs), also known as security futures, are the newest entry among equity-based futures contracts. As part of the so-called Johnson-Shad Accord that set the ground rules to let stock index futures begin trading in 1982, futures on individual stocks and narrow-based stock indexes were not allowed to trade unless approved by both the Commodity Futures Trading Commission (CFTC) and the Securities and Exchange Commission (SEC).

When Congress passed the Commodity Futures Modernization Act in December 2000, the legislation opened the door for SSFs. As a result, two new exchanges—OneChicago, a joint venture of the Chicago exchanges, and NQLX, a wholly owned company of Euronext.liffe—began trading SSFs in November 2002. After two years of slow trading and lack of support from the equities industry, NQLX stopped trading single-stock futures in December 2004.

OneChicago lists futures on about 100 individual stocks as well as several sectors and the DIAmonds exchange-traded fund (ETF). All trading is electronic, and all contracts are based on 100-share lots. Volume is still relatively thin in many SSFs, and OneChicago continues to make adjustments to what it lists, so you will need to check with your broker to see if an SSF contract is available on a stock that interests you.

SSFs provide many of the advantages of futures over stocks, such as greater leverage and the ability to go short, but not the same tax benefits. Many securities firms have been hesitant about offering and marketing SSFs, so the concept, while showing volume that makes it successful compared to other market start-ups, has not yet blossomed as much or as fast as advocates anticipate it will.

International Stock Index Futures

In today's electronic world, you can trade stock indexes based on stocks from many different countries. Firms such as Dow Jones and Morgan Stanley Capital International have developed a number of indexes incorporating the shares of international companies.

Futures on the Nikkei 225, Japan's leading stock index, are traded at the CME. It includes 225 top-tier Japanese companies listed under the first section of the Tokyo Stock Exchange. The price-weighted index, introduced in 1949, is computed and distributed by publisher Nihon Keizai Shimbun.

In addition, stock index futures and options contracts traded on a number of foreign exchanges are available to U.S. traders. Some are traded in open-outcry sessions, but most are traded completely electronically. For a list of the major international stock index markets on which the CFTC has approved futures and options trading, visit the CFTC web site at www.cftc.gov/opa /backgrounder/opapart30.htm.

FINANCIAL INSTRUMENTS

Financial instruments can be divided into two main categories: those instruments related to interest rates and those connected to the value of a country's currency. Many of the same factors that affect one market also affect the other, as well as the stock market. These factors include reports on the current status of leading economic indicators, industrial production, employment, and other matters influenced by the growth rate of the economy. In fact, almost anything linked to a nation's economic health, inflation expectations, monetary policy, political trends, and so forth is likely to have some bearing on these markets.

Interest Rates

As with most supply/demand factors in a free market, a greater demand for money is likely to drive up the price of money—that is, the interest rate. Demand depends on factors such as a nation's economic health, the level of government borrowing to support budgets, and people's perception of inflation (when they think inflation is rising, they may be more likely to borrow, thinking they can repay loans with cheaper money later). In theory, an interest rate should take into account the real rate of interest, inflation premium, and risk premium.

The Federal Reserve Board plays an extremely important role in determining the direction of U.S. short-term interest rates, and the meetings of the Federal Open Market Committee about every six weeks are often market-moving events. The Fed, as the U.S. central bank, controls the supply of money, mainly through direct market trading (buys Treasuries and increases bank reserves to send interest rates lower; sells Treasuries and decreases bank reserves to raise interest rates) but also by adjusting reserve requirements and the discount rate at which banks can borrow money from the Fed.

An important element in the interest rate market is the yield curve—that is, a picture that shows the relationship of rates from short-term to long-term. Typically, the curve should be sloping upward as in Figure 8.2 because the longer the lender is exposed to the risks of the marketplace, the higher the rate the lender will want for providing the money to the borrower. In contrast, a strict monetary policy when the Fed is tightening credit and trying to cool the economy typically results in an inverted yield curve with short-term interest rates higher than long-term rates (see Figure 8.3).

U.S. Treasury Bonds   T-bonds are long-term debt issues of the U.S. government with maturities of more than 10 years. U.S. economic strength, inflation rate, and monetary policy are the major influences on T-bonds. Demand for money in a strong and/or inflationary economy typically causes interest rates to rise; conversely, demand weakens and rates tend to fall in a weak economy.

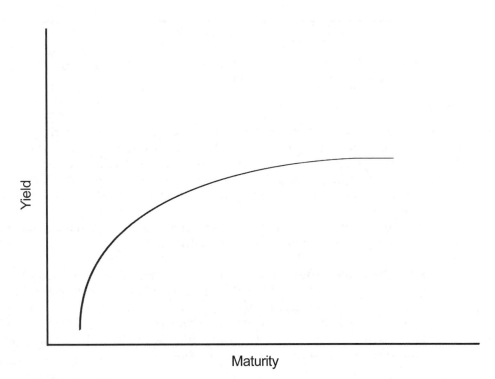

FIGURE 8.2   Traditional yield curve. (*Source:* Copyright 2003 Investopedia, Inc., www.investopedia.com)

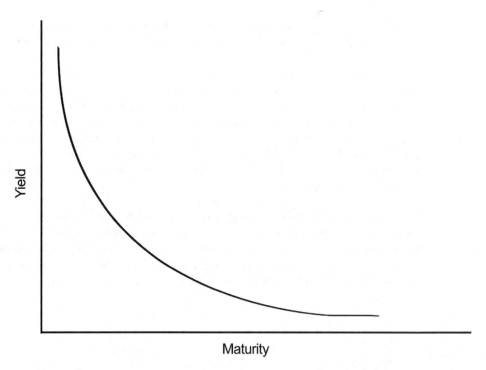

FIGURE 8.3   Inverted yield curve. (*Source:* Copyright 2003 Investopedia Inc., www.investopedia.com)

Government spending (and resulting issuance of debt securities) also influences the level of interest rates. The Federal Reserve Board, which controls monetary policy, adjusts the money supply and the fed funds rate (the overnight rate at which banks lend funds to each other, which acts as a floor for short-term interest rates) as part of an effort to keep economic growth stable without high inflation.

Futures on T-bonds are traded both in an open-outcry setting and electronically at the CBOT with the electronic contracts gaining market share quickly.

U.S. Treasury Notes   T-notes are medium-term debt obligations of the U.S. government, typically issued at the end of each month, with maturities ranging from 1 to 10 years. Futures are traded on 2-year, 5-year, and 10-year T-notes. As the government has shortened the maturities of its debt issues, 10-year T-note futures have taken over the volume leadership from T-bonds, which was the most active futures contract for many years. T-note futures also trade at the CBOT.

U.S. Treasury Bills   T-bills are U.S. government debt issues with maturities of up to one year. T-bills are the most widely issued government debt security and are auctioned weekly and monthly. The T-bill interest rate is considered the risk-free rate of return available to investors. Thirteen-week T-bill futures trade at the CME.

Eurodollars   A Eurodollar is a U.S. dollar on deposit in a foreign bank, mainly in Europe, commonly used to settle international transactions. Eurodollar deposits are not guaranteed by any government but rather are the obligation of the bank holding them. Eurodollar futures, which track the interest rate on 90-day Eurodollar deposits, are the most widely traded financial futures instrument in the world.

Futures on Eurodollars are traded on the floor and electronically at the CME, also with the electronic venue making quick inroads into trading dominance.

Currencies

When you trade currencies or foreign exchange (forex or FX), everything is relative. You are not trading just one currency such as the U.S. dollar but a currency pair based on the relationship of one currency to another currency. Currency futures are traded at the CME; cash forex trading occurs at a number of firms (see Chapter 10).

A number of factors go into determining the strength or weakness of currencies vis-à-vis each other, but it usually comes down to comparing one nation's economy to another's. Generally, expanding economies have strong currencies while recessionary economies have weak currencies. Statistics such as gross domestic production (GDP) comparing the economic growth rate of two nations influence a currency's value, as does the trade balance between countries. The current account balance and money flows from one country to another reflect a currency's supply and demand, so traders are always watching each country's trade balance to see changes in surpluses or deficits.

A strong currency may mean a country's exports become more expensive and result in fewer sales, cutting into corporate profits and weakening an economy. In some cases, the situation may become serious enough that a nation's leaders decide intervention in the currency markets is necessary—that is, a country buys its own currency when weak and sells its currency when it is strong to keep its currency in line with a value that is perceived to be acceptable.

A country's fiscal policies are important in determining a currency's value. An expansive fiscal policy (total government debt relatively high versus money supply) that stimulates both growth and inflation will likely lead to a rise in interest rates. Relative real (inflation-adjusted) interest rate differentials between two countries will affect currencies because capital tends to move toward the highest real rate of return, thus increasing the demand for the currency of the higher-rate nation. However, if interest rates are high because of inflation expectations or other problems, then demand for that currency will weaken.

Political leadership and events such as elections can also make a difference to a currency because they may influence the direction of the economy, monetary policy, trade policy, and capital flows. Generally, the U.S. dollar has been considered to be a safe haven during times of international crisis.

In addition to these overriding factors that affect all currency relationships, here are some factors that may have more of an impact on specific currencies.

Australian Dollar   The Australian dollar market is particularly sensitive to commodity prices because Australia exports wheat, wool, and gold. Strong commodity prices will tend to boost the A-dollar as long as they don't get too high to discourage buyers and reduce export demand. What happens to Asian economies is particularly important to the A-dollar, as 40 percent of Australia's exports go to Asia. Central bank policies on gold reserves can affect not only gold prices but also the A-dollar.

British Pound   The United Kingdom has not adopted the euro as its currency yet, but the British pound often takes its lead from what happens to the European Union. However, it has some unique characteristics that cause it to chart its own course. For example, the European Union economies and the euro are sensitive to oil prices as an importer whereas the United Kingdom and the pound are sensitive to oil prices as an exporter from the North Sea oil field.

Canadian Dollar   Like the Australian dollar, the Canadian dollar is especially sensitive to developments in commodity prices because of the natural resources that it exports. It is especially sensitive to anything that happens to the U.S. economy because 60 percent of Canada's exports go to the United States. The saying "When the United States sneezes, Canada catches cold" might apply here.

Euro   The European Union is affected by many of the same things domestically that affect the United States, but the additional challenge is that it brings together a number of different governments and economies with potentially different agendas and not always heading in the same direction. Strength or weakness in the German economy may not be reflected in the Italian economy in the same way, for example, and analysts have a number of diverse economic factors to consider to put together a composite outlook for the euro. The addition of 10 former Eastern bloc nations on May 1, 2004, does not make the task of trying to get one reading on multiple economies and political policies any easier. The emergence of an apparently strong European Central Bank does provide a central focus for interest rate decisions that may affect the euro's relationship to other currencies.

Japanese Yen   Trade issues are a major factor in Japan, which typically has run a huge trade surplus with the rest of the world. A rising trend in the current account surplus has produced a natural rising trend in the value of the yen. The challenge for the Japanese government and the Bank of Japan is how to keep the yen's value at a level that will maintain the nation's competitive edge in export markets. With 40 percent of its exports going to Asian markets, the health of those markets is important for Japan's economy, as the Asian currency crisis of 1998 emphasized. On the other side of the trade picture, Japan is a major oil importer, making the yen sensitive to oil price developments. Japan's banking system also has struggled since the excesses of the early 1990s, and any bank failures could have a damaging effect on the economy and the value of the yen.

Swiss Franc   Switzerland has a long history as an independent nation and, true to form, is not a part of the European single-currency plan. Helped by the country's secretive banking policies and a reputation for maintaining an interest in gold, the Swiss franc continues to be regarded as a safe-haven currency in times of uncertainty or currency crisis. With this status, the value of the Swiss franc depends more on perception and less on economic fundamentals than most other currencies. Traditionally, the Swiss franc's closest relationship was with the deutsche mark because about 60 percent of Swiss trade is with Germany, and this has carried over to the euro.

COMMODITIES

Until the 1970s, futures markets and commodities were synonymous because the markets were all about those physical products that you could touch, taste, grow, mine, consume, or deliver. Although the types of markets traded as futures have changed considerably since then, physical commodities still are a major component of the futures and options industry and are still the markets with which many traders are most familiar.

Like other segments of the futures industry, commodities can be broken down into several categories: metals, energy, grains, livestock, and food and fiber. These are not paper assets. In general, they are all produced and they are all consumed at a price that is discovered in a central marketplace based on the forces of supply and demand. Except for metals and energy, which are taken from reserves in the ground, they are renewable resources. Many of these markets exhibit seasonal price patterns because of climate, and weather often plays a major role. Aside from those generalities, each market has unique factors that affect its pricing.

Metals

Metals have a unique status among commodities in that all of the metals traded in futures markets are produced and consumed like other commodities, but prices tend to be dictated by influences other than supply and demand. The metals all have industrial uses, but views about the health of the economy or the metal's role as a storehouse of value are more likely to set the tone of prices. Metals such as gold or silver are not really consumed like grains or livestock, for the most part, but are converted into some other form and can be recovered if desired.

Copper   Copper is one of the world's major industrial metals, ranking third behind iron and aluminum in use. Nearly half of copper demand is for electrical purposes, including telecommunications; it also is used in construction and industrial machinery manufacturing. Chile is the world's largest producer, accounting for about 25 percent of the world's output. The United States is the world's second largest producer at 18 percent. As an alloy component, copper combines with tin to produce bronze and with zinc to produce brass.

With electrical wiring and construction accounting for so much of its use, the price of copper is sensitive to statistics related to economic growth, particularly reports such as housing starts. China has also become a large importer in recent years, and economic statistics there are important for copper prices as well.

Gold   Gold is a precious metal used worldwide not only as a store of monetary value (both coins and bars) but also in jewelry, electronics, and dentistry. The yellow metal has long been considered a hedge against economic or political uncertainties, and many central banks back their currency with gold reserves. South Africa not only is the world's largest gold producer but also holds about half of the world's estimated gold reserves. The United States is the world's second largest producer, with the most output coming from Nevada.

The physical supply of gold takes a backseat to the many demand factors that influence gold prices. Gold prices are most sensitive to political and economic factors that may cause central banks and individuals to change the amount of gold they hold as an investment or safety asset.

Platinum   Platinum is the principal metal of the platinum group of metals, which also includes palladium, rhodium, ruthenium, osmium, and iridium. As an industrial metal, nearly half of the world's consumption of platinum is for catalysts. Automotive catalytic converters are the largest source of demand; other catalytic uses are in the chemical and petroleum refining industries. Annual platinum production runs less than 10 percent of gold production, with nearly 75 percent of the world's supplies concentrated in South Africa.

Even though platinum is largely used for industrial purposes, prices can move in sympathy with the gold and silver markets. Political and labor activities in South Africa are always of prime concern to the platinum market.

Palladium   Palladium is the second largest metal of the platinum group of metals; it also is produced as a by-product of nickel production. Russia and South

Africa account for about 90 percent of world production. Palladium is used in electronic applications, for dental alloys, automotive catalysts, and jewelry.

Economic and political conditions in Russia, the largest producer, are of prime importance because of their effect on mine production, inventory levels, and shipment policies.

Silver Silver, sometimes called "poor man's gold," is primarily used in industry, photography, jewelry, and silverware. Coinage uses usually account for less than 5 percent of annual consumption. Mexico and Peru are the world's largest producers. The United States ranks first in the recovery of silver from secondary supplies, such as scrap and old coinage.

Silver prices react to many influences, including warehouse stocks, inflation fears, price of gold, and economic health as it affects industrial demand.

Energy

Although futures on most commodities existed for a number of years prior to the introduction of financial and equity-based futures, futures on energy did not begin trading until 1978 when the New York Mercantile Exchange (NYMEX) launched trading in heating oil. Crude oil futures followed in 1983. The energy market today has become one of the most important gauges of world economic and political developments.

The value of the U.S. dollar is significant because much of the world's crude oil is priced in dollars. U.S. energy prices are also quite sensitive to statistical reports detailing production, imports, and especially stocks released weekly by the American Petroleum Institute and the U.S. Department of Energy.

Crude Oil Crude oil is the "black gold" that comes from the depths of the earth as a raw material to be refined into heating oil, gasoline, and other petroleum products. Crude oil can be classified as "light, sweet" or "sour." NYMEX offers futures on both types, but the light, sweet contract is considered to be the international pricing benchmark. The size of the NYMEX contract is 1,000 barrels, but NYMEX also offers a half-sized miNY version of 500 barrels traded electronically on Globex and cleared by NYMEX.

The world's three largest crude oil producers are Saudi Arabia, Russia, and the United States (North Sea oil production is about the same as U.S. output but is split up among several nations). The world's supply of crude oil depends largely on the politics surrounding the Organization of Petroleum Exporting Countries (OPEC), which accounts for a little over 40 percent of world production. OPEC members include Algeria, Indonesia, Iran, Iraq, Kuwait, Libya, Nigeria, Qatar, Saudi Arabia, United Arab Emirates, and Venezuela.

Demand for crude oil filters up from the demand for its two main products, heating oil and gasoline. Thus, winter weather conditions (particularly in Northeast

United States) can influence heating oil demand. Driving patterns, vehicle types, and a country's economic health affect gasoline demand. The profitability of refining products also can influence crude oil prices.

Gasoline   Unleaded gasoline is the refined petroleum product used to fuel cars and trucks and accounts for almost half of U.S. crude oil consumption. About half of the gasoline produced in the United States originates on the Gulf Coast. New York Harbor handles both imported and domestic supplies, and NYMEX lists futures and options on New York Harbor unleaded gasoline.

In addition to the worldwide factors that influence the supply of crude oil, the gasoline market pays particular attention to gasoline inventories, refinery margins, and refinery maintenance schedules. (The market can be edgy during hurricane season if the storms threaten Gulf Coast production.) Gasoline demand depends on the weather, speed limits, retail pump prices, trends in vehicle fuel efficiency, and economic conditions. Demand typically picks up going into and during the summer when travel increases.

Heating Oil   Heating oil, also known as No. 2 fuel oil, is used to heat homes and businesses, primarily in the Northeast United States. It is the second largest refined product, accounting for about 25 percent of the crude oil barrel yield.

Winter weather conditions in the Northeast United States are a prime demand factor. Demand typically picks up as distributors begin to stock heating oil supplies in late summer and fall and can spike sharply higher during frigid spells in the winter. On the supply side, refinery margins and operating schedules play a role, as does the level of distillate inventories.

Natural Gas   Natural gas is a combustible fuel found in the earth's crust and is used for industrial purposes as well as to generate electricity, heat homes, and fuel cooking stoves. Natural gas accounts for about 25 percent of U.S. energy consumption. Louisiana and Texas are the two largest producing states.

Weather conditions in the main usage areas—U.S. Midwest (heating) and U.S. Southwest (cooling)—are among the main demand factors for natural gas. The potential for hurricanes disrupting production in the Gulf of Mexico also is a price consideration. Natural gas cannot be imported as easily as crude oil, so pipeline capacity and the number of domestic working rigs drilling for natural gas affect U.S. supplies as well.

Environmental policies, particularly concerning air pollution standards, are a background factor for natural gas.

Grains and Soybeans

Grains and soybeans are essential to food and feed supplies, and prices are especially sensitive to weather conditions in growing areas at key times during the crop's development and to economic conditions that affect demand. Monthly reports issued by the U.S. Department of Agriculture summarize these key variables for both U.S. and world crops:

- Ending stocks or carryover from the previous season.
- Production for the current season.
- Domestic usage expectations.
- Potential export shipments.
- Projected ending stocks or carryover at the end of this season.

All crop production figures are estimates or projections but are based on surveys, actual measurements, technology such as satellite images, and other means to provide assessments that attempt to be as accurate as possible. The ending stocks-to-usage ratio is a key figure reflecting overall supply/demand pressures that influence prices (see Table 8.3).

Corn Corn is the world's foremost feed grain and is used in rations for cattle, hogs, and poultry. It also has food and industrial uses, such as high-fructose corn syrup used to sweeten carbonated beverages and ethanol to fuel vehicles. Most of the world's corn is grown in the United States, primarily in the Midwest. Other producers include China, France, Argentina, and South Africa.

The area planted to corn and weather during the growing season are the two main factors that determine supply each year. The corn market is particularly sensitive to weather conditions when the plant pollinates, typically during July and early August in the United States, the most critical period for determining yield (bushels per acre) and the crop's overall production size.

Demand considerations include not only the number of animals in the United States for determining potential U.S. feed demand but also the livestock population around the world, which influences U.S. export demand. Food and industrial uses for this high-carbohydrate crop also have grown sharply around the world. Consumption of corn for fuel ethanol used as a gasoline volume extender, octane booster, and oxygenate has increased dramatically in recent years to account for nearly 10 percent of annual U.S. corn production. Thus, in addition to food and livestock feed usage, corn futures traders now need to watch U.S. energy legislation closely as well as developments in the production of ethanol from other sources to determine the impact of this growing usage category on corn demand and prices.

Soybeans Soybeans are an oilseed crop grown mainly for processing into soybean meal for animal feed rations and soybean oil for food purposes. In the United States, soybeans are grown in roughly the same areas as corn. Production in South America has become increasingly important to the world soybean market, exceeding the size of the U.S. crop in recent years. Combined output from Brazil, Argentina, and Paraguay has become the market's second harvest,

TABLE 8.3 U.S. Soybeans and Products Supply and Use (Domestic Measure)[1]

Item	2002–2003	2003–2004 Est.	2004–2005 Projections October	November
Soybeans:		Million Acres		
Area				
Planted	74.0	73.4	75.1	75.1
Harvested	72.5	72.5	74.0	74.0
		Bushels		
Yield per harvested acre	38.0	33.9	42.0	42.6
		Million Bushels		
Beginning stocks	208	178	112	112
Production	2,756	2,454	3,107	3,150
Imports	5	6	6	6
Supply, total	2,969	2,638	3,225	3,269
Crushings	1,615	1,530	1,645	1,645
Exports	1,044	885	1,025	1,010
Seed	89	92	89	89
Residual	41	19	61	64
Use, total	2,791	2,525	2,820	2,808
Ending stocks	178	112	405	460
Average farm price ($/bushel)[2]	5.53	7.34	4.70–5.50	4.55–5.35
Soybean Oil:		Million Pounds		
Beginning stocks	2,358	1,491	1,061	1,057
Production	18,438	17,077	18,425	18,425
Imports	46	307	105	105
Supply, total	20,843	18,875	19,591	19,587
Domestic	17,089	16,881	17,250	17,300
Exports	2,263	937	1,150	1,100
Use, total	19,352	17,818	18,400	18,400
Ending stocks	1,491	1,057	1,191	1,187
Average price (¢/lb)[2]	22.04	29.97	21.50–24.50	21.50–24.50
Soybean Meal:		Thousand Short Tons		
Beginning stocks	240	220	225	212
Production	38,213	36,318	39,160	39,173
Imports	166	270	165	165
Supply, total	38,619	36,808	39,550	39,550
Domestic	32,379	32,256	33,900	33,900
Exports	6,019	4,340	5,400	5,400
Use, total	38,399	36,596	39,300	39,300
Ending stocks	220	212	250	250
Average price ($/s.t.)[2]	181.57	256.05	150.00–180.00	145.00–175.00

Note: Reliability calculations at end of report.

[1]Marketing year beginning September 1 for soybeans; October 1 for soybean oil and meal.

[2]Prices: soybeans, marketing year weighted average price received by farmers; for oil, simple average of crude soybean oil, Decatur; for meal, simple average of 48 percent, Decatur.

Source: U.S. Department of Agriculture World Agricultural Supply and Demand Estimates (WASDE-416-13).

coming to the world market when U.S. farmers are planting their crops in the spring.

Acreage and growing weather conditions, especially when the plants are setting and filling pods (August in the United States and January–February in South America), are the two main supply factors that influence the market, but they keep market watchers busy year-round because of the importance of production in the United States (northern hemisphere) and in Brazil, Argentina, and Paraguay (southern hemisphere).

Demand for soybeans stems from demand for soybean oil, used in food processing and fast-food preparation, and soybean meal, a primary ingredient in hog and poultry rations.

Soybean Oil: Soybean oil is a product of soybean processing when the oilseed is crushed to make oil and meal. Soybean oil is used in food processing for products such as salad dressing and in the fast-food industry as cooking oil.

The size of world soybean and other edible oil crops (palm, canola, peanut, sunflower-seed, and cottonseed) are the major supply factors. Expanding personal income is a strong demand factor in expanding the world's demand for edible oils each year in line with population growth.

Soybean Meal: Soybean meal is the other product produced when soybeans are crushed at a processing facility. Soybean meal is used mainly as a feed ingredient to boost the protein level of hog and poultry rations. It also is the basis for textured vegetable protein, used in food products.

The supply of soybeans determines the potential output of soybean meal production each year. Demand is determined by the feed needs of hogs and poultry, which can be influenced by the number of animals and demand for pork and poultry at grocery stores around the world.

Wheat Wheat is the most widely grown crop in the world, with special varieties used to make bread, crackers, noodles, and pasta. Hard red winter wheat, traded at the Kansas City Board of Trade, is milled to make many breads. Soft red winter wheat, traded at the CBOT, is used for crackers. Hard red spring wheat, traded at the Minneapolis Grain Exchange (MGE), also is used to make bread flours. Because of their specialty use within the wheat flours and their smaller production, durum, the primary wheat in pasta, and white wheat, used in the making of noodles, have more independent market situations than the other wheat categories.

Wheat traders need to have a good grasp of where each variety of wheat is grown so they can effectively evaluate the impact of weather conditions on the variety they are trading. China is the world's largest wheat producer but consumes most of its output domestically. Europe, Canada, Australia, and Argentina are major exporters, and a number of other countries such as Russia, Ukraine, Kazakhstan, and India can have an impact on the export market at times, depending on their production during any given year. However, many importing countries look to the United States, the world's second largest producer, as their residual wheat supplier. Demand for wheat is driven by expanding world incomes and population as well as nutritional trends.

Millers use various blends of wheat to produce flour for numerous wheat-based foods. Therefore, the three major types of wheat being traded on U.S. futures exchanges are influenced not only by their own supply/demand factors but also by the status of the other two markets. For example, all three markets will be affected by total acreage planted to wheat, but individual varieties may react more bearishly or bullishly, depending on their own statistics. Wheat also must compete with corn, soybeans, and other crops for acreage, so prices of all the crops tend to maintain an economic relationship with each other.

Livestock

Prior to the 1960s, futures trading was limited to commodities that were storable. That included butter and eggs traded since 1898 at the Chicago Butter and Egg Board, which evolved into the CME in 1919. The CME expanded into frozen pork belly futures in 1961, the first futures contract based on frozen, stored meats, and began to develop its reputation as an innovative marketplace in the mid-1960s when it introduced futures on live cattle, the first nonstorable commodity, and then live hogs (changed to lean hogs in 1997). After becoming a world leader in financial futures and electronic trading over the next 30 years, the CME returned to its roots with a revised milk futures contract in 2000.

Prices in this sector tend to be quite sensitive to concerns about diets and health, as reflected by the nitrite issue in bacon some years ago and, more recently, various mad cow disease scares.

Live Cattle   Live cattle are market-ready beef animals. The term stems from the cash market practice of quoting prices to producers based on the animal's weight instead of quoting prices to meat buyers based on carcass weight.

Consumer demand for beef is a long-term factor that influences the live cattle market and can be influenced by the supply of competing meats (primarily poultry and pork). On the supply side, it is also important to know how many cattle are in the feedlots and when they may be coming to market, decisions that are influenced by cattle prices, feed prices, and weather.

Health concerns may influence cattle prices in either direction, as seen with diet fads that promote beef as a protein source or reported incidences of bovine spongiform encephalopathy (BSE), sometimes known as mad cow disease, a disease of cattle first identified in 1986. The number of animals infected with BSE generally has been small and isolated, but publicity about even one case can send prices sharply lower because of worries about the effect on domestic consumption and import restrictions imposed by other nations.

Feeder Cattle   Feeder cattle are young animals that will be fed to reach market weight. Feedlot operations buy feeder cattle when they weigh between 600 and

800 pounds with the intention of feeding them until they reach a market weight of 1,100 to 1,200 pounds.

From the supply side, the number of cows in the United States determines how many calves will be born each year. Also, the long-term outlook for cattle prices and feed prices may influence how many heifer calves are held back for breeding purposes rather than sent to feedlots.

Demand for feeder cattle varies with the outlook for live cattle prices and the cost of feeding the animals to reach market weight.

Lean Hogs The value of the meat produced by market-ready hogs that have been fed to the packers' desired weights of about 230 to 260 pounds is the difference between "lean" and "live" hog prices. Because bones and waste represent about 26 percent of a typical hog, live prices are normally 74 percent of a lean hog price quote. Increasingly, the cash hog market is being quoted in lean values rather than live-weight prices.

Consumer demand is the major long-term factor that drives the lean hog market. Personal income, the supply of competing meats (primarily poultry and beef), and health concerns influence individual purchases. It's also important to know how many pigs are being farrowed and fed to market weight and when they may be sold, decisions that are influenced by lean hog prices, feed prices, and weather.

Pork Bellies A pork belly is the underside of a hog (beneath the ribs) that is used to make bacon. Each hog produces two pork bellies that are then cured, smoked, and cut into strips of bacon.

The supply of pork bellies, both fresh and frozen, is a key market factor. Demand remains relatively steady throughout the year except for a blip up during "BLT" season as home garden tomatoes ripen in late summer. The CME started a fresh pork belly contract in April 1997, but the previous frozen belly contract remains the dominant futures contract in this market so far.

Milk The CME replaced its Basic Formula Price (BFP) milk futures contract with a Class III milk contract in January 2000 to reflect the price of milk used in the manufacturing of cheese under the federal government's revised milk price classification system. Volume in milk futures, a 200,000-pound contract, at times matches or exceeds activity in pork belly futures. Traders watch cash cheese and butter markets to get pricing indications for futures.

Food and Fiber

Also known as tropical commodities because of where they are grown, this group of commodities is traded at the New York Board of Trade and in London on Euronext.liffe. Production is concentrated in less-developed countries, sometimes influenced by political factors, and demand comes primarily from Western developed nations, with interaction between the two mostly responsible for determining prices in this sector of the commodities market.

Cocoa   Cocoa is a tropical commodity that is the basis for manufacturing chocolate candy and other cocoa products, including cosmetics and pharmaceuticals. Cocoa trees usually are planted within 20 degrees of the equator. Beans are first produced on the trees after four to five years, but the tree does not reach maximum productivity until it is eight to 10 years old. Africa's Ivory Coast is the world's foremost cocoa producer, with its neighbor Ghana a distant second.

Weather conditions, disease, insects, and producer crop management techniques have a direct impact on the size of the cocoa crop. Political and economic conditions in the producing countries can sway production plans. Demand is strongest in the Netherlands, followed by the United States, Germany, and the United Kingdom.

Coffee   The coffee that many people need to get their day started gets its start as a coffee bean grown on trees or bushes in subtropical climates. Trees begin to bear two to three years after planting, reaching their full potential in four to eight years; trees may produce for 20 to 30 years. The world's primary type of coffee, arabica, is grown mainly in the western hemisphere, with Brazil and Colombia the leading producers. Robusta coffee, which has a stronger flavor than the arabicas, is produced in Asia and Africa. Vietnam has emerged as a major coffee producer and exporter in recent years.

Coffee demand is largely inelastic, with consumption changing significantly only when prices rise or fall dramatically. Still, with an expanding number of gourmet coffee shops, U.S. coffee consumption is on an upswing, according to coffee industry statistics.

Weather conditions, particularly the potential for a killing freeze, in the primary growing areas can influence prices. Long-term health of the coffee trees and harvesting practices also affect the supply of coffee. Government policies in the producing countries and producer groups also influence long-term production decisions and export quotas.

Cotton   Cotton is a fiber crop grown annually for fabric for clothes and other cotton goods, with cottonseed oil being an important by-product. The United States and China are the world's two largest cotton producers. Cotton has a long history in international trade, including the relationship between England and the Colonial United States. Cotton reached its record high price of $1.89 per pound during the Civil War; cotton futures first opened for trading in 1870.

Acreage planted to cotton in the main producing countries as well as growing season weather are the main factors to watch for their effect on prices. Government policies controlling the amount of imports into the United States also influence prices. Demand for cotton-based clothes and goods is sensitive to consumer preferences and economic conditions.

Frozen Concentrated Orange Juice (FCOJ) FCOJ is what millions of Americans pull out of the frozen food section at their grocery stores and mix with water to make orange juice for the breakfast table. The process that eliminated the need to squeeze fresh oranges for juice every morning was developed just after World War II ended. The United States and Brazil dominate world orange production and world FCOJ trade. Newly planted orange trees produce marketable fruit in three to five years but don't reach their peak until they are 15 to 20 years old.

FCOJ prices are more weather sensitive than other markets. From December through March, a frost or freeze in Florida can have a disastrous effect on both the current crop size and long-term production prospects. Similarly, Brazilian orange trees are at risk from drought from July through November.

Shifts in consumer preferences among juices and other beverages influence demand for FCOJ. Internationally, exchange rates versus the U.S. dollar affect demand. Processing capacity also is a consideration, particularly as a short-term factor.

Sugar Sugar is a sweetener used in the baking and confectionery industries as well as in the home. It also can be converted into industrial alcohol fuel. Sugar comes from both cane and beets. Sugar cane is a bamboo-like grass grown in semitropical regions of the world. Sugar beets are grown mainly in Europe, Russia, and Ukraine.

Production of both sugar cane and sugar beet crops can be affected by weather, disease, insects, and cultivation practices. World trade in sugar is highly dependent on government policies, such as import tariffs. Sugar demand is affected by consumer income, candy and confectionery sales, and competing sweeteners, such as high-fructose corn syrup. Demand for industrial alcohol production can reduce the amount of sugar processed for sweetener purposes.

CHAPTER 9

Options
on Futures

A Flexible Trading Tool

If you're surprised to find a chapter on options in a book about futures, you're not alone. Clients new to futures are often unaware they can invest in futures options. In fact, they sometimes doubt they heard right: "Options on futures—how can that be? I thought they were two different things." This confusion will arise because one of the first lessons taught about futures is "they are not the same as options."

Futures and options are indeed different investment vehicles—just as futures are different from real estate, bonds, or stocks. But these latter four investment classes share one common feature: Each can have an option based on it.

For instance, if you have found a house to buy, you may first negotiate to buy an option on the property, which will give you the sole right to buy that house at a certain price and by a specified time in the future. That is an option on real estate. If you are looking to invest in a local business you can instead purchase an option to buy, allowing time to fully analyze the books. That is an option to buy into an ownership interest.

Perhaps you're more familiar with options on stocks, a mature and popular industry considered mainstream by many investors. Buying a call option provides the right to *purchase* the underlying stock at a specified price and time; buying a put option gives you the right to *sell* it at a particular price and time. Options in many forms abound, and each can have a role to play in an efficiently diversified portfolio. And so it is with options on futures as well.

Futures options are just what they sound like—an option based on price changes of an underlying futures contract. They trade on regulated exchanges side by side with the futures on which they are based. Their value is calculated using the same variables as other types of options (more on that later). Any futures contract can have options traded on it, although not all do.

The futures industry is growing by leaps and bounds, and more significantly, options on futures are expected to enjoy an even greater rate of growth in the coming years. Any book about futures would be lacking indeed without a chapter on futures options.

Now that you're over the initial shock of "options on futures," let's explore the subject a bit more.

ISSUES TO CONSIDER WHEN INVESTING IN FUTURES OPTIONS

If you're new to options, don't worry. This chapter will review the basics and will describe exactly what an option is. You'll learn the difference between calls and puts, and the essentials on how they are valued. You'll gain an overview of how different factors, such as changes in interest rates or volatility, can affect option values.

This chapter has three sections. We'll cover the mechanics of options in section two and then review some common trading strategies in section three. We begin first with some general discussion on issues important to options investors.

Think Like an Options Trader

It has been said that options traders don't think like the rest of us. Maybe that's just some industry humor, but there's always a bit of truth in humor. Options investors not only care about *where* a market is going, they are equally concerned with *how* it will get there.

The reason is twofold. First, an option price depends in part on the volatility of the instrument it's based on. If a volatile market rallies for two months but with ever-smaller ranges (decreasing volatility), an option buyer who picked the direction correctly may still lose money on the investment because options are priced lower on calm markets than on volatile markets.

Second, and equally significant, is the fact that options lose value over time. All things being equal, every week that goes by means the options have lost more time value. Considered another way, at any given moment an option has priced into it the *probability* that the underlying market will move in its favor. Every week that passes where the market fails to move favorably is another week where the option has lost some of that value. These two issues—volatility and time value—will be explored further in the section on the mechanics of options, but understanding these concepts is an important first step in learning about options.

Why Trade Options?

Like futures markets, organized options markets are an integral part of an advanced and developed economy. Any business faces both risks and costs of business, and an efficient economy will have mechanisms in place for business to lay off those risks and costs. Options markets provide valuable hedging and balancing functions for institutional and commercial enterprises with real business needs. But what about you, the average individual investor?

You're simply looking to make money, and there's nothing wrong with that. In fact, much of the daily trading volume comes from speculators like you, who add liquidity and efficiency to the marketplace. It takes many participants, all trading for their own valid reasons, to create a marketplace. But the process is never easy. Let's dispel some common myths about options.

Some Common Options Myths

Investors new to options often learn from the school of hard knocks some of the lessons addressed here. It's best to consider these matters early in the chapter to provide some context to the mechanics and strategies sections. Here is a short list of what we consider to be some of the more common myths about options investing.

If the Underlying Market Goes My Way the Option Will Gain in Value

In other words, in rising markets the call options will naturally increase in value, and in falling markets the puts will make money. This is not always the case.

Choosing the market direction is a very important factor, of course, but equally crucial can be those issues of time value and volatility. You don't want to be an options investor surprised by losses because you focused only on the price of the underlying futures contract and not on the option price as well.

Buying Options Has Limited Risk and Therefore Is Safer than Selling Options

While it's true that buying an option has a limited amount of risk, the amount of that risk is quite substantial—100 percent of the option value! Does this limited-risk feature of buying an option mean the strategy is less risky than one of selling options (also known as "writing" or "granting" options)? Not necessarily. Perhaps a better mind-set is to say that by buying an option you can *define* your risk.

The reason is that risk and safety can be measured in different ways. Many options have a high probability of expiring worthless. In such instances, some will argue it is option buyers who take the greater risk because they will have to suffer through many losses before hitting upon the windfall profit they hope will arrive.

Conversely, while it's true that some option-writing strategies can have less volatility and a higher probability of positive returns than option-buying strategies, the risk is unlimited. In fact, options writers could lose more than the value of their account! One big surprise loss could wipe out many months' worth of winners in a single stroke of misfortune.

Options strategists apply one method rather than another (options buying or options selling) depending on circumstances, but ultimately the outcome of any given trade is unknowable and inherently risky, regardless of whether you are an option buyer or a seller.

Options Are Very Complicated and Difficult to Understand As you know by now, several factors influence the value of an option. What's more, different options can be matched in combinations to create unique and varied strategies. However, the good news is that each individual strategy is usually very straightforward and easy to understand.

To understand a particular strategy simply plug in and solve the profit or loss of that strategy for a variety of different scenarios—the market is higher, lower, or somewhere in between, or the market is unchanged after two weeks have passed. You'll find examples of how to do this in the strategies section later in the chapter.

Successful Options Trading Requires Fancy Computers to Evaluate Opportunities Don't get hung up on the mathematics and the "Greeks" of options trading. We'll mention them in this chapter but much of what you need as a practical matter can be gleaned by tracking both the option price itself and the price of the underlying future. Besides, even the most advanced option pricing models are only as good as the data fed into them—the human part of the equation.

More importantly, every option strategy—from the simplest outright option purchase to the most complicated option spread—relies ultimately upon the investor forecasting the market.

Buying Underpriced Options and Selling Overpriced Ones Provides a Valuable Edge in Trading Options Would you like a surefire way of knowing what an option is worth? Experienced traders have this terrific way of knowing what something is worth, and we share with you now this powerful technique. In fact, you can use this simple, universal formula to also discover what your home, automobile, or time-share is worth.

Using your home as an example, here is the formula: *Your home is worth what someone is willing to pay for it.*

Think about this a bit. You may believe your home is worth more than what buyers are offering, but until the marketplace agrees with you there is little you can do about it. As the old adage says, "The market is always right." How often have you seen a market move seemingly too high or too low only to see the move double or triple from there? Markets can trend, especially in futures markets, for a surprisingly long time.

The market will price options for a reason. Even if that reason is not readily apparent to you, if prices diverge from their theoretical value that in itself is valuable information. For instance, if stock index puts are overpriced when compared against the calls, the market is saying the risks of a big sell-off are high. The sell-off may or may not happen, but puts should not be sold short just because they are expensive. Equally, if overall volatility is at an all-time low then options will be cheap, but that in itself does not indicate the time has come for prices to break out actively.

Buying Options Is a Good Way to Protect Against the Risks of Existing Futures Positions Investing is a risky business. And where there are risks, there are often ways of protecting against those risks. You may have heard that buying an option can help safeguard against risks you may be facing. Unfortunately, some investors overestimate the extent and nature of the protection achieved from buying options.

If you're trying to avoid the risks of corrections that are typical in daily and weekly market activity, buying options may actually be a needlessly expensive way to lower your exposure in a position. For example, if you are long 10 euro currency futures and are worried about a sell-off, you might choose to buy 10 puts to help shield the position. In a worst-case scenario where the futures position goes terribly wrong against you, at some point the puts will fully defend you against additional losses. This is an example where buying options does indeed provide protection against a big loss becoming a catastrophic loss.

But, what about the more common everyday risks of trading? In our example, buying the puts may hedge the long 10 futures contracts into a net long position of only 7.2 futures. But, if you're buying puts to lighten your exposure in the event that futures might drop back to last week's lows, why not start out with only seven long futures? Why buy 10 futures and then *pay money* to decrease the risk of that position back to about seven contracts?

Don't get the wrong idea here; if you are truly concerned about the risk of a catastrophic loss, then buying puts will certainly provide you with protection from that worst-case scenario. However, buying puts to avoid typical market volatility can wind up being an added expense that doesn't really work, anyway. Although the smaller, unhedged position (seven contracts in our example) still has unlimited loss potential in the event of a catastrophic meltdown, some investors will choose instead to manage the risks with active money management.

To think like an options trader, you must always be careful that you are buying options for the right reasons. The cost of an option, referred to as its premium, can definitely be thought of as an *expense*. You pay monthly premiums for automobile, life, and mortgage protection because you have a real and preexisting need to do so. But, if choosing to have a position of 10 contracts means you'll then need to spend money to lessen that risk, perhaps the better choice is to simply begin with a smaller position.

Options Strategies and Decision Making

In Chapter 2, "Becoming a Futures Trader," you read about the issue of art versus science and how it ties in with achieving your goals as an investor. The issue is especially germane when discussing futures options. Because options take into account variables other than just the direction of the underlying market, an investor has more details to learn when studying the mechanics of options. That's the "science" part of the equation, and much of this chapter deals with these essential details.

The "art" part of the equation is a little more difficult to master and may be what separates the beginners from the experts. While this chapter introduces you to some of the key issues and concepts about when certain strategies are best used, it will be your task to develop the art of decision making further over time.

The general issues discussed so far can be helpful as you begin investing in futures options. Still, you'll need a basic appreciation of the *mechanics* of futures options to build a foundation for understanding options *strategies*. The last part of this chapter introduces you to some of the more popular and well-known of those strategies. But now let's take a look at the basic mechanics of how options work.

MECHANICS OF FUTURES OPTIONS

If you understand stock options you'll have no problem with futures options, because they operate in exactly the same way. The only distinction is they are based on a different underlying instrument—in this case a futures contract, not a stock.

What Are Futures Options?

There are two types of options—call options and put options. With both types it is the buyer who gains rights and the seller who is assigned the obligation to fulfill those rights. We'll state the obvious by pointing out these rights and obligations are incurred only when a position is on. In a liquid market, options may be bought and sold as frequently as the investor deems appropriate, and offsetting a position is the most common way of removing an obligation or a right.

A *call* option gives the buyer the right to *purchase* the underlying futures contract at a specified price (the strike price) and within a certain time (on or before the expiration date). A *put* option gives the buyer the right to *sell* the underlying futures contract at the strike price on or before the expiration date. Clearly, the call buyer expects a market rally and the put buyer seeks a pullback.

As with any transaction, there is a seller for every buyer. Just as the call buyer expects a market rally, the one who sells it hopes the rally does not occur. The call seller is obligated to sell the underlying futures at the agreed-upon strike price—even if it has rallied considerably from the time the deal was originally made.

And just as the put buyer expects a market to drop, the put seller is hoping this does not happen. From the seller's view, a put option is an obligation to buy the underlying futures at the agreed-upon strike price—even if the market has subsequently dropped.

The option buyer pays money for the option and the seller receives that money. So the most the option buyer can lose is the cost of the option (the premium paid). The most the option seller can make is the amount of premium received. Of course, the option can increase in value an unlimited amount, which the buyer hopes will happen and the seller hopes will not. So the option buyer has unlimited profit potential and the seller has unlimited corresponding risk of loss. Why then would someone be willing to sell options if the gain is limited and the risk is unlimited?

The reason is that each position (long options or short options) is really just a different reward/risk profile. Stated another way, one position is not necessarily more risky than the other, only different. As you'll see, factors work to keep the risks balanced. For instance, time decay works in favor of the options seller, so there may be many winning trades in a row before a setback from a large loss comes along. In theory, the market prices the options so that an investor should be indifferent about whether it is better to be a buyer or seller.

Since everyone already knows the rights and obligations, the only issue left to negotiate is, how much money should the option be worth? Of course, different options will have different values, and those values depend on the particulars of each option. Luckily, for exchange-traded options these terms are standardized, simplifying the process of trading. Let's consider now how those different terms factor into the value of an option.

Determining the Value of an Option

A detailed discussion of the math behind options is beyond the scope of this chapter. Many excellent books are available on this topic, and anyone serious about investing in options should become familiar with the mathematics of options pricing. By avoiding much of the math, this chapter will instead explain option variables in terms that are both intuitive and practical.

On the most basic level, an option price is determined primarily by three things: the price of the underlying instrument it is based on, the volatility of that underlying instrument, and the amount of time remaining on the option. Prevailing interest rates also factor into the option pricing formula. And the big wild card in valuing options is the supply and demand situation in the marketplace. We'll consider each of these in order.

Price of the Underlying Futures Contract   Clearly, the price of the underlying futures is the main factor in an options price. You know this intuitively; as prices rally you will be willing to pay more for the right to buy (call options) and you will be offering less for the right to sell (put options). Indeed, forecasting rallies and breaks in the underlying futures is the whole point of options investing! But what is the exact relationship?

More precisely, it is the option's strike price in relation to the underlying futures that influences the option price. Again, this is intuitive. You will be willing to pay more for the right to buy gold futures at $400 than at $450. In the case of puts it is the opposite; you are willing to pay more for the right to sell at the higher price of $450 than to sell at only $400.

You'll need to know some important terminology to consider further this relationship between strike price and underlying futures. A call option with a strike price that is *above* the price of the underlying futures is said to be out-of-the-money. A call with a strike price that is *below* the price of the underlying market is said to be in-the-money, and for a strike at or around the same price of the underlying it is at-the-money.

For a put it is reversed. With a strike price that is *below* the price of the underlying futures a put is out-of-the-money, and for a strike price *above* the underlying market it is in-the-money. However, as with calls, a strike around the same price of the underlying is referred to as being at-the-money.

Those terms can be confusing on the first read-through, but here's why they are mentioned. An option's value consists of two elements—time value and intrinsic value. As long as some time remains until expiration, an option's price will have some time value in it (although it might be barely measurable).

But this intrinsic value depends on the relationship of the option's strike price to the underlying. An in-the-money option will have intrinsic value, as it could be exercised and turned into an underlying futures position at a favorable price. For instance, if S&P 500 futures are trading at 1195.00, the 1190 calls are in-the-money by 5.00. The 1190 calls will be worth 5.00 *plus* any time value (time value is discussed further later). In contrast, the 1200 calls are out-of-the-money, have no intrinsic value, and will be worth only the time value remaining in the options.

Perhaps you're wondering how much the option will gain or lose for a given change in the underlying futures price. This is a good point to introduce some of the option Greeks, the mathematical relationships inherent in options. Without going into the details of the math, here is what you need to know. Delta is the measurement of how much the option will move for a given change in the underlying price. For instance, if gold futures rally $10, from $410 to $420, the 400 strike price call might increase $6. In this example the delta is .6, because the call increased 60 percent of the change in the underlying ($6 = 60 percent of the $10 rally in gold).

Different options have different deltas, and the delta of an option changes both over time and as the underlying futures move up and down in price. The good news is that professional market makers spend their entire days making sure that options remain in line with each other, a process called arbitrage.

Your quote service will likely list for you the deltas of options you're interested in. Check the deltas to see how volatile your options are—to get an idea of how much they might move if your forecast of the underlying market is correct. In our example, if you predict a $10 rally in gold, then all things being equal, the 400 strike call with a delta of .6 should increase in value about $6.

But, remember that other factors are in play—volatility and time decay, to name two. Let's consider this example under other conditions. What if your predicted $10 rally takes many weeks to occur? What if it happens unexpectedly?

Volatility An option on a volatile market is worth more than an option on a quiet market. Again, you know this intuitively; a market characterized by sharp swings and sudden spikes has a greater chance, simply from random movement, of moving in a favorable direction for the option buyers. You will be willing to pay more for such an option; or looked at another way, you would demand greater compensation (a higher price) to be the seller of this more volatile option.

In our gold futures example, if the $10 rally happened in two minutes because of some surprise news, the 400 strike call might increase much more than the expected $6 (60 percent delta). It might instead rally by $7.60, $8.20, $9.00, or more, and its new, higher delta would reflect the new increase in volatility. After all, if gold futures just rallied suddenly on surprise news, who knows what is going to happen next? Uncertainty about the price of gold has suddenly increased, and now all options reflect a new consensus on higher volatility. This new "volatility premium" may cool off in a few days, or it might continue to increase as the surprise event develops further.

Notice that an increase in volatility increases the value of both calls and puts, helping options owners and hurting options sellers. Conversely, decreasing volatility lowers options values, helping those investors who have sold calls and puts. In options jargon, investors can be categorized as being "long volatility" or "short volatility"—that is to say, either owning options or having sold them. Taken to an extreme, complex delta neutral spreads can be crafted that have little or no exposure to changes in the direction of the market, but, rather, focus on changes in volatility only.

Volatility can be determined in several ways. Implied volatility can be calculated with the options math formula (most typical is the Black-Scholes option pricing model) used to value options. Instead of solving the formula for the option price, an analyst can plug in actual current market prices and solve instead for volatility. The true volatility can also be measured directly from the underlying futures contract and plugged into the option pricing formula. Small differences of opinion can occur about volatility because different time periods will produce different results. Regardless of how volatility is obtained, it can be compared against historic volatility to determine generally if it is high or low.

Notice also how delta increased when the volatility increased. This points out the interdependence of all the Greeks. A change in one measurement will cause changes in the others. Again, without getting into the math, just consider it logically; if volatility is higher, then an option is going to change more rapidly for a given move in the underlying future. It would also stand to reason that with a higher-volatility premium, the option will have more time value to lose each week (discussed next). A somewhat esoteric Greek worth mentioning is vega (sometimes known as kappa), which is the change in option price given a one-percentage-point change in volatility.

We've just discussed examples of a price move occurring suddenly and in the process affecting volatility premiums. Now consider what happens when a price move takes weeks to occur.

Time Value   An option with a great deal of time remaining is worth more than an option that is close to expiring. As with the other factors discussed so far, time value can be proven and measured mathematically. But disregard the math for now and consider this instinctively; an option with only two days remaining will have less of a chance of experiencing a large favorable move than one with two months remaining. You will be willing to pay more for an option with more time remaining on it. As a seller, you will demand more money to write an option that exposes you to several more months of risk.

Remember, at any given time an option has priced into it the probability that the underlying market will move in its favor, and this depends heavily on the amount of time remaining. With every week that passes, the time premium of the option is lessened. You can easily imagine a scenario where any gains from the market price moving favorably might be completely offset by the decay of time value.

Perhaps you're wondering just how much time value an option will lose each week. Theta is the component from the option pricing formula that measures time decay, and is the change in option price given a one-day decrease in time to expiration. But how would you like a quick nonmath estimation to view your time decay risk? Simply look up the number of weeks remaining before expiration and calculate what percentage one week represents. With seven weeks to go, one week later the option will have lost about one-seventh of its time value.

Notice that we did *not* say it will lose one-seventh of its *total* value. In some cases the total value of the option will indeed be all time value, but not always. Remember, the price of in-the-money options will also include intrinsic value. *Only the time value portion of an option's price will decay over time.*

Here's another important feature you need to know about time decay. It is nonlinear, that is to say, time decay erodes more quickly in the final days and weeks before expiration than with many months remaining. Walk yourself through the estimation trick in the earlier paragraph to prove this intuitively. With 10 weeks remaining, one week of decay is a 10 percent loss in time value; with only two weeks remaining the same one-week decay represents a 50 percent loss. Not surprisingly, this is an important factor when considering your options strategies.

Continuing with our gold futures example, let's say gold futures are trading at $425.00, the 450 calls settled at a price of 10.50 (worth $1,050), and the 400 calls settled at 35.50 (worth $3,550). The 450 calls are out-of-the-money, so the entire 10.50 is time value. Notice the 400 calls are in-the-money by 25.00 points, and so the value of 35.50 equals 25.00 (intrinsic value) plus 10.50 (time value). Only the 10.50 time value portion of each option's price is subject to time decay.

One final note: Time decay is steepest for at-the-money options. This is because they have the greatest amount of time value and therefore the most to lose each week.

Futures price, volatility, and time value are the three most important factors affecting the price of an option. However, you need to be aware of two other elements important to an option's value—interest rates and marketplace supply and demand.

Interest Rates The prevailing interest rates in the economy impact the value of an option. Indeed, interest rates are an element in formal option pricing models. The reason is that options are highly leveraged, so they tie up only a portion of the money that would otherwise be required to invest in the underlying futures contract. This means institutional investors save on their cost of capital, and that factor influences the option price.

The interest rate Greek is rho, which is the change in option price given a one-percentage-point change in the risk-free interest rate. The sensitivity of options to changes in interest rates is generally very low, especially at low interest rate levels.

Supply and Demand As discussed earlier, ultimately it is the marketplace that determines the price of an option. For this reason, options often trade at levels above or below their theoretical value (as determined by comparing them to other related options).

When this occurs, the mathematical explanation is simply that the market is pricing in a different volatility premium for those mispriced options. This difference in pricing may continue for some time or may unwind itself quickly, but while it occurs it is difficult to say the price is wrong.

Another important marketplace issue is liquidity. A general rule for any financial instrument is that the more participants who are trading it the better the liquidity will be. You know this intuitively; more participants in a market can mean greater competition among buyers and sellers. Accordingly, the spread between the bids and offers will become tighter and thus the quality of fills likely will improve.

As with any exchange-traded instrument, supply and demand is the big wild card in pricing of options. During hectic periods, both opportunities and risks can increase.

Reading Futures Option Quotes

Investors new to futures options are sometimes intimidated by the simple task of determining what the different options will cost. Unlike stock options, where each one is priced the same (dollars per share), futures options require you to find out the different tick values of each underlying commodity. Being unsure of the tick value of any particular market is a terrible reason to miss the opportunities that market may be offering you.

Table 9.1 lists some common futures options markets and explains the tick values for each. Notice the table includes the size of the underlying contract to

TABLE 9.1 Common Futures Options Markets

Market	Contract Size	Value of Full Point	Value of 1 Tick	Option Quote Example
Financials				
Big S&P 500 futures	$250 × Index	1.00 = $250	0.10 = $25	"1350" = 13.50 = $3,375 (13.50 × $250)
E-Mini S&P 500 futures	$50 × Index	1.00 = $50	0.25 = $12.50	"825" = 8.25 = $412.50 (8.25 × $50)
Mini-Sized Dow futures	$5 × Index	1.00 = $5	1.00 = $5	"160" = 160 = $800 (160 × $5)
Euro Currency futures	125,000 Euro	$12.50 per point	0.0001 = $12.50	"180" = .0180 = $2,250 (180 × $12.50)
Japanese Yen futures	12,500,000 Yen	$12.50 per point	0.000001 = $12.50	"238" = .000238 = $2,975 (238 × $12.50)
U.S. 10-Year Note futures	$100,000 Face Value	1-00 = $1,000	1/64 = $15.625	"3-48" 3 48/64 = $3,750 (3 48/64 × $1,000)
Metals				
Gold futures	100 oz.	1.00 = $100	0.10 = $10.00	"310" = 31.0 = $3,100 (310 × $10)
Copper	25,000 lbs.	$2.50 per point	5 points = $12.50	"230" = 2.30 = $575 (230 × $2.50)
Energies				
Crude Oil futures	1,000 barrels	1.00 = $1,000	0.01 = $10	"60" = .60 = $600 (60 × $10)
Heating Oil futures	42,000 gallons	1 point = $4.20	1 point = $4.20	"90" = 90 = $378 (90 × $4.20)
Unleaded Gasoline futures	42,000 gallons	1 point = $4.20	1 point = $4.20	"260" = 260 = $1,092 (260 × $4.20)
Agricultural				
Soybean futures	5,000 bushels	1 cent = $50	1/8 cent = $6.25	"8 6/8" = 8.75 = $437.50 (8.75 × $50)
Live Cattle futures	40,000 lbs.	$4 per point	2.5 points = $10	"170" = 170 = $680 (170 × $4)
Cocoa futures	10 metric tons	1 point = $10	1 point = $10	"70" = 70 = $700 (70 × $10)
Sugar futures	112,000 lbs.	1.00 = $1,120	1 point = $11.20	"140" = 1.40 = $1,568 (140 × $11.20)

help you understand how the different pricing for each option came about. Don't fall into the common beginner's trap of agonizing over where the decimal point should go for each commodity quote; even the financial newspapers don't always follow the same conventions. As a practical matter, industry professionals know the contract size of each market but they focus instead on the individual point values and think in terms of how much money is being made or lost for a given move. Accordingly, the table provides you with a real-world example of how each option value can be calculated.

Now that you have reviewed the mechanics of futures options, let's see how those principles can be used in specific strategies.

BASIC FUTURES OPTIONS STRATEGIES

Options themselves can be very straightforward. Still, beginners will sometimes be overwhelmed because options strategies, especially options used in combinations, can be very powerful. We'll begin first with basic strategies and build from there. In all of these examples, the cost of commissions and fees have not been included.

Trading a Bullish View

If you are interested in a particular market and believe prices will go higher, your decision is pretty simple with futures, stocks, and many other investment vehicles: You just buy. If the price of the market goes up as you expect, you make money; if the price of the market goes down, you lose money. For these instruments it's a straight-line profit/loss profile (see Figure 9.1).

Options give you other ways to invest according to your opinion about rising prices, and most do not involve a simple straight-line profit/loss profile. Let's consider now a simple buy-call strategy.

Buy a Call If you believe a market's price will go up but wish to avoid the unlimited risk of a futures position, you can buy a call option. Let's assume you buy a call with a strike price of 100 and pay a premium of 6 points.

As the profit/loss diagram illustrates (see Figure 9.2), the advantage of a call option is that your profit is unlimited while the amount of loss is predefined to the amount of premium you paid for the option. The disadvantage of the call is that the price of the underlying market must be higher than 106 for you to make a profit. Therefore, you must be rather confident in your analysis that the price will exceed 106 prior to the option's expiration.

Let's plug in and solve the profit or loss of the call-buying strategy for a variety of different scenarios. Keep in mind that in this example, and for all of the profit/loss profiles shown, we are calculating the numbers *on expiration day*. This

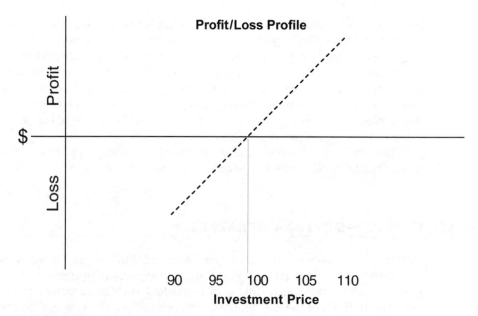

FIGURE 9.1   Typical nonoptions profit/loss profile. For futures, stocks, and many other investment vehicles, buying is a straight-line profit/loss profile. In this graphic, the purchase price is 100; above 100 is the profitable zone, and below is the area of loss.

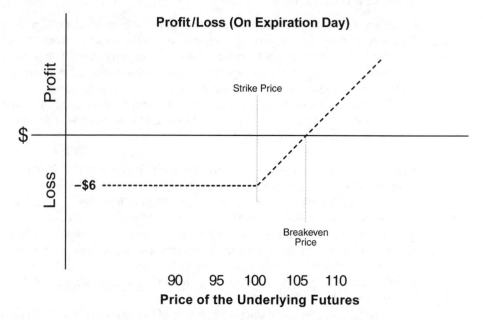

FIGURE 9.2   Buy a call. No matter how much the underlying futures contract drops in price, the loss will never exceed the cost of the option, in this case $60. Add the option cost to the strike price to determine the breakeven (6 + 100 = 106 breakeven).

means that time value has dropped to zero and only intrinsic value will be considered. (Remember, though, that you don't have to hold the option all the way until expiration day if a short-term move in the right direction produces enough profit that you choose to offset the trade.)

To review, in our example we bought the 100 strike call for a price of 6. For simplicity we'll say that each point is worth $10, so the cost is $60. We'll also assume this trade was placed when the underlying futures were trading at 100, so this was an at-the-money call when it was purchased.

Now then, to plug in and solve, simply determine if it is profitable to exercise the right to buy the futures at the strike price. On expiration day, if the underlying futures close at 110, then you can exercise the call (buy the futures) at 100 (the strike price), which means the option is worth $100 ([110 – 100] × $10/point). Since we paid $60 our profit is $40. If the futures close at 106, the option is worth $60, exactly what we paid, so 106 is our breakeven point.

Notice that on expiration day if the futures settle at 100, there is no benefit to exercising the call, so the option is worth zero and the trade is a $60 loss (the cost of the option). Finally, on expiration day, at any price below the strike price of 100, the option is worthless and the trade is a $60 loss. Why is the option worthless? Because the option provides the right to buy at 100, and at any level below that you can simply go directly into the marketplace and buy the futures at a better price.

Sell a Put   When you sell a put, you are not necessarily concluding that prices are going higher but rather, you just believe prices will not go any lower. This is a subtle but important distinction between option buyers and option sellers. As long as the market price settles above the strike price on expiration, the put will expire worthless and you will keep the entire premium that the put buyer paid you. (As always, you can choose to offset your short position at any time and you don't have to hold it all the way until expiration.)

For example, if you sell a 100 strike put for 6, the market would have to close below 94 on expiration day for the position to lose money (see Figure 9.3).

Let's plug in and solve for values in this put-selling strategy. On expiration day, if the underlying futures close at 90, the investor who bought the put from you will exercise the put (force you to buy the futures from him or her) at 100 (the strike price), which means the option is worth $100 ([100 – 90] × $10/point). Since you sold it for $60, your loss is $40. If the futures close at 94, the option is worth $60, exactly where you sold it, so 94 is your breakeven point.

Buying a call and selling a put are both bullish views, but the two strategies are very different indeed. In the case of selling a put:

- Your profit is limited to the premium received. Even if the market rallies to 120 or above, the option expires worthless and you get to keep the $60 you collected from the buyer.

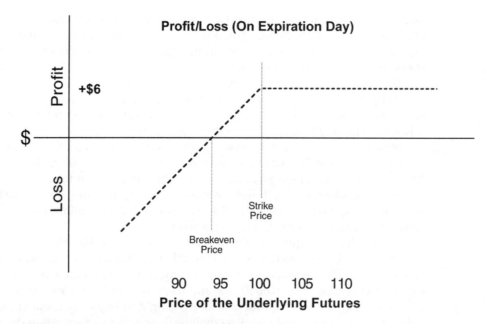

FIGURE 9.3 Sell a put. The put seller has unlimited loss potential in the event of a market sell-off and has a fixed maximum profit, in this case the $60 received for selling the put. However, the strategy has a low breakeven (100 – 6 = 94 breakeven) and therefore a better chance of being profitable.

- Your risk is unlimited should prices fall below the breakeven point. The short put is just like being long the underlying instrument.
- However, the strategy has a lower breakeven (100 – 6 = 94 breakeven) and therefore a higher probability of being profitable.
- Also, time decay works in your favor by eroding the value of the option each week.

Buy a Call, Sell a Call   This is also called a bull call spread or, more generically, a vertical spread. If you think prices are more likely to go a little higher but aren't convinced they will make a big move, you may not wish to risk buying a call or a futures contract outright. In this type of situation, some options traders like to establish a bull call spread.

For example, with the underlying futures near 100, let's say you buy the 95 call for 7 ($70 in our example) and at the same time you sell the 105 call for 3 ($30). You pay out 7 and take in 3, so the net outlay for you is $40 ($70 – $30). Figure 9.4 diagrams the results.

Let's plug in and solve for values in this bull call strategy. On expiration day, if the underlying futures close at 105, the 95 calls you own are worth 10 (105 – 95) and the 105 calls you sold are worth zero (105 – 105), which means your total

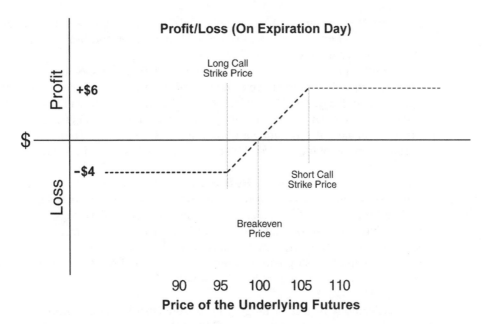

FIGURE 9.4 Bull call spread. Selling a higher-strike call against a call you own limits the upside profit of the trade. The benefit is that you lower your total investment in the trade, lower the breakeven point, and decrease somewhat the effect of time decay.

spread is worth $100 ([10 – 0] × $10/point). Since you paid $40 for the spread, your profit is $60. Plug in values for the underlying futures at levels above 105 and you will discover the most this spread will ever be worth is $100. If the underlying futures settle on expiration day at 95 or lower, both options are worthless and you have lost the total amount you spent on the spread, in this case $40. The breakeven point for this trade is a price in the underlying futures of 99 (95 + 4).

The rationale for a bull call spread can be thought of in several ways. If you forecast only a moderate rally then you will be willing to limit the potential profits of the call you buy by selling a call against it. But even if you believe prices may go quite a bit higher, you may still like the idea of selling the higher-strike call. By doing so, you not only lower your total investment in the trade, but lower your breakeven point as well.

Or looked at another way, part of what you pay for when you buy a call is the chance the underlying future will rally an *unlimited* amount. But as a practical matter, some level of profit exists where you will choose to offset the trade. For some, that may be a relatively small profit and for others it may be quite large, but what is the chance someone will hold a call to infinity? If you know in advance you will be offsetting the position on a rally to some level, why pay for that portion of the call that represents the profit area you won't participate in anyway? By *selling* the higher-strike call, you are simply selling back those rights (to the higher portion of the move) to another and helping to pay for the option you are buying.

Another more obvious benefit is gained in a bull call spread as well. Selling a higher-strike call not only lowers the cost of the trade, it provides some protection against time decay, too. Time decay erodes the value of the call you *own* but also the call you *sold*. Of course, the net position will still experience some time decay, but the sell side of the trade can provide significant relief. The next strategy is a variation on the bull call spread that actually benefits from time decay.

Buy a Futures Contract, Sell a Call   Also called a covered call or a synthetic short put, this is a variation on the bull call spread. Instead of owning a call and then hedging with a short call, the covered call strategy starts first with a long futures position and sells a call against that. The covered call is a well-known stock option strategy often presented as a method of generating income on an existing bullish position. This is because the investor receives money for selling the call. Of course, this is in exchange for limiting the potential upside of the trade.

Basically, with this strategy you are bullish the underlying futures but are agreeing in advance to sell the position at the strike price in the event of a rally. Just as with the bull call spread, selling a call lowers the breakeven point of the trade. Equally important is the fact that because the buy side of the trade (the futures) is not a wasting asset, time decay works in your favor by eroding each week the value of the call option you sold.

The profit/loss diagram of this strategy looks identical to the short put strategy shown in Figure 9.3—limited upside profit, unlimited downside risk, and a lower breakeven. One reason to use this covered call strategy instead of a simple short put is the ability to leg into or to leg out of the trade. For instance, an investor who was originally long the futures during a rally may wish to then sell a call against the position. By waiting for the rally, he or she may be able to sell the call at a higher price.

Trading a Bearish View

If you believe market prices are headed lower, your decision again is pretty simple with futures, stocks, or many other investment vehicles: You just sell. If the price of the market goes down as you expect, you make money; if the price of the market goes up, you lose money. The profit/loss profile of a short position in futures is a straight-line projection (see Figure 9.5).

Buy a Put   All things being equal, a put will increase in value as the underlying futures market drops. If the market price collapses, your profit potential is unlimited.

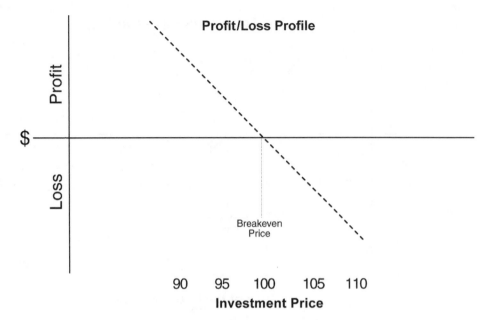

FIGURE 9.5 Profit/loss profile of a typical nonoptions bearish trade. For futures, stocks, and many other investment vehicles, selling short is a straight-line profit/loss profile. In this graphic, the market is sold short at 100; below 100 is the profitable zone and above is the area of loss.

Let's plug in and solve the profit or loss of the put-buying strategy shown in Figure 9.6, where the purchase is $60. Again, all figures are calculated on expiration day, which means that time value is zero and only intrinsic value is considered.

If the underlying futures close at 90, then you can exercise the put (sell the futures) at 100 (the strike price), which means the option is worth $100 ([100 – 90] × $10/point). Since we paid $60 our profit is $40. If the futures closed at 94, the option is worth $60 ([100 – 94] × $10/point), exactly what we paid, so 94 is our breakeven point.

Sell a Call When you sell a call, you are not necessarily positioning for prices to go down, but rather, you just believe prices will not go any higher. As long as the market price stays below the strike price at expiration, your profit is the premium that the call buyer paid. In the example, if you sell a 100 strike call for 3, the market would have to close above 103 on expiration day for the position to lose money (see Figure 9.7).

Let's plug in and solve for values in this call-selling strategy. On expiration day, if the underlying futures close at 105, the investor who bought the call from you

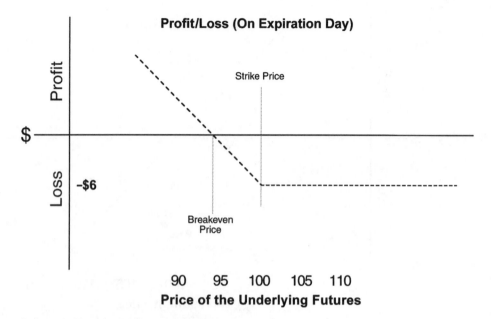

FIGURE 9.6 Buy a put. All things being equal, a put will increase in value as the underlying futures market drops. The loss on this trade will never exceed the cost of the put, in this case $60. Subtract the option cost from the strike price to determine the breakeven (100 – 6 = 94 breakeven).

will exercise the call (force you to sell the futures to him or her) at 100 (the strike price), which means the option is worth $50 ([105 – 100] × $10/point). Since you sold it for $30, your loss is $20. If the futures closed at 103, the option is worth $30, exactly where you sold it, so 103 is your breakeven point.

As Figure 9.7 illustrates, the short call is a bearish position but with several big differences from the long put:

- Your profit is limited to the premium received. Even if the market drops to 90 or below, the option expires worthless and you get to keep the $30 you collected from the buyer.
- Your risk is unlimited. It's just like being short the underlying instrument if prices should rally above the breakeven point.
- However, the strategy has a higher breakeven (100 + 3 = 103 breakeven) and therefore a greater chance of being profitable.
- Also, time decay works in your favor by eroding the value of the option each week.

Buy a Put, Sell a Put Also called a bear put spread or, more generically, a vertical spread, this is the counterpart of the bull call spread. In this bearish

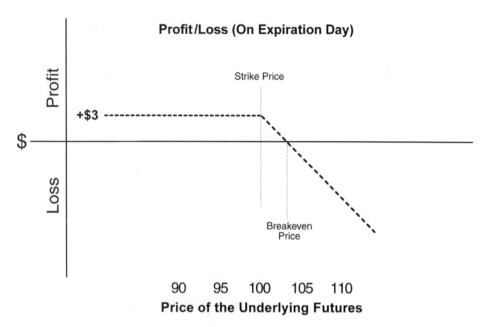

FIGURE 9.7 Sell a call. The call seller has unlimited loss potential in the event of a market rally and a fixed maximum profit, in this case the $30 received for selling the call. However, the strategy has a higher breakeven (100 + 3 = 103 breakeven) and therefore, a better chance of being profitable.

strategy you buy a put and help offset the cost of it by selling a cheaper out-of-the-money put.

For example, with the underlying futures at 100 let's say you buy the 100 put for 9 ($90 in our example) and at the same time you sell the 90 put for 4 ($40). You pay out 9 and take in 4 so the net outlay for you is $50 ($90 – $40). Figure 9.8 diagrams the results.

Let's plug in and solve for values in this bear put strategy. On expiration day, if the underlying futures close at 90, the 100 puts you own are worth 10 (100 – 90) and the 90 puts you sold are worth zero (90 – 90), which means your total spread is worth $100 ([10 – 0] × $10/point). Since you paid $50 for the spread, your profit is $50. For any levels below 90, the most this spread will ever be worth is $100. If the underlying futures settle on expiration day at 100 or higher, both options are worthless and you have lost the total amount you spent on the spread, in this case $50. The breakeven point for this trade is 95 (100 – 5).

The benefits of a bear put spread are similar to those of the bull call spread. In exchange for limiting your profit (in this case during a sell-off) you lower your total investment in the trade, improve your breakeven point, and gain some protection against time decay.

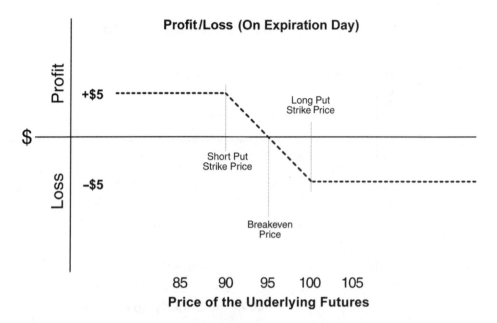

FIGURE 9.8 Bear put spread. Hedging a put by selling a less expensive put against it limits the maximum profit of the trade. The benefit is that you lower your total investment in the trade, improve the breakeven point, and gain some protection against time decay.

Sell a Futures Contract, Sell a Put Also called a covered put or synthetic short call, this is the bearish counterpart of the covered call strategy. With this strategy you would sell short the underlying futures and hedge the position by selling a put.

With this strategy you are bearish the underlying futures but are agreeing in advance to buy the position back at the strike price in the event of a sell-off. In exchange for limiting the potential profit of the trade, you gain a more favorable breakeven point and enjoy favorable time decay erosion. In a profit/loss diagram, this strategy looks identical to the short call strategy (see Figure 9.7)—limited maximum profit, unlimited risk of loss, but a more favorable breakeven.

Options strategies discussed so far are for investing with a bias to either the upside or the downside. But what about investing for a sideways market?

Trading a Sideways Market

Markets can trend up or down, but they can also trend sideways. Some options positions are designed for just this type of market condition.

Sell a Call, Sell a Put Commonly called a short straddle (when using the same strikes) or a short strangle (when using different strikes), these strategies seek to profit during a sideways-trending market by collecting the time decay on both sides of the market.

For example, with the underlying futures at 100 let's say you sell the 100 call for 6 ($60 in our example) and at the same time you also sell the 100 put, also for 6 ($60), for a total of $120. Notice that exactly at-the-money puts and calls will have the same value. If your forecast of a trendless market is correct, time decay will work in your favor by eroding the value of the options on both sides of the market. Figure 9.9 diagrams the results of this short straddle.

Let's now plug in and solve for values in the short straddle. If the market price settles exactly at 100 on expiration day, both options expire worthless and you keep the entire premium. Chances are small that a market will settle exactly on a strike price, but the closer the price is to 100 at expiration, the more money you retain.

For a settlement price of 88, the 100 strike put is worth 12 (100 – 88 = 12) and the 100 strike call is worth zero, for a total spread value of 12 (12 + 0), which is exactly what was received for the straddle. So 88 is the lower breakeven point; for any closes on expiration day below 88 the short straddle will have lost money. The upper breakeven is calculated similarly and works out to be 12 points above the strike price, or 112.

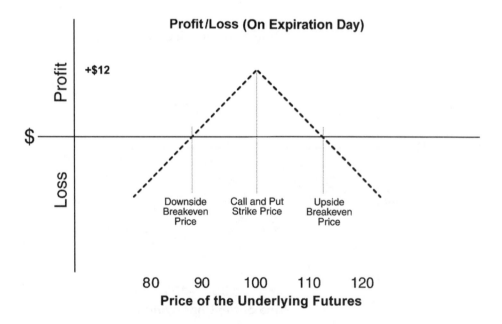

FIGURE 9.9 Sell a straddle. Simultaneously selling both a call and a put is a way to collect time decay on both sides of the market. By selling options at the same strike price (a straddle) the profit zone is narrowed, but the maximum potential profit is raised.

A variation similar to the short straddle is the short strangle. The only difference with this strategy is that the two options sold have different strikes—a higher-strike call and a lower-strike put. Accordingly, the short strangle has a wider and flatter profit zone, which increases the chance that the trade will be profitable on expiration day. Of course, the trade-off for getting this wider range of profitability is that the maximum potential profit is less than with the short straddle.

For instance, with the underlying futures at 100 let's say you sell the 105 call for 4.5 ($45 in our example) and at the same time you also sell the 95 put, also for 4.5 ($45), for a total of $90. Just as with the short straddle, in a trendless market, time decay will work in your favor by eroding the value of the options on both sides of the market. Figure 9.10 shows the profit/loss profile of the short strangle strategy.

Let's plug in and solve for values in the short strangle in Figure 9.10. If the underlying futures market settles at 95 on expiration day, both options expire worthless and you keep the entire $90 premium received. This is also the case for settlement up to 105. For a settlement price of 86, the 95 strike put is worth 9 (95 – 86 = 9) and the 105 strike call is worth zero, for a total spread value of 9 (9 + 0), which is exactly what was received for the strangle. So 86 is the lower breakeven point; for any settlements on expiration day below 86 the short

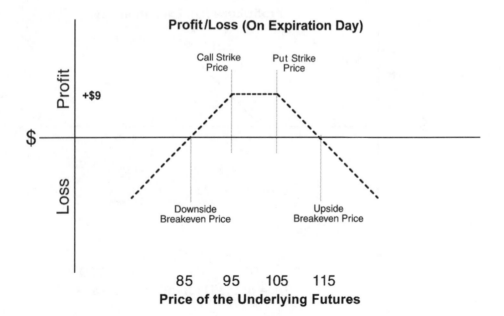

FIGURE 9.10 Sell a strangle. The short strangle is similar to selling a straddle, but sells options of differing strikes. The strategy still collects time decay on both sides of the market, but with a wider profit zone and a slightly lowered maximum potential profit.

strangle will lose money. The upper breakeven is calculated similarly and works out to be 9 points above the upper strike price, or 114.

Trading a Breakout View

Just as some options strategies are designed for a sideways-trending market, reversing the positions provides a way to trade a market that is expected to break out.

Buy a Call, Buy a Put   This is the inverse of the previous two strategies. With a long straddle you buy both a call and a put with the same strike price, and with a long strangle the options have different strikes. As expected, with these strategies you hope the market will move sharply in one direction or another. Perhaps there may be an important report or event (like a Fed meeting) coming up, the outcome of which might cause a sharp price movement in either direction, but you have no preference whether the move will be up or down. Figure 9.11 shows the profit/loss profile for the long straddle.

Using as an example the same prices from the earlier short straddle example, we get the following plug-in-and-solve values. With both the call and put costing $60 each, the total investment for buying the straddle is $120. If the market price settles exactly at 100 on expiration day, both options expire worthless and you

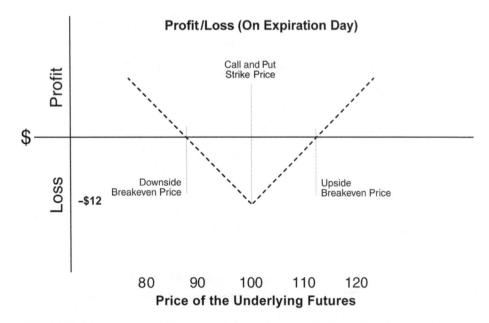

FIGURE 9.11   Buy a straddle. By simultaneously buying both a call and a put, you seek a market move in either direction. This long straddle is the inverse of the short straddle.

lose the entire premium paid. Just as before, the lower breakeven point is 88 and the upper breakeven is 112. Clearly, you hope to see the market move considerably away from the 100 strike price—and the further the better. Keep in mind that you don't have to hold any of the options strategies discussed in this chapter all the way until expiration day. Even a short-term move in the right direction can produce enough profit that you might choose to offset the trade.

A long strangle is similar to a long straddle in that it is positioned for a breakout in either direction. The strangle is more affordable and therefore has less money at risk. However, the market price has to move further to make your position profitable.

Let's now plug in and solve for values in the long strangle in Figure 9.12, using as an example the same prices from the short strangle earlier. If the underlying futures market settles between 95 and 105 on expiration day, both options expire worthless and you lose the entire $90 premium paid. Just as with this strategy's inverted cousin, the lower breakeven point is 86 and the upper breakeven is 114.

Other Options Strategies

As you may have guessed by now, options can be combined to craft many other useful strategies, each with unique and fascinating properties. For instance, with a bull call spread you could overwrite the short call side by selling two or more calls

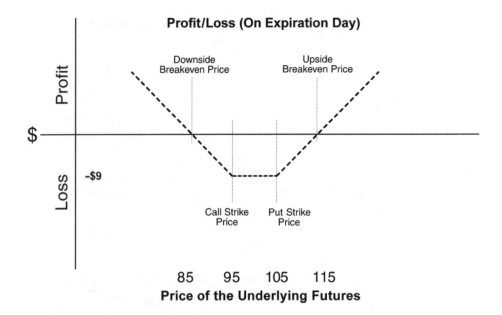

FIGURE 9.12 Buy a strangle. This long strangle is the inverse of the short strangle. By buying a call and a put with different strikes, you tie up less money in the trade.

in a strategy called a ratio write. Straddles and strangles can be turned into butterfly spreads.

Strategies already discussed can be used in ways not shown here. For example, the short straddle and short strangle strategies can be done with strikes that create a strong directional bias in the underlying futures. Legging into and legging out of options can be an integral part of a strategy as well. For instance, in a variation on a bull call spread you can first buy the call side of the trade and then wait for a rally before selling the higher-strike call. If you are able to get enough of a rally, the higher-strike option can sometimes be sold for the same price that you paid for the buy side, creating what is called a free trade.

Follow-up strategies can be employed to readjust a position from time to time. For example, a short straddle or strangle can sometimes become skewed to an unfavorable directional bias. In such instances one leg of the spread could be rolled out to a further strike, or alternatively, additional out-of-the-money options could be added to the winning side to get the trade back closer to delta neutral.

This section has covered only the more common and popular options strategies. Perhaps you'll have established enough of an interest to explore the subject in more detail. You may wish to visit the education tab of our web site, available at www.lind-waldock.com, for periodic updates on a variety of options-related materials.

Are You Thinking Like an Options Trader?

In this chapter you learned the distinctions of how to "think like an options trader." Unlike other investment vehicles, options require you to consider not only *where* a market is going, but also *how* it will get there. The reason is that options values involve not only market direction, but time decay and volatility as well.

While the mechanics and terminology of options can be daunting at first, each strategy is actually very straightforward. It's just that what options do can be very powerful indeed, especially when done in combination strategies. Perhaps the best way to understand and master each strategy is to plug in and solve for a variety of scenarios—the market is higher, lower, or unchanged on expiration day. You can also quickly estimate the effects of time decay by simply finding the amount of time value remaining in any given week.

Defining and controlling your risk can be two of the most important factors in achieving your goals as an investor, and options are perhaps the most flexible investment vehicle available for doing just that. With a foundation built upon the content of this chapter, you can consider options on futures as another valuable edge as you seek to achieve your investing goals.

CHAPTER 10

Forex

*Another Opportunity
for Traders*

In addition to the rapid growth of trading in the electronic stock index futures markets, one of the hottest new trading venues in recent years has been the development of trading in cash currencies or the foreign exchange market (more commonly known as the forex or just FX markets). With the prominent role of the U.S. dollar in the world forex market, in interest rates, and in the pricing of many other markets such as gold, oil, grains, and soybeans, fluctuations in the value of currencies against the dollar have provided attractive opportunities for traders for a number of years.

The ability of individual traders to participate in this market has expanded greatly with the establishment of a number of new cash forex firms since the late 1990s, thanks to new regulations and advances in technology that make trading and record keeping on a smaller scale possible. Some of these firms have many of the same regulatory requirements as futures and options brokerage firms. However, there are some important differences, particularly because cash forex firms do not trade on an exchange. Therefore, forex trading is worthy of a chapter of its own in any book on trading.

WHAT IS THE FOREX MARKET?

If the world existed with a single currency, there would be no need for a foreign exchange market. But that is not the case; most nations have their own national currencies.

The forex market plays the key role of providing the mechanism for making payments across borders. It is the vehicle for transferring funds and purchasing power from one currency to another and determining that all-important price, the exchange rate. Any nation whose residents conduct business abroad or engage in financial transactions with persons in other countries must have a mechanism for providing access to foreign currencies so that payments can be made in a form acceptable to both parties. In other words, there is a need for forex transactions—exchanging one currency for another. This is the forex market.

Every successful market must have two key participants: those who want to eliminate risk and those who are willing to take on risk. Broadly speaking, these are called hedgers and speculators. The financial institutions that facilitate transactions between these participants are called dealers. Dealers may be commercial banks, merchant banks, investment banks, broker/dealer firms, or simply trading companies specializing in foreign exchange.

A hedger is a person or business that buys or sells goods, services, or investments denominated in a currency other than their native currency. Hedgers are looking to offset the risk of fluctuating exchange rates so they can lock in the final economic effect of a transaction.

A speculator may be a bank, investment fund, trading company, or individual trader. Until recently, speculators in the cash forex market were large traders; a retail market didn't exist in any viable way. Now, however, technology and regulation have created the opportunity for even small individual investors to participate directly in the forex market. Here are some key features of that market.

Birth of the Modern Forex Market

Prior to the early 1970s, the Bretton Woods accord, established in 1944, was the basis for the international monetary system. The goal was to keep exchange rates stable and provide for small adjustments by governments from time to time when necessary. The U.S. dollar and gold were used as world financial reserves.

The Bretton Woods system fell apart as a result of increasing U.S. balance-of-payments deficits and other countries' reluctance to hold increasingly large quantities of U.S. dollars. Under the accord, the U.S. dollar was convertible into gold at $35 per ounce, meaning the United States had to take back its dollars in exchange for gold at a rate of $35 per ounce. By August 1971, the demand from foreign central banks to exchange their dollars for gold became so great that the United States could not continue to honor this agreement. The so-called gold window was closed—the dollar was no longer convertible, and the U.S. dollar was officially devalued.

The subsequent Smithsonian Agreement realigned currencies and created wider bands for fluctuation. This proved to be a useless attempt to perpetuate the adjustable peg system with a new currency alignment. The Smithsonian Agreement fell apart in February 1973, and other currencies were left to float against the dollar.

Thus was born what has become the largest international trade and investment market in the world.

Evolution of the Forex Market

A series of significant events helped to develop today's forex market:

1972—Chicago Mercantile Exchange (CME) introduces currency futures trading. Recognizing the significance of fluctuating exchange rates and their possible negative effects on international business, the exchange sought to provide a marketplace for business to shift this risk to speculators. These were the first financial futures contracts, and they allowed individuals access to the forex market.

1978—International Monetary Fund articles are officially amended, sanctioning floating exchange rates. Subsequently, the U.S. Federal Reserve shifted its policy away from targeting interest rates. In effect, this was the birth of the modern-day international fixed-income markets. Interest rates were allowed to fluctuate, thus creating large international money flows as investors sought greater returns on their assets.

1985—The Plaza Accord. Demand for U.S. dollar investments had pushed the value of the dollar to such levels that the Group of Major Industrial Nations (the United States, Britain, France, Germany, and Japan, known as the G5) worried about a so-called dollar bubble. The goal of the G5's Plaza Accord was to achieve an orderly appreciation of the main nondollar currencies against the dollar. G5 countries cooperated in selling the U.S. dollar, precipitating a large decline.

1987—The Louvre Accord. The U.S. dollar had lost more than 40 percent of its value from the highs in 1985. There was general agreement among the G6 countries (the G5 countries and Canada) that current levels of their currencies were broadly consistent with underlying fundamentals. They agreed to cooperate closely to maintain stable exchange rates around those levels. This understanding among the group of major central banks and finance ministers continues to be the basis for cooperative central bank intervention in the marketplace.

1992—Electronic trading begins. Globex, CME's global electronic trading system, began providing after-hours trading in currency futures.

1999—Introduction of the euro. The euro began trading as the international currency of exchange for 11 countries in the European Union. It replaced the deutsche mark, French franc, and Italian lira among others. The euro is progressively becoming more important as an international benchmark currency.

2000—Commodity Modernization Act of 2000. After many years of debate among the Federal Reserve, the Commodity Futures Trading Commission (CFTC), and the Securities and Exchange Commission (SEC), Congress officially defined the retail forex marketplace in the United States, providing the definition of a retail investor and what types of institutions can deal with those retail investors. It also authorized the CFTC as regulator of the retail forex marketplace. This has enabled U.S. forex dealers to open this market to retail investors and has led forex trading to become the fastest-growing market segment of the U.S. investment community.

Largest and Most Liquid Market in the World

Worldwide turnover is estimated at more than $1.8 trillion a day. Market liquidity is truly impressive. Large trades of $200 million or more are not uncommon. Likewise,

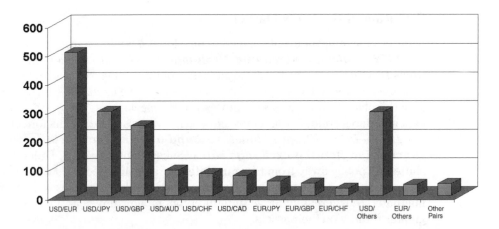

FIGURE 10.1   Daily FX volume by currency pair, 2004. (*Source of data:* Bank for International Settlements)

small trades of $100,000 are also a staple of the market. Some currency pairs trade several hundred billion dollars per day (see Figure 10.1). Yet studies have shown that prices tend to move in relatively small increments, a sign of a smoothly functioning and liquid market.

A 24-Hour Market

With the exception of weekends, the forex market follows the sun around the world. Banks and other financial institutions provide continuous markets to their clients around the clock via a network of branches, affiliates, correspondents, and 24-hour trading desks.

International Network of Dealers

The forex market consists of approximately 2,000 dealer institutions that are actively trading foreign exchange—trading with their customers and with each other. Here is a simplistic view of a typical trade:

Dealer A buys a foreign currency in exchange for U.S. dollars from Customer C.

Dealer A then sells that currency to Dealer B.

Dealer B then sells that currency to Customer D.

In this manner, the risk of a fluctuating exchange rate has been shifted from Customer C to Customer D. The dealers have acted as the conduit and have provided the market to the customers.

These dealer institutions are geographically dispersed, located in financial centers around the globe (see Figure 10.2). Banks account for the largest share of trading, but investment firms have become more active in recent years (see Figure 10.3). All of these dealers are linked together by a progressively sophisticated electronic network of computers, telephones, and other electronic communications systems. The forex market is probably the only truly global market, linking the various foreign exchange trading centers around the world into a single, unified, cohesive worldwide market.

EXCHANGE RATES AND CENTRAL BANKS

Market forces of supply and demand determine exchange rates for the major currencies. Occasionally, central bank intervention influences prices, but this is done in a way that is consistent with free-market activity.

Like any other buyer or seller in the market, a central bank is motivated to act based on the economics with which it is faced. Central bank intervention is merely the buying or selling of one currency against another conducted by the central

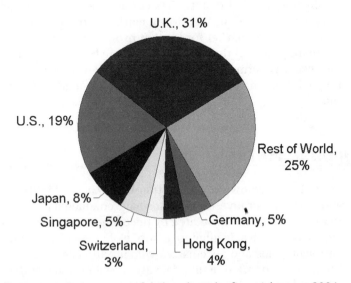

FIGURE 10.2 Estimated percentage of daily volume by financial center, 2004. (*Source of data:* Bank for International Settlements)

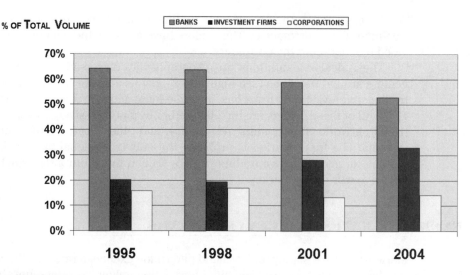

FIGURE 10.3   Daily global volume by counterparty type. (*Source of data:* Bank for International Settlements)

banks of one or more of the major industrialized countries. If exchange rates are influenced by a central bank's activities, it is because that entity is injecting either supply or demand into the marketplace.

   In essence, that country has certain types of risk to mitigate. One way it attempts to do so is through forex market activities. But it doesn't always work. Sometimes, the market forces that propel exchange rates in a certain direction are more powerful than can be overcome by even a group of central banks. Just because a government or governments want a currency to stay in a particular range doesn't mean it's going to do so. Free-market forces determine exchange rates.

THE TRADING INSTRUMENT

Since the breakdown of the Bretton Woods accord in the early 1970s, speculators and cross-border investment funds have conducted progressively more trading activity. This has been facilitated by the open-market policies adopted by the world's largest economies, leading to a more global view of investments by most large investment funds and speculators who are the customers of dealers and generally do not need or want actual delivery of the currencies that are traded. However, when a dealer trades with a commercial customer or when dealers trade with each other, actual settlement of the transaction generally takes place.

So what is actually traded? A foreign exchange dealer buying U.S. dollars is actually buying a dollar-denominated deposit in a bank located in the United States. This is the case even if the trade is conducted in Japan or any other financial center. Likewise, a dealer buying British pounds is actually buying a pound deposit in a bank in Great Britain. The same scenario holds true for all foreign currencies.

So, if Dealer A buys British pounds from Dealer B in exchange for U.S. dollars, the following takes place: Dealer A deposits the agreed amount of U.S. dollars into a bank account held by Dealer B in the United States (most likely in New York). On the same day, Dealer B deposits the agreed amount of British pounds into a bank account held by Dealer A in Great Britain (most likely in London).

The U.S. dollar is by far the most widely traded currency. In the 1998 survey of foreign exchange dealers conducted by the Bank for International Settlements, the U.S. dollar was estimated to be one of the two currencies involved in 87 percent of global forex transactions.

Currency Pairs and Spot Pricing

Foreign exchange rates are always quoted in terms of one currency against another. The two currencies involved in the transaction are called the "currency pair." Most transactions involve a foreign currency exchanged for U.S. dollars—for example, USD/CHF (U.S. dollars versus Swiss francs). However, many transactions occur as an exchange of one non-U.S. currency against another non-U.S. currency. An example of this would be EUR/JPY (euro versus Japanese yen). Nondollar currency pairs are called "crosses," and their exchange rates are called "cross rates."

Most trading activity is done as spot transactions. *Spot* is a term used to describe the current market rate—the benchmark price. A spot transaction, by market convention, is a trade with a value date two business days after the date on which the trade is made. The two-day period provides time for the two parties to confirm the agreement and arrange the settlement of the currencies into the specified bank accounts in the various international locations. An exception to this rule is the currency pair USD/CAD (U.S. dollars versus Canadian dollars). *Spot* means only one day forward in this currency pair.

Spot prices are quoted as a bid and an offer. The bid is the price at which the market maker is willing to buy the base currency in exchange for the "terms" or "counter" currency. Because every forex transaction involves two currencies, it is important to keep straight which is the base currency and which is the terms or counter currency. A trader always buys or sells a fixed amount of the base currency. The amount of the terms currency will vary as the exchange rate fluctuates.

Another way of looking at it is that the base currency is always quoted as a quantity of the terms currency. So the exchange rate (spot rate) can be described as the quantity of the terms currency that can be exchanged for one unit of the base currency. For example, USD/CHF means the quantity of Swiss francs needed to purchase one U.S. dollar.

In oral and electronic communication, the base currency is always stated first, for example "dollar/swiss." Bids and offers quoted by dealers are the prices at which they would either buy or sell the base currency in exchange for the terms currency.

Pips

A pip is the smallest amount by which an exchange rate normally changes. For most currency pairs, this is the fourth decimal place. For example, if EUR/USD is traded at 1.2600 U.S. dollars per euro, a one-pip increase in the value of the euro would make the exchange rate 1.2601. For certain currency pairs, a pip is defined as the second decimal place. These pairs involve currencies whose units are relatively small in absolute value, such as the Japanese yen.

Rollovers

Because most speculative and investment customers of the forex market do not want to make or take delivery of foreign currencies, the typical practice of most dealers is to roll over their customers' spot positions each day. There are two ways to do this.

Traditional Method   The rollover can be done in the traditional way of offsetting the position for the original value date and reinstituting the position for the next spot date. The price differential between those two value dates is largely determined by the interest rate differential between the deposit rates of the two currencies.

Depending on certain factors, this price differential may be in the customer's favor (he or she will earn the differential) or to his or her detriment (he or she will pay the differential). Generally speaking, if the interest rate of the base currency is higher than the interest rate of the terms currency, forward value dates will be priced at a discount to the nearer value dates. Conversely, if the interest rate of the base currency is lower than the interest rate of the terms currency, forward value dates will be priced at a premium to the nearer value dates.

As an example, assume a customer is long 100,000 euros against U.S. dollars. Market convention is to quote euros as the base currency in terms of the amount of U.S. dollars it takes to exchange for one unit of euros. An exchange rate of 1.2600 means it takes 1.26 U.S. dollars to purchase one euro. Let's also assume that the interest rate on euros is 2 percent while the interest rate on the U.S. dollar is 1 percent. When the dealer rolls the position forward one day, the forward-date price will be at a discount to the near-date price. Therefore, the client will sell a position in euros on the near date and simultaneously buy back a position in euros at a discount for the one-day-forward date, thereby earning the differential.

Here is the formula for approximating this differential:

$$[(Ti \div 360) - (Bi \div 360)] \times R$$

where Ti = interest rate of the terms currency
Bi = interest rate of the base currency
R = rate in number of units of the terms currency per unit of the base currency

If the interest rate on short-term euro deposits were 2 percent, the interest rate on short-term U.S. dollar deposits 1 percent, and the spot rate for EUR/USD 1.2600, the forward differential would be calculated as follows:

1% ÷ 360 = 0.00002778

2% ÷ 360 = 0.00005556

0.00002778 – 0.00005556 = –0.00002778

–0.00002778 × 1.26 = –0.00003500

A pip value in EUR/USD is the fourth decimal place. So, given the preceding parameters, the nominal differential in a one-day EUR/USD rollover would be a discount of 0.35 pips. If the rollover were done at this differential and the original value date of the trade were July 5, the rollover transaction would be:

Customer sells 100,000 EUR/USD for value date July 5 at 1.2600.

Customer buys 100,000 EUR/USD for value date July 6 at 1.259965.

Therefore, the customer has liquidated and then reinstated a position at a more favorable price. If the customer had been short EUR/USD, the rollover would have resulted in a reinstatement of the position at a less favorable price.

Alternative Method Traditional rollovers are done based on exchange rates that exist on the date of the rollover. This means that, if the customer holds the position for any length of time, the original trade price is lost in the midst of all the rollover transactions that flow through the account. The overall economic effect of the transaction does not change, but it is difficult to track the actual profit and loss of a given position that may be on the books today but was initiated some time in the past.

However, another way to handle this position maintenance necessity is particularly attractive to retail investors. The positive or negative effect of the rollover transaction can be calculated automatically and simply credited or debited to the customer's account. If we use the previous example, the credit to the customer's account would be calculated as follows:

$100,000 \times 1.2600 = 126,000.00$
$100,000 \times 1.259965 = 125,996.50$
$126,000 - 125,996.50 = 3.50$

So, in this example, the customer's account would simply be credited $3.50.

When this procedure is followed, the original trade price remains on the position that is carried in the customer's account. This will then allow the customer's account statement to reflect the *gross* profit or loss of the trade, comparing the original trade price against current market valuations. Of course, in calculating the *net* profit or loss of the trade, debits or credits from rollovers would need to be considered as well.

Because of the nature of what is actually being traded (currencies on deposit), the foreign exchange market is inextricably tied to the fixed-income markets. These rollover transactions are the equivalent of overnight repurchase agreements commonly done in the world's money markets. These trades are done by banks all over the world, and the actual rates (differentials) are determined within the framework of a highly competitive marketplace. There is a bid and an offer for any two value dates in all currency pairs. So it is relatively easy for a dealer to price these rollovers every day.

SPOT MARKET VERSUS FUTURES MARKET

Although there are similarities in some functions, spot forex trading and futures forex trading have some differences. Here are some of the main issues.

Principal versus Exchange

Spot forex trades are contractual obligations between two counterparties. A trade between a dealer and a customer is a principal transaction between those two parties. No other entity is involved in clearing or guaranteeing the performance of the parties.

Futures market trades are executed on a centralized exchange through a futures broker who also performs the role of the customer's clearing firm. The other party to the transaction is anonymous, and the trades are guaranteed by the exchange's clearing organization.

Contract Terms

Spot forex trades can be done in any size and are usually for value two business days after the trade date. Either currency can be the base currency.

Futures market trades must be done in standardized units for specific value dates in the future. The base currency is fixed.

Price Quote Conventions

Spot forex trades are quoted in European terms. This traditionally means that most currencies, when traded against the U.S. dollar, are quoted as the number of currency units per one U.S. dollar. For example, "USD/CHF at 1.2150" means it takes 1.2150 Swiss francs to buy one U.S. dollar. Exceptions are the euro, British pound, Australian dollar, and New Zealand dollar. For example, EUR/USD at 1.2510 means it takes 1.2510 U.S. dollars to buy one euro. Trading terms and conventions in the spot forex market have historically been geared to the sophisticated institutional or commercial user. In recent years, however, some dealers have created account structures and electronic trading platforms that simplify the process and make it more convenient and less confusing to retail investors. For example, some of the trading platforms feature a standardized contract size and specific currency pair conventions.

Many futures market contracts are quoted in American terms. A currency is quoted in the quantity of U.S. dollars per unit of foreign currency. For example, a Swiss franc futures contract at .8283 means it takes .8283 U.S. dollars to purchase one Swiss franc.

Dealer versus Broker

Futures market customers often refer to their account representatives as their brokers. The firm that carries the futures customer's account is called a brokerage firm because it charges fees for brokerage and clearing services. Those fees pay for facilitating the customer's trading activity on futures exchanges and for the fiduciary services of carrying the customer's account.

A forex dealer is not a brokerage firm; it is a market maker and a principal to all transactions. Sometimes a forex dealer will offer services similar to a brokerage firm's services, but the key difference is that the dealer is a direct trading counterparty to the customer. A dealer may have relationships with brokers for the purpose of introducing customers. Mostly, this occurs when a broker has a value-added service to offer the customer. This could be in the form of investment planning, trade recommendations, or even the introduction of professional trading companies to act as third-party traders for customers. In these cases, a commission fee is usually added to the customer's trading activity and paid to the introducing broker. Typically, though, these brokers are not employees of the dealer.

ELECTRONIC TRADING

Until about 1992, "electronic trading" was a description of any trading activity by two counterparties conducted via a mechanism other than the telephone—in essence, electronic messages between two counterparties. Then the market-place saw the development of several "electronic broking" systems—the Globex system at the CME, the Reuters Matching system, and Electronic Brokerage Systems (EBS).

Futures brokerage firms and their clients use the Globex system to trade futures contracts on currencies. The other two systems are used by forex dealers to trade among themselves. These systems allow for the continuous posting of bids and offers available to participants on the system. Counterparties are anonymous until after transactions are made.

As this technology has advanced, it has also become more practical for individual dealers to provide electronic trading capabilities to their customers. In the late 1990s and early 2000s, several dealers developed their own systems to provide this service to their customers. By early 2004, any forex dealer serious about serving its customers' best interests had developed and implemented systems to enable customers to enjoy the ease and convenience of trading electronically, utilizing the Internet.

These systems, or trading platforms, provide the customer a constant stream of bid/offer quotes. Some of these platforms allow transactions to be executed with only a couple of mouse clicks. Others use a process known as "request for quote," which means that the rates quoted are only indications, and a specific request has to be made to get a bid and offer for any deal. Some platforms are more sophisticated than others and provide for straight-through processing, charts, news, and online, real-time account statements. Trades done on these platforms are principal transactions between the customer and the dealer.

COSTS OF TRADING

The first thing a trader should consider when assessing the costs of trading forex is the spread between the bid and offer. This is because the spread is the first thing that needs to be overcome for a position to be profitable. Large institutional customers, such as investment and hedge funds, demand and get the narrowest spreads. These are typically three to four pips wide in the major currency pairs. Individual investors generally see bid/offer spreads of five pips or more.

The dealer provides liquidity to customers by maintaining a constant stream of bid/offer prices. The dealer makes money when a customer hits the dealer's price and the dealer is able to lay off that position somewhere else (usually another dealer) at a more favorable price.

Brokerage Fees

A commission is usually charged as a dollar amount per standard quantity of currency traded. This standard quantity can be $100,000, $1,000,000, or any other quantity that makes sense to the client and the broker. For instance, futures brokers often like to have the commission be the same as it would be on a futures contract.

However, a markup, which is another form of transaction fee, is not discernible to a client once the trade has hit the account statement. The bid/offer spread may be widened to accommodate the markup. Alternatively, the markup could be applied to the price at the time the trade hits the back-office processing system. In either case, the markup is done in pips.

In general, the dealer does not participate in commissions or markups unless it performs regulatory oversight of the broker.

Regulation

For many years, U.S. regulators hotly debated who should have jurisdiction over the forex market. The CFTC and the SEC were primarily concerned about protecting the public, while the Federal Reserve fought against any attempt to implement regulations that might affect the way commercial banks do business. The core of the issue was how to provide adequate customer protection while maintaining a basic framework allowing banks to conduct their normal banking activity unfettered by unnecessary constraints.

While this debate was going on, unscrupulous forex investment schemes were being chased down by local and state law enforcement agencies that got no help from federal guidelines and business practice regulations.

The Commodity Modernization Act of 2000 clarified much of the uncertainty that had existed in the U.S. forex markets. It provided a definition of a "retail investor" in the forex marketplace and specifically identified what type of institutions can deal with those retail investors. It also appointed the CFTC as the government agency with regulatory oversight of the retail forex markets in the United States.

Today, specific rules and business practice guidelines that are similar to those that exist in the commodities and securities markets are being applied to forex firms that deal with retail investors. Any investor can review these rules and guidelines as well as check up on investment firms, dealers, and brokers at the National Futures Association web site at www.nfa.futures.org.

CHAPTER 11

Deciding
to Trade

By now you probably have formed some opinions about whether trading futures, options on futures, or forex should be part of your overall investment portfolio as an alternative asset class. You have read about the advantages that these trading instruments offer, how and where they are traded, what you can trade, and whether it is feasible with the size of trading account you can fund.

If you do decide to add futures to your portfolio, here are some of the critical matters that you need to consider:

- How much money will you be trading in your futures account?
- How much time do you have to devote to futures trading?
- How much knowledge do you have about futures, about trading, and about the marketplace in general?
- What is your trading personality?

Answers to these interrelated questions will go a long way in determining what futures markets you trade and how you may want to trade them.

THE MONEY FACTOR

Money is a primary prerequisite for any trading program. The first money issue, of course, is the amount you put into your trading account. The second involves covering your expenses to conduct trading.

An overriding money issue, whether for your account or for trading expenses, is the source of your trading funds. The money you use to trade should be money you can afford to lose without having it affect your lifestyle. You should not be tapping into your retirement or college fund or your household budget to fund your trading experience. The money you put into your trading account should be considered money at risk, and it should not be a factor in how you live if you lose it.

Your Trading Account

Brokerage firms typically require a minimum of at least $5,000 to open a futures trading account, but both you and the firm will probably be more comfortable if you start trading with at least $10,000 or $20,000. The larger your account, the more diversified your positions can be and the more staying power you have, increasing your chances for trading success.

Starting with $5,000 may preclude you from trading markets you would like to trade or know best. For example, you might like to trade S&P 500 index futures, but the full-size contract has a margin requirement that is about four times the size of your starting amount, making it impossible to trade that contract, no matter how well you think you might be able to master trading. Even trading the E-mini S&P, your initial $5,000 will limit your trading to one contract whereas trading multiple contracts might be more suitable to your trading program—in effect, all of your eggs are in one basket and you have no possibility for diversification.

Of course, most futures contracts do not have such large margin requirements, and it is possible to begin trading with as little as $5,000. But the main point is that you should have a realistic view of what you can accomplish with the amount of money you do have available for trading. The discussions about leverage, risk, and margins in earlier chapters should provide some guidelines for the amount of money your trading plan requires.

Your Trading Expenses

The amount of money you need to cover your trading expenses can vary widely, depending on how simple or sophisticated you want your trading setup to be. More than likely, your initial expenses will include some or all of these items:

- Computer to receive quotes, analyze prices, and convey orders to a broker.
- Internet connection through an Internet service provider, preferably a high-speed alternative.
- Information sources, such as news, charts, research, or advisory services.
- Price quotes. You may need only end-of-day, snapshot, or delayed quotes, but many active traders prefer real-time quotes, which not only involve data vendor fees but also exchange fees for each exchange providing a real-time data feed.
- Commissions. Compared to some of the other costs of trading, this may be one of your least concerns.

The brokerage firm you choose may provide a number of these resources (see Chapter 6), but you should be aware that getting set up to trade may require spending an amount of money over and above the amount you actually need for funding your trading account.

TIME FOR TRADING

If you have a $5,000 or a $20,000 account, trading may be a sideline for you while you maintain your day job. Even if you have a substantially larger account, you may have a business that requires much of your time. Or you may prefer to spend much of your time with family, hobbies, or some other activities that are important to you.

How much time do you plan to devote to: (1) learning how to trade futures, (2) monitoring prices and analyzing markets to find trading opportunities, and (3) actually making the trades? In your initial enthusiasm for trading, you may believe you have enough time to handle everything associated with trading, but time is a critical element of trading that should not be overlooked any more than the amount of money you need.

KNOWING THE MARKET

What you already know about futures, market analysis, and the trading process may determine how much time you need if you hope to trade successfully. Or it may determine how much money you decide to put into your trading account, depending on the confidence you have in your trading skills based on your knowledge of the market.

Is this your initial exposure to the futures market? Are you familiar with the fundamentals of the market you want to trade? How much do you know about technical analysis? What type of education do you think you need so that you feel comfortable that you are prepared to begin trading? How much trading experience do you have? Do you know when and how to use various orders or when to exit a bad position?

WHO ARE YOU?

You can probably give pretty definite answers to the questions about how much money you want to put into a trading account, how much time you want to devote to trading, and how well you know the markets and trading. But the most difficult question of all involves the personal traits you bring to trading.

How suited are you to deal with the stresses of trading? What is your tolerance for risk? How would you react if you had a big losing trade—or, almost as important, a big winning trade? What is behind your decision to trade futures? What makes you think you can succeed as a trader?

You may think you have the answers to these questions, but how you think and how you actually react in the heat of a trade may be totally different. That is why it is very important to analyze yourself as carefully as you would analyze any trade and to find a trading style and situation that are most compatible with your personality.

YOUR TRADING PLAN

Money, time, knowledge, and personality are all interrelated issues that have a bearing on what you can trade and how you will trade. You can't really deal with one of those matters without considering them all.

The next decision is where you will implement your trading program. Perhaps you are unsure as to whether you should trade yourself, work with a broker to assist in the trade selection process, or have your money managed by a professional trader. This question is very important, and you need to determine what works best for you. Let's examine each scenario.

Do It Yourself

If you are thinking about becoming a self-directed trader, ask yourself the following questions:

- Do you have a trading plan? This plan starts with your motive for trading in the first place and encompasses your whole trading approach—the time frame you will trade, what markets you will trade, your criteria for entering a position, how much money you will risk on each trade, what factors will determine when you exit a trade, and so on.
- Do you have time to devote to the markets to execute the trading plan you have formulated? This includes acquiring knowledge about trading and doing the research you need to make each trading decision as well as to do the actual trading itself.
- Do you have the personal risk tolerance to sit with a position when you have to make the decision to exit a trade? You can train your brain, but controlling your heart may be another matter. Simulated trading is an excellent way to learn the mechanics to prepare yourself for trading, but your emotions may

react differently when real money—your money—is on the line. Will you be able to make a rational decision when you have to make the call to take a loss or a profit?

If you answered yes to all of these, then you may just have what it takes to trade futures on your own in a self-directed account. If you answered no to any of these, then other alternatives may be more suitable for you.

Work with a Broker

If you like everything about futures but have some shortcomings when it comes to time or knowledge, you may want to seek some help from a full-service broker. There is nothing like experience to help avoid some of the most common pitfalls and mistakes in trading, and that, among other things, is what a seasoned broker can bring to the table.

If you have some basic ideas about what you want to trade or how you want to trade or you want to make the call on what positions to take but aren't sure how to execute the order, the help of a broker can be invaluable. He or she can help you in timing your trade entry, controlling your risk by assessing your risk management, or producing ideas about refining your entry and exit points. In short, the experienced broker can enhance any trading program you may have by explaining how to put it into action in a variety of ways.

In addition, a broker can offer some creative strategies you may not even be aware of or provide you with trading recommendations, backed up by the information and research capabilities of a large firm. With a broker-assisted account, you may be able to receive a complete course on trading or trading tips via a web site, e-mail, newsletter, or some other means. The broker can be your trading mentor and can tailor his/her input to exactly what you need.

Have a Professional Trade Your Account

You may have decided that you want futures to form part of your portfolio but that it might best be left to someone else to make all of the trading decisions for you. Many investors lack the time, knowledge, or personality to trade an account themselves, so turning their futures account over to a professional may indeed be the best route to go for those who are more comfortable investing rather than trading.

You may also decide to trade your own futures account but to place some of your funds with a professional futures trader as a way to spread your risk or achieve diversification. Even professional traders sometimes have other professionals manage a portion of their trading funds because that gives them exposure to a different trading method or removes their emotional involvement from making trading decisions with that money.

There are several ways to get professional trading help, depending on the amount of money you have to commit. Your brokerage firm can introduce you to many commodity trading advisors or to a trading method that can be traded automatically by a broker. In either case, all of the trading is done on your behalf. Instead of making a trading decision, your decision is which professional program to choose after evaluating a variety of trading styles and track records. Then you simply monitor the performance of the professionally traded program.

PICKING A BROKERAGE FIRM

Whether you decide to put your money into a self-directed account, trade with a full-service broker, or place your futures account in the hands of a professional, you will need to find a brokerage firm to execute your trades. The brokerage firm is your link to the exchanges where the trading actually takes place, and you should find a firm that can handle all the things you need to trade in the manner you have determined.

I can't think of the last time I went an entire day without seeing an ad in the newspapers, on television, or on the Internet from one of the hundreds of brokerage firms offering "the best service possible," "commission-free trading," "free everything," or some similar enticement. Although you can choose from among numerous firms, many of which do provide excellent service, you still need to make the important decision about where to open your trading account based on which one best meets your needs and not which one is cheapest.

My philosophy in selecting a futures broker is the same philosophy I use in everyday life: You get what you pay for. When I pay top dollar for something that I know is important to me, I get the best product or the best service. If there is a problem, I know the company will stand behind its product. But when I try to cut corners and save a few bucks, I am invariably sorry.

While saving money is a worthy goal in general, when it comes to something important (and I believe your brokerage service is), I recommend finding the best there is and worrying about price later. Saving a few dollars in commissions is not relevant when you are talking about the type of trade support you need from your brokerage firm when navigating these markets.

In making that selection, you need to make some basic decisions about your own trading situation first and then do a little research to find the right brokerage firm and perhaps the right broker within that firm. You need to look at the trading support tools the firm provides, the trading platform, the markets and products you can trade, and the help you can expect to get if trading becomes hectic or disrupted.

The history and stability of a firm can be quite telling. There's a reason that some firms are larger than others and have been in the business longer. It's generally because the firm has found a way to provide the best possible service. Find out how long a firm has been in business, how many clients it has, and the amount of customer-segregated funds it has on deposit.

The previous chapters should have given you more insights into what to expect and what you need, whether your account is self-directed, broker-assisted, or professionally managed. Refer to them for help in determining what type of broker and brokerage firm is best suited to you.

CHAPTER 12

Opening an Account

If you have ever purchased any real estate or a new vehicle or applied for a loan, you may have been overwhelmed by the paperwork and wondered how all those forms could possibly be necessary for what seems to be a relatively straightforward transaction. When you open a futures account, be prepared for more of the same. All of the paperwork does have a purpose for both the client and the brokerage firm, also known as a futures commission merchant (FCM).

For the client:

- Discloses the risks associated with futures trading.
- Describes the rights and responsibilities of each party to the transaction.
- Educates the client about the process of futures trading.

For the FCM:

- Provides information regarding the client's finances.
- Discloses the client's level of knowledge and experience in markets the client intends to trade.
- Describes the rights and responsibilities of each party to the transactions.

When you trade, you want to know that every person on the other side of your positions will fulfill the terms of the transactions into which you have entered. Other traders expect the same thing of you and deserve to know that you have been screened and found acceptable to participate in trading. The Commodity Futures Trading Commission (CFTC) and National Futures Association (NFA) require FCMs to have complete information on file prior to opening an account as part of their due diligence. This paperwork also serves to protect both you and the FCM.

OPENING ACCOUNT INFORMATION

FCMs have standard opening account documentation that must be filled out before an account can be opened. The forms are different, depending on the type of account—for example, individual versus corporate. The CFTC also specifies what information needs to be obtained from customers and what risk disclosures have to be provided to clients.

Forms include a customer account application, which asks for basic identifying information (name, address, telephone number) and, for an individual, employment status (see Figure 12.1). Customers also need to provide financial information such as annual income, net worth and estimated liquid net worth, amount of capital available, banking information, and trading experience. Customers will need to disclose if they have any affiliations or employment with any company associated with the futures or securities industries.

The customer agreement is the contract between an FCM and its customer. The customer agreement:

- Authorizes the FCM to purchase and sell futures contracts upon the customer's oral or written instructions, subject to the rules and regulations of the exchanges and other markets.
- Requires the customer to provide and maintain margin requirements.
- Authorizes the FCM to liquidate the customer's positions in certain circumstances.
- Obligates the customer to pay specified charges and fees.
- Requires the customer to report discrepancies in statements.
- Requires the customer to acknowledge that investment in futures contracts is speculative and involves a high degree of risk.

There may also be one or more agreements about the customer's anticipated use of an electronic trading platform. Other provisions in a customer agreement may limit the customer's ability to file a lawsuit to a certain jurisdiction or venue, shorten the time allowed for filing claims, or require the customer to waive the right to a jury trial.

RISK DISCLOSURES

Futures trading involves a substantial risk of loss, and customers must acknowledge that they are aware of this risk and will accept responsibility for any losses that result from taking this risk. Customers also must acknowledge that they understand that, because of the low margins normally required in futures trading, price changes in futures contracts may result in significant losses, which may

FOR OFFICE USE ONLY
Salesman Name and/or #:_____
Acct. #: _____
Date: _____
$: _____

IF JOINT: Primary Person to Contact _____

Phone no. (_____) _____

ACCOUNT APPLICATION

Account owner _____ ❑ Mr. ❑ Miss ❑ Mrs. ❑ Ms. Social Security no. _____

Home street address _____ Home telephone no.(_____)_____
Please, street address only - list P.O boxes below.

City _____ State _____ Zip _____ Country _____

Complete only if mailing address is different than home street address above:

Address _____ City _____ State _____ Zip _____ Country _____

Date of birth _____ U.S. citizen? ❑ YES ❑ NO Marital status _____ Number of dependents _____

Employer _____ Nature of business _____ Position _____

Business address _____
Please include City, State, Zip and Country.

Business telephone no. (_____) _____ Fax number _____

E-mail address_____ Portable/Cellular phone no. (_____) _____

Annual income:
❑ $25,000-$49,999   ❑ $50,000-$100,000
❑ more than $100,000 ❑ if less than $25,000, please specify exact amount:
_____

Net worth (excluding equity in home):
❑ $50,000-$99,999   ❑ $100,000-$249,999
❑ $250,000-$499,999 ❑ $500,000-$1,000,000
❑ more than $1,000,000 ❑ if less than $50,000, please specify exact amount:
_____

Estimated liquid net worth (excluding residence):
❑ $25,000-$49,999   ❑ $50,000-$100,000
❑ $100,001-$500,000 ❑ more than $500,000
❑ if less than $25,000, please specify exact amount: _____

Residence: ❑ Own ❑ Rent ❑ Other

Is this a joint account? .... ❑ YES ❑ NO
If YES, account will be Joint Tenants with Rights of Survivorship unless
you indicate here for ❑ Tenants in Common ❑ Tenants in Common

**Does any person other than the owner(s) of the account have authority
to trade this Account?** .... ❑ YES ❑ NO
If YES, please list their name(s) and submit the separate book called
MANAGED ACCOUNT AUTHORIZATION.

**Are you related to any employee of Man Group plc or any other broker-
age firm?** .... ❑ YES ❑ NO
If YES, please write name, firm and position:
_____
_____

**Do you now, or did you ever, have an interest in a futures or options
account?** .... ❑ YES ❑ NO
If YES, please list:
Firm _____ account ❑ open ❑ closed
Firm _____ account ❑ open ❑ closed

Are you a member of any exchange? .... ❑ YES ❑ NO

Investment experience: .... YES   (# of years)   NO
Stocks/Bonds   ❑   _____   ❑
Funds   ❑   _____   ❑
Futures/Options   ❑   _____   ❑

Affiliations:
Are you affiliated with or employed by a futures or securities
exchange, NFA, NASD, a member firm of either of those entities,
or by Man Group plc.
❑ YES, with_____ ❑ NO
Are you a "control person" or "affiliate" of a public company as
defined in SEC Rule 144? This would include, but is not necessarily limited to, 10% shareholders, policy-making executives, and
members of the Board of Directors.
❑ YES, Trading symbol: _____
Company _____ ❑ NO

Primary trading objective: ❑ Speculation ❑ Hedging

**Do you intend to trade security futures or narrow-based index prod-
ucts?** .... ❑ YES ❑ NO

**Date you received the Risk Disclosure Statement For Security Futures
Contracts** _____

Security futures and narrow-based index products trading objective:
❑ Speculation ❑ Hedging

Current Bank/Money Market accounts:
Firm _____ ❑ Checking
City _____ ❑ Saving
Acct. # _____ ❑ Money market

Firm _____ ❑ Checking
City _____ ❑ Saving
Acct. # _____ ❑ Money market

Are you now or were you ever an NFA member? .... ❑ YES ❑ NO
Registration status and sponsor _____
_____

What online trading system(s) do you intend to use?_____

**Please send free trial subscriptions for new clients. I understand
Lind-Waldock will disclose my contact information only to companies
that have agreed to keep such information confidential.** ... ❑ YES ❑ NO

Please send me Lind eWire e-newsletter .... ❑ YES ❑ NO

Please send me special offers by email .... ❑ YES ❑ NO

FIGURE 12.1 Account Application Form Book 2, page 1. (*Source:* Lind-Waldock)

substantially exceed the margin deposits that the customer has made. Finally, customers must indicate that they have read and understood the risk disclosure document that the FCM sends to each customer.

If a customer is a novice to futures trading, is retired, or is over the age of 65, the FCM will require the customer to sign an additional risk disclosure. The customer must acknowledge that the funds in the trading account are pure risk capital and that the loss of those funds will not jeopardize the lifestyle or retirement program of the customer.

Many FCMs use online trading platforms, and many customers prefer to use them to enter their own orders online. Consequently, electronic trading agreements are often included in an FCM's opening account documents. These outline many of the risks associated with online trading such as technical problems, system capacity issues, Internet-related problems, security breaches, theft, and unauthorized access.

If the customer decides to have a broker at the FCM trade the account with a trading system or wants to open a managed account, the customer will also be required to sign a document acknowledging receipt of a disclosure document containing the system or broker's performance data, as well as some additional disclaimers and risk disclosures.

If a customer intends to trade single-stock futures, an additional risk disclosure document will be provided. Trading in security futures contracts requires knowledge of both the securities and the futures markets. In addition to the substantial risk involved in trading futures products, the customer may be unable to liquidate if trading is halted due to unusual trading activity in either the security futures contract or the underlying security, if a system failure occurs on an exchange or at the firm carrying the position, or if the position is in an illiquid market. If a customer holds a position in a physically settled security futures contract until the end of the last trading day prior to expiration, the customer will be obligated to make or take delivery of the underlying security, which could involve additional costs.

TYPE OF ACCOUNT

Customers are categorized according to the type of account to be opened. Most FCMs accept individual accounts in the name of one person, joint accounts in the name of two individuals, as well as corporate, trust, limited liability company, and retirement accounts. The last-named accounts require the submission of additional paperwork, as the FCM will want to assure itself that these entities are authorized to trade in commodity futures. The FCM will request corporate resolutions, copies of trust documents, or documents relating to the organization and operation of the entity or retirement plan demonstrating that trading in futures is authorized.

POWER OF ATTORNEY

A customer may decide to leave the trading decisions in their account to another person or entity, giving authority to trade to a friend or relative, a broker, or a commodity trading advisor. If so, the customer must give written power of attorney to that person to allow him or her to trade the account. The FCM will want written assurance that the customer accepts full responsibility for all trading decisions in the account and agrees to hold the FCM harmless from any loss that the manager incurs trading the customer's account. For more information, see Chapters 4 and 5 on managed futures and auto-executing trading systems.

CUSTOMER IDENTIFICATION (PATRIOT ACT REQUIREMENTS)

Prior to September 11, 2001, many FCMs performed a preliminary credit check, making sure that the forms were completely filled out and that the name on the account was the same as the name on the check or bank account that was funding the account. Their compliance departments made sure that any third persons trading the account were registered, if so required. The accounts were also screened to make sure that a corporation or a trust, for example, had authorized the opening of an account on its behalf and that the trader was authorized to place the trades. Finally, the accounts were screened to identify persons with either a criminal or regulatory history.

Since September 11, 2001, and the passage of the Patriot Act, the new accounts department, in conjunction with the compliance department, must screen accounts more closely. FCMs require customers to furnish proof of identity and address, so customers must now provide a picture ID and proof of address. FCMs are also now required to enter customer information into several databases maintained by the U.S. government. Accounts of persons who are residents of countries that have been identified as "noncooperative" by U.S. law enforcement officials must now, by law, be rejected outright. Persons whose names appear in databases identifying suspected money launderers must also be rejected as customers.

SINGLE-STOCK FUTURES

Additional paperwork may be required for customers who express an interest in trading single-stock futures, which are regulated by both the CFTC and the Securities and Exchange Commission. Rules that were implemented when this new product first began trading in November 2002 required additional information and additional risk disclosures not contained in most FCMs' original account opening documents. Although some FCMs may now have incorporated all of this required information into their account forms, the more extensive risk disclosures for single-stock futures will usually be contained in a separate document.

ACCOUNT FUNDING REQUIREMENTS

Once the account has been approved, it must be funded. Customer funds must originate from a bank account with the same title as that of the trading account. Funds delivered by wire are considered "good funds," and customers can trade as soon as these funds are credited to their accounts. If the account is funded with a personal check, many FCMs will not allow a customer to trade until the check clears the bank. FCMs will usually not accept third-party checks, funds originating from a source different than the account owner, or funds drawn on credit.

Although customers' funds are not insured, FCMs are required to segregate customer funds from the rest of the firm's money and are limited in how they may invest those funds to earn interest when they are not being used by the customer.

MARGIN CALLS

Financial integrity is vital to the futures market. Under the current system, all trades executed on a U.S. exchange are cleared through an exchange clearinghouse. Instead of a specific trader on the other side of a customer's trade, the clearinghouse actually becomes the buyer to every seller and the seller to every buyer. Because of this arrangement, a customer need not be concerned about the financial condition of the person on the other side of his trade. Rather, the clearinghouse stands in the middle of the transaction and looks to each individual customer's FCM to be financially responsible for their respective side of the trade.

Because futures trading is highly leveraged (i.e., the margin deposit that a customer makes is very small relative to the value of the underlying contract), a small price movement may result in the FCM being required to send additional funds to the clearinghouse. Consequently, the FCM must be able to receive these funds from its customers quickly in order to satisfy its obligation to the clearinghouse. If a margin call cannot be met on a timely basis, the FCM may be forced to liquidate a customer's position. This protects the customer from incurring a debit balance, and protects the FCM from having to send its own money to the clearinghouse when a customer has no intention of sending additional money to the FCM.

Customers should be aware that FCMs are very serious about margin calls and the preservation of their right to liquidate. The customer account agreement gives the FCM the right to liquidate a customer's positions for various reasons, including but not limited to a customer's failure to maintain adequate margin or a customer's unavailability to receive a margin call. Should your FCM notify you of a margin call, you have a limited time to meet this request for additional funds. Should you fail to send the funds in a timely basis, you may discover your position has been closed out. Foreign customers may wish to use the services of a U.S. bank to ensure that money can be wired on a timely basis. Margin calls are generally initiated during normal market hours in the United States, which may require foreign customers to meet a margin call in the middle of the night in their time zone.

The rules regarding margins and margin calls are very strict and rigidly enforced, but, to the credit of the futures industry, no customer has ever lost money due to the failure of an FCM.

RESOLVING DISPUTES

Unlike the securities industry, FCMs cannot require customers to agree to arbitrate disputes. Customers may bring claims to the CFTC through its reparations program or to NFA arbitration. Customers can also choose to arbitrate their disputes at the exchange on which the trade was executed or at an organization such as the American Arbitration Association. Both FCMs and customers may commence actions in state or federal court, although customers may have waived their right to a jury trial in their customer agreement, and may also have agreed to litigate in a jurisdiction selected by the FCM.

A customer who is seeking restitution for alleged violations of the Commodity Exchange Act may file a reparation claim with the CFTC within two years of the time the claim arose. The customer can file pro se (without an attorney) and the cost is minimal. Reparations decisions are often appealable, but this may increase the costs and the time it takes to finalize the decision. Although a customer can contractually agree to a one-year limitation on bringing a claim in any other forum, this does not alter his or her right to commence a reparation claim for two years from the date of the alleged violation.

NFA offers an arbitration program. Should a customer commence an action against a member of the NFA (and all FCMs and introducing brokers are required to be members of NFA), the member is obligated to respond. Again, a customer can file an arbitration demand pro se; however, the filing fees are higher than in reparations. The various exchanges also offer arbitration programs for disputes involving contracts traded on that exchange.

Both reparations and arbitration matters are usually decided faster than they would be in court. Depending on the amount of the claim, the matter may be decided within a year. Large claims normally require oral hearings, and a customer may want an attorney to represent him or her if the claim is for a substantial amount of money. Both the CFTC and the NFA will usually schedule a hearing in a location selected by the customer. The aforementioned forums may allow testimony by telephone with prior approval.

Customers should be aware that FCMs routinely file actions in state or federal court to collect on debit balances that a customer may incur. Due to provisions in the customer agreement, a customer may be forced to defend a claim in the state where the FCM is located. This could involve the cost of travel, as well as the cost to hire an attorney to represent the customer's interests.

CHAPTER 13

The Tax Factor
for Traders

W hen newcomers begin to trade futures, taxes probably are not at the top of their list of concerns. But there are tax advantages with futures trading, in addition to the benefits of leverage, short selling, and the like that futures offer.

Several caveats should be mentioned before getting into a discussion on the tax treatment of futures and currency transactions:

- Tax laws are subject to change by Congress at any time and are constantly evolving. For current-year tax regulations, you should consult an accountant or tax adviser.
- This chapter covers only federal income tax provisions. Various states may have applicable rules that could affect your total tax picture as it relates to trading.
- This chapter covers only the general rules for taxing the results of futures and currency trading by the typical individual trader and does not get into other tax issues such as achieving trader status or complex trading arrangements. You should definitely find an accountant or tax specialist to advise you on those matters.

SECTION 1256 CONTRACTS

For tax purposes, it is important to determine whether a contract comes under Section 1256 of the Internal Revenue Code (IRC) because gains or losses from these contracts are treated differently than those from stocks or interest-bearing instruments.

Section 1256 includes any regulated futures contracts, foreign currency contracts, nonequity options, and dealer equity options. A regulated futures contract is a futures contract that is traded subject to the rules of a qualified domestic commodities exchange. Regulated futures contracts can also include futures contracts traded on a foreign exchange if the foreign exchange employs a cash flow system similar to the variation margin system used in the Unites States and if the foreign exchange has been designated by the U.S. Secretary of the Treasury as a "qualified board or exchange," as stated in IRC Section 1245(g).

The key features of Section 1256 status include:

- *The mark-to-market rule.* All Section 1256 contracts held at the end of a tax year are marked to market at year-end and deemed to have been sold at the market's year-end closing price. The actual gains and losses on dispositions of the Section 1256 contracts throughout the year are aggregated with the deemed gains and losses on the year-end positions. The mark-to-market rule applies to all Section 1256 contracts, whether they have been held for minutes or months and is similar to the daily mark-to-market practices in the futures industry.
- *The 60/40 tax treatment.* All gains and losses on Section 1256 contracts, regardless of time held, receive 60/40 treatment—60 percent of the net gain (or loss) is considered long-term capital and 40 percent is considered short-term capital gain (or loss).

Example: On May 5, 2005, you buy a regulated futures contract with a value of $50,000. On December 30, 2005 (the last day of business of your tax year), the fair market value of the contract was $60,000. Because you are deemed to have sold the contract at the market's year-end closing price, you recognize a $10,000 gain on your 2005 tax return, treated as 60 percent long-term and 40 percent short-term capital gain. On February 14, 2006, you sell the contract for $65,000. Because you recognized a $10,000 gain on your 2005 tax return, your tax basis in the contract is increased to $60,000 and you recognize only the additional $5,000 gain ($65,000 − $60,000) on your 2006 tax return, which is also treated as 60 percent long-term and 40 percent short-term capital gain.

How much difference does this tax treatment make for the investor? Using the same example, let us assume you had a net gain of $10,000 to report for Section 1256 contracts and were in the 35 percent tax bracket in 2005. If the total were taxed at short-term ordinary income rates, your tax liability for futures profits would be $3,500.

With the 60/40 tax treatment, your tax liability would break down as follows:

60% × $10,000 = $6,000

$6,000 × 15% maximum long-term capital gains rate = $900 tax due

40% × $10,000 = $4,000

$4,000 \times 35\%$ short-term capital gains rate = $1,400 tax due

Total tax due $900 + $1,400 = $2,300

In this scenario, the maximum blended tax rate is 23 percent instead of 35 percent, the top tax rate on profits from similar investment gains from securities or other instruments. You save more than $1,000 on taxes with the 60/40 treatment for futures profits compared to what you would have to pay on profits from other investments taxed at the short-term capital gains or ordinary income rates.

One other point should be noted about the marked-to-market provision. It is possible that you could pay tax on the $10,000 gain as of the end of the year and then have an adverse market move after the first of the year reduce those profits—in other words, you have paid taxes on profits that no longer exist. You can factor the loss into the new year's net result calculations, of course, but if your overall capital loss for the year is greater than $3,000, the excess could not be recognized that year and would have to be rolled forward another year; it may take several years to deduct the total loss.

Note: The mark-to-market and 60/40 rules do not apply to Section 1256 contract transactions that are made for the purposes of hedging. A hedging transaction is entered into in the normal course of a trade or business primarily to reduce an investor's amount of risk or exposure. Any gain or loss from hedging transactions involving Section 1256 contracts will result in ordinary income or loss.

Cash forex transactions that are part of a taxpayer's international business operations are not covered by Section 1256 treatment, either, but rather by Section 988 of the IRC. However, an individual cash forex trader can elect Section 1256 treatment instead, just as the futures trader can.

HOW TO REPORT GAINS OR LOSSES

Anyone who bought or sold a regulated futures or foreign currency contract during the tax year or is holding such a contract at the end of the year has to report this activity to the Internal Revenue Service (IRS). You should receive a Form 1099-B or an equivalent statement from your broker with your trading results (Box 9 on Form 1099-B). See Figure 13.1.

The net gain or loss from Section 1256 regulated futures contracts is reported on Form 6781, Part I, line 1. See Figure 13.2.

The net gain or loss amount on Form 6781 is then reported on Schedule D (Form 1040). No special election needs to be made to have marked-to-market 60/40 treatment. See Figure 13.3.

If trading in Section 1256 contracts results in a net loss for the year, a noncorporate taxpayer can use up to $3,000 of net capital losses to offset ordinary income ($1,500 if the taxpayer is married and filing separately). Any unused net capital loss can be carried forward into subsequent tax years until it is used up.

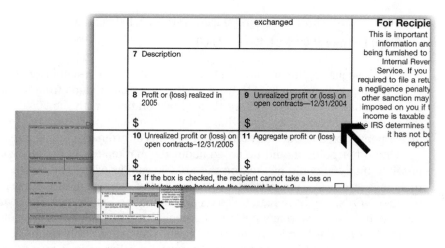

FIGURE 13.1 Form 1099-B: Proceeds from Broker and Barter Exchange Transactions. (*Source:* IRS)

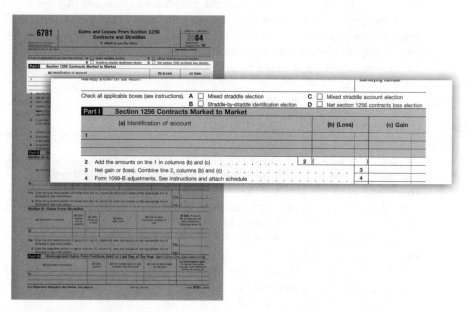

FIGURE 13.2 Form 6781: Gains and Losses from Section 1256 Contracts and Straddles. (*Source:* IRS)

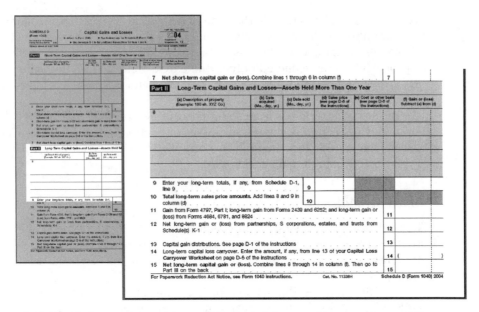

FIGURE 13.3 Schedule D (Form 1040): Capital Gains and Losses. (*Source:* IRS)

SPECIAL CONSIDERATIONS

There are other types of futures transactions that are reported differently than Section 1256 contracts.

Securities Futures Contracts

Securities futures contracts, also known as single-stock futures, are contracts for the sale for future delivery of a single security or of a narrow-based securities index. These are not Section 1256 contracts (unless they are dealer securities futures contracts, a separate issue not covered here) and receive different tax treatment than other futures contracts.

Gains (or losses) from offsetting or terminating a single-stock futures contract are taxed under Section 1234B and have the same character as the gain or loss from transactions in the underlying security (stock, options, and narrow-based indexes). As a result, there is no 60/40 tax treatment for these futures contracts.

Straddles

A straddle is any set of offsetting positions on personal property. These offsetting positions substantially reduce the investor's risk of loss from holding another position. A straddle may be in the form of a physical commodity, a commodity futures or options contract, or a financial futures or options contract.

Losses are subject to the loss deferral rule. That is, losses on the disposition of property can be deducted only to the extent that the loss is greater than the offsetting unrecognized gain position. Any unused losses are carried over to the next period.

The net gains or losses from straddle positions are also reported on Form 6781 but in Part II, Section A, line 10, for losses or Section B, line 12, for gains as seen earlier. The gain or loss amount on Form 6781 is then reported on Schedule D (Form 1040), "Capital Gains and Losses."

Mixed Straddles

A mixed straddle is a straddle in which some, but not all, of the positions in the straddle are Section 1256 contracts. There are two methods to account for mixed straddles: You can open a mixed straddle account or you can make an election for straddle-by-straddle identification.

In both instances, the net gain or loss from the mixed straddle attributed to the Section 1256 contract is treated as 60 percent long-term, 40 percent short-term, the same 60/40 treatment as futures contracts. If the net gain or loss from the straddle is attributed to the non-1256 position, the gain or loss is treated as short-term. In addition, there are annual limitations that apply in the case of a mixed straddle account. You should consult your tax adviser if you are trading mixed straddles, as the analysis of whether a mixed straddle account would be beneficial to you is complex and beyond the scope of this discussion.

CHAPTER 14

The Business of Futures

Who Does What

P ublic confidence is the cornerstone of the financial services industry. We've all seen what can happen to markets when the public loses its confidence in them or when the public loses confidence in analysts making recommendations or in corporate accounting or management practices.

The best way to create and preserve public confidence is to ensure that the highest levels of integrity are demanded of each and every market professional. Customers need to know that the firms and individuals with whom they are transacting business are properly licensed, are sufficiently knowledgeable about the products and services they offer, and have the best interests of their customers at heart.

The futures industry attempts to preserve the integrity of trading with several levels of participants: Regulators, exchanges, brokerage firms and, finally, the individual brokers and advisors who deal directly with customers.

REGULATORY STRUCTURE

Regulation is the single most effective way to ensure the public's confidence in the integrity of the marketplace. In the United States, regulation is provided by a combination of federal oversight agencies and self-regulatory organizations. Unlike most other countries throughout Europe, Asia, and the rest of the Americas, where there is a single regulatory authority with responsibility for the entire financial services community, the United States currently has similar, but distinct, regulatory structures for the securities and commodity futures industries.

This dual approach evolved, in part, because of the inherently different purposes of the marketplaces. The securities market serves to enable capital formation; the futures market facilitates price discovery and risk transfer, as explained in Chapter 1.

Timing is another key reason for the structure. During the Depression that followed the stock market crash of 1929, Congress held hearings that resulted in the passage of the Securities Act of 1933 and the Securities Exchange Act of 1934. As an outgrowth of this legislation, the Securities and Exchange Commission (SEC) was created in 1934 and given a mandate to enforce new securities laws, promote stability in the markets, and protect investors.

Although U.S. futures markets trace their origins to 1848 when the Chicago Board of Trade was founded, the first piece of comprehensive federal futures legislation was not enacted until 1936. At that time, only agricultural products were being traded on the futures exchanges, so regulatory oversight was placed with the U.S. Department of Agriculture. As futures markets expanded, Congress created the Commodity Futures Trading Commission (CFTC) as a separate agency in 1974.

The U.S. regulatory structure has four components:

1. At the federal level are the SEC and the CFTC. These agencies are charged with protecting investors and ensuring the integrity of the securities and commodity futures industries, respectively. Their operations are funded by federal appropriations. The SEC and the CFTC, in turn, report to Congressional oversight committees.

2. Industrywide self-regulatory organizations (SROs) are the second component. The National Association of Securities Dealers (NASD) and National Futures Association (NFA) deliver private-sector regulation at no cost to the taxpayer. NASD and NFA have similar duties. They're responsible for registering industry professionals, writing rules to govern their behavior, examining them for compliance, bringing enforcement actions when appropriate, and operating dispute resolution forums. These self-regulatory programs are funded, for the most part, by assessment fees paid by the users of the marketplace. Additional revenues come from various fees paid by members. The activities of these SROs are overseen by their respective federal agencies. The NASD came into existence in 1938; NFA, in 1982.

3. Securities and futures exchanges also are SROs and are the third component of the regulatory structure. They are responsible for ensuring that their respective member communities follow prescribed exchange rules and relevant federal regulations. Exchange activities are also subject to review by federal oversight agencies.

4. The fourth level is the futures commission merchant (FCM) or broker/dealer. FCMs and broker/dealers both hold customers' funds. Consequently, they are responsible for ensuring that their employees and agents are properly licensed to do business with the public and for monitoring that business.

These are all important participants in the business of regulation. Their involvement ensures that there is no point in the order process that is not subject to scrutiny.

FUTURES EXCHANGES

Futures exchanges, or boards of trade, are officially designated by the CFTC as contract markets. The CFTC currently identifies 14 exchanges as "active" and another half-dozen or so that it classifies as "dormant" because their contracts haven't traded for at least six months. Most of the active exchanges are traditional bricks-and-mortar exchanges, but some are electronic.

Historically, futures exchanges have been structured as not-for-profit organizations that are owned and governed by their members. Most exchanges are still member organizations, but the Chicago Mercantile Exchange (CME) became the first financial exchange to demutualize into a shareholder-owned corporation in December 2002.

In the traditional not-for-profit model, membership on an exchange is limited to a specific number of individuals, although some exchanges permit members to hold multiple memberships. Each membership carries with it a percentage of ownership and trading rights.

In the publicly held model, members of the public purchase shares in the exchange, just as they do in any other publicly held enterprise. At the CME, traders who satisfy certain requirements can either purchase shares of Class B common stock, which gives them rights to trade at the CME, or lease rights to trade at the CME from other Class B shareholders.

Although futures and securities exchanges are both auction markets, the way business is conducted on the floors of futures exchanges can differ from how it is conducted on the floors of securities exchanges. For example, the New York Stock Exchange currently uses a specialist system to maintain an orderly order flow and to guarantee that public customers receive a fair price. However, futures exchanges typically rely on independent floor brokers to represent customer orders and "locals" to make a market for those orders.

CLEARINGHOUSES

The purpose of clearing trades is to guarantee all contracts traded on the exchanges. In effect, the clearinghouse becomes the seller to every buyer and the buyer to every seller.

The clearinghouse ensures that trading is conducted in an orderly fashion by matching and recording trades, collecting and maintaining margins according to the positions of the clearing member firms, matching open short with open long positions for delivery, allocating delivery notices, and generating trading and delivery statistics. The clearinghouse also acts as a fiscal transfer agent, transferring money from the margin funds of traders who have incurred a loss in the market on any given day to the margin funds of traders who have generated a gain.

Here's how the typical order process works:

1. A customer places an order through a brokerage firm.
2. The brokerage firm sends the order to an exchange.
3. The order is filled at an exchange.
4. The order is then transmitted to the clearinghouse. If the brokerage firm isn't a member of a clearinghouse, it clears through another firm that is a clearinghouse member.
5. The clearinghouse confirms the order, guarantees the trade, and adjusts the clearing firm's account based on the gain or loss that results from the transaction.
6. The FCM then credits or debits its customer accounts accordingly.

This cash flow allows for the daily settlement of accounts, which is known as marking to the market. Marking to the market is one of the single most distinguishing features of futures markets and the most vital procedure for maintaining the financial integrity of the markets. Daily settlement prior to the market's opening the next morning serves to confirm that each clearing member firm is solvent and can continue to conduct business.

This process also reduces the risk of defaults by FCMs. In fact, no clearing member of the Clearing Corp., formerly known as the Board of Trade Clearing Corporation, nor the CME's clearinghouse has ever experienced such a default.

Settling transactions in the securities industry is handled differently. The current standard is T+3, which means that stock transactions must be settled within three days of transaction. The SEC is working on a plan to move to T+1 and to automate every step in the settlement process, creating what is commonly referred to as straight-through processing (STP). The implementation of STP would actually bring the settlement process in the securities industry closer to the norm in the futures industry.

The clearing process itself is also handled differently in the securities and futures industries. Although securities take three days to settle, all trades are cleared in one place, as are securities options trades. Until recently, futures exchanges steadfastly maintained their own closed and proprietary clearing systems, which was cumbersome and expensive for FCMs. However, the threat of competition from new exchanges finally drove the CBOT and CME, who between them clear upwards of 85 percent of all futures contracts in the United States, to create a Common Clearing Link. Implementation of the Common Clearing Link began in November 2003 and was completed successfully in January 2004.

In addition to U.S. clearinghouses, international organizations—or Central Counterparty Clearing Houses, as they are known in Europe—perform similar functions. One example is the LCH.Clearnet Group, which serves major international exchanges and platforms, equity markets, derivatives markets, energy markets, international swaps markets, and the majority of the euro-denominated markets. LCH.Clearnet Group is overseen by the Financial Services Authority, the agency with responsibility for regulating the financial services industry in the United Kingdom.

FUTURES INDUSTRY PROFESSIONALS

With a few exceptions, any individual or firm that conducts futures business with the public is required by the Commodity Exchange Act to become registered with the federal government. Registration is intended to serve two purposes: (1) to screen for the applicant's fitness to engage in business as a futures professional, and (2) to identify those individuals and organizations whose business activities are truly subject to federal regulation. There are nine official registration categories (many of which we've already referenced), but we'll describe only the ones you're most likely to encounter as a trader. Details about the registration exemptions can be found in Part 4 of the regulations of the Commodity Exchange Act.

Futures Commission Merchant

A futures commission merchant (FCM) is an individual or organization that solicits or accepts orders to buy or sell futures contracts or options on futures and accepts money or other assets from customers to support these orders. An FCM is frequently referred to as a brokerage firm. As of December 2004, approximately 200 firms are registered as FCMs.

Introducing Broker

An introducing broker (IB) is an individual or organization that solicits or accepts orders to buy or sell futures contracts or options on futures but does not accept money or other assets from customers to support the orders. Instead, the IB introduces the accounts to an FCM, which handles the customer's funds. Approximately 1,500 IBs are registered and operate much like an FCM branch office or a full-service brokerage firm.

Commodity Pool Operator

A commodity pool operator (CPO) is an individual or organization that operates a commodity pool or solicits funds for a commodity pool—that is, an enterprise in which funds contributed by a number of persons are combined for the purpose of trading futures contracts or options on futures or to invest in another commodity pool. There are approximately 1,800 CPOs. If you decide to put money into futures but would prefer to have it traded by professionals rather than trade it yourself, you may use the services of a CPO to help you find the right pool for you.

Commodity Trading Advisor

A commodity trading advisor (CTA) is an individual or organization that for compensation, or profit, advises others as to the value of, or the advisability of, buying or selling futures contracts or options on futures. These can be brokers or, most often, those who trade commodity pools. Today there are approximately 800 CTAs. As with the CPO, if you decide to put money into futures but would rather have it traded by a professional, you may want to have a CTA trade it for you or want to trade the CTA's recommendations yourself. Brokerage firms can often help you find a CTA whose trading philosophy matches your investment goals.

Associated Person

An associated person (AP) is an individual who solicits orders, customers, or customer funds (or who supervises persons so engaged) on behalf of an FCM, IB, CPO, or CTA. An AP is anyone who is a salesperson or who supervises salespersons for any of these categories of individuals or firms. The registration requirements apply to any person in the supervisory chain of command and not just to persons who directly supervise the solicitations of orders, customers, or funds. There are approximately 53,000 registered APs.

National Futures Association Members and You

Any registered FCM, IB, CPO, and those registered CTAs who manage or exercise discretion over customer accounts must also become members of the NFA to conduct futures business with the public. The futures exchanges also are voluntary members of the NFA.

These are the primary categories of futures professionals. It's a large and diverse community, and sometimes it's difficult to know what type of business relationship might make the most sense for you. However, one thing is certain: If you're going to participate in the futures markets, you need to work with a professional who is properly licensed, is registered in one of these categories, and is an NFA member. The reason is simple: As an NFA member, the firm or individual is subject to a set of consistent financial requirements and sales-practice rules designed to protect your best interests as an investor.

Certain types of futures-related activities do not require registration and NFA membership. For example, authors, newsletter providers, and professionals who develop courses, teach seminars, and create web sites but who don't otherwise directly solicit customers typically aren't required to register. Although registration isn't required, in some instances these professionals register anyway.

Background Affiliation Status Information Center (BASIC)

If you're new to futures and you don't already have a business relationship, the Background Affiliation Status Information Center (BASIC) system offered by the

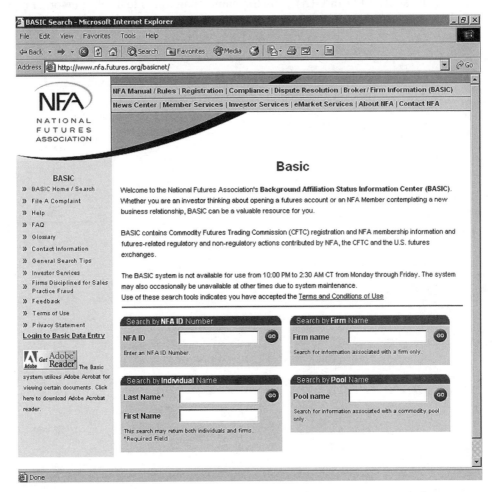

FIGURE 14.1 NFA BASIC home page. (*Source:* National Futures Association)

NFA can be a particularly valuable resource. It can tell you a great deal about the professional with whom you may be considering working.

BASIC includes CFTC registration status, NFA membership information, and futures-related regulatory and nonregulatory actions contributed by the CFTC, the NFA, and the nation's futures exchanges. Futures-related regulatory actions are typically disciplinary actions taken by the CFTC, NFA, and the exchanges. Nonregulatory actions refer to business disputes that have been resolved either through the NFA's arbitration program or the CFTC's reparations program.

To access the BASIC system, visit the NFA web site at www.nfa.futures.org (see Figure 14.1). The most efficient way to search the system for an individual or firm is by unique NFA ID number. You also can search by firm name (whether an FCM, IB, CPO, or CTA) or by the name of an individual salesperson or a particular commodity pool.

Domestic and International Futures Contract Volume

The Futures Industry Association compiles and reports the trading volume on domestic and international exchanges. The data presented here, which represents trading for January through December of 2004, illustrates how extensive and diverse these markets have become.

Domestic Exchanges Futures, Options, and Options on Equities Volume, January–December 2004

	Unit	Commodity Group	Dec. 2003	Dec. 2004	Jan.–Dec. 2003	Jan.–Dec. 2004
AMEX						
Airline Index (XAL)	$100 × Index	Equity	2,401	2,228	13,576	35,058
Amex China Index (CZH)	$100 × Index	Equity		81		1,629
Biotechnology Index (BTK)	$100 × Index	Equity	9,140	11,203	185,921	142,136
Computer Tech Index (XCI)	$100 × Index	Equity	572	161	6,566	4,597
Defense Index (DFI)	$100 × Index	Equity	122	4	369	192
Disk Drive Index (DDX)	$100 × Index	Equity	70	3	595	945
Eurotop 100 Index (EUR)	$100 × 1/10 Index	Equity	679	650	6,469	2,729
Gold BUGS Index (HUI)	$100 × Index	Equity	6,821	3,601	12,085	79,611
Hong Kong (floating rate) Index (HKO)	$100 × Index	Equity	4		1,416	331
Interactive Week Internet Index (IIX)	$100 × Index	Equity	1,426	21	13,823	6,833
Japan Index (JPN)	$100 × Index	Equity	31,871	9,238	210,880	73,071
Major Market Index (XMI)	$100 × Index	Equity	251	96,120	214,726	290,789
Morgan Stanley Commodity Index (CRX)	$100 × Index	Equity	122	49	1,240	975
Morgan Stanley Consumer Index (CMR)	$100 × Index	Equity	14	74	3,299	4,797
Morgan Stanley Cyclical Index (CYC)	$100 × Index	Equity	2,417	5,915	35,675	135,401
Morgan Stanley Internet Index (MOX)	$100 × Index	Equity	441	10	2,013	1,030
Morgan Stanley High Tech 35 Index (MSH)	$100 × Index	Equity	5,611	629	63,050	31,816
Nasdaq Biotech Index (NBI)	$100 × Index	Equity	254	36	1,361	330
Nasdaq Non-Financial 100 Index (NDX)	$100 × Index	Equity	117,676	273,378	832,034	2,671,379
Mini Nasdaq Non-Financial 100 Index (MNX)	$100 × Index	Equity	273,617	249,075	2,436,756	3,506,891
Natural Gas Index (XNG)	$100 × Index	Equity	4,581	16,966	8,440	38,889
Deutsche Bank Energy (DXE)	$100 × Index	Equity	159	314	1,719	4,133
Oil Index (XOI)	$100 × Index	Equity	7,389	12,095	40,686	140,263
Pharmaceutical Index (DRG)	$100 × Index	Equity	8,938	4,841	53,372	35,963
Securities Broker/Dealer Index (XBD)	$100 × Index	Equity	2,241	2,904	14,462	57,128
S&P MidCap Index (MID)	$100 × Index	Equity	503	1,746	112,207	11,939
All Options on Individual Equities		Indiv. Equity	14,260,874	16,155,828	175,802,038	195,402,074
AMEX Index Total			**14,738,194**	**16,847,170**	**180,074,778**	**202,680,929**
BOSTON OPTIONS EXCHANGE						
All Options on Individual Equities		Indiv. Equity		3,359,028		20,741,271
BOX Total				**3,359,028**		**20,741,271**

BROKERTEC FUTURES EXCHANGE

	Contract Size	Type		Trading ceased 11/03		
Ten-Year T-Notes	$100,000	Interest			654,800	
Five-Year T-Notes	$100,000	Interest			327,910	
BTEX Total					**982,710**	

CHICAGO BOARD OPTIONS EXCHANGE

	Contract Size	Type				
S&P 100 Index Options (OEX)	$100 × Index Level	Equity	1,326,937	1,276,031	14,343,992	16,426,392
S&P 100 European Exercise (XEO)		Equity	146,479	145,701	1,933,355	1,800,574
S&P 500 Index Options (SPX)	$100 × Index Level	Equity	3,761,302	4,805,137	36,754,720	49,472,117
Dow Jones Industrial Index (DJX)	$100 × Index	Equity	649,673	568,931	10,193,708	7,347,145
Exchange Traded Funds	$100 × Index Value	Equity	3,694,813	3,932,310	41,146,233	51,259,036
Sectors Total	$100 × Index	Equity	20,504	39,623	175,210	431,099
NYSE Composite (NYA)	$100 × Index	Equity			55	
Nasdaq-100 (NDXCBO)	$100 × Index	Equity	220,404	277,568	1,622,687	3,528,556
Nasdaq-100 Mini (MNX)	$100 × Index	Equity	452,425	600,021	4,034,201	5,503,345
Russell Midcap Growth Index (RDG)		Equity		320		35
Russell Midcap Index (RMC)		Equity		370		492
Russell Midcap Value Index (RMV)	$100 × Index	Equity		90		570
Russell 1000 Index (RUI)	$100 × Index	Equity	1,519	353	2,271	6,170
Russell 1000 Value Index (RLV)	$100 × Index	Equity	205	100	955	6,777
Russell 1000 Growth Index (RLG)	$100 × Index	Equity	645	856	1,525	2,633
Russell 2000 Value Index (RUJ)	$100 × Index	Equity	56	163	337	2,691
Russell 2000 Growth Index (RUO)	$100 × Index	Equity	53		53	766
Russell 2000 Options (RUT)	$100 × Index	Equity	92,395	84,536	612,790	889,448
Russell 3000 Value Index (RAV)	$100 × Index	Equity		120		487
Russell 3000 Growth Index (RAG)	$100 × Index	Equity		10		412
Interest Rate Composite	$100 × compLevel	Interest	7,150	8,325	90,438	90,608
All Options on Individual Equities		Indiv. Equity	16,832,628	18,914,089	173,033,965	224,317,421
CBOE Total			**27,207,188**	**30,654,654**	**283,946,495**	**361,086,774**

CBOE FUTURES EXCHANGE

	Contract Size	Type				
CBOE Volatility Index (VIX)	$100 × Index	Equity	4,772			89,622
CBOE China Index (CX)	$100 × Index	Equity	104			581
S&P 500 Three-Month Variance (VT)	$50 per point	Equity	200			1,129
CFE Total			**5,076**			**91,332**

CHICAGO BOARD OF TRADE

Futures

	Contract Size	Type				
Wheat	5,000 bu	Agricultural	465,405	402,286	6,967,416	7,955,155
Mini Wheat	1,000 bu	Agricultural	1,962	1,063	22,288	31,044

(continues)

Domestic Exchanges Futures, Options, and Options on Equities Volume, January–December 2004 (Continued)

	Unit	Commodity Group	Dec. 2003	Dec. 2004	Jan.–Dec. 2003	Jan.–Dec. 2004
Corn	5,000 bu	Agricultural	1,364,332	1,169,616	19,118,715	24,038,233
Mini Corn	1,000 bu	Agricultural	4,755	4,587	53,404	86,771
Oats	5,000 bu	Agricultural	27,170	20,650	318,898	416,448
Soybeans	5,000 bu	Agricultural	1,538,505	1,526,109	17,545,714	18,846,021
Mini Soybeans	1,000 bu	Agricultural	34,172	31,516	250,447	362,829
Soybean Oil	60,000 lbs	Agricultural	618,502	599,294	7,417,340	7,593,314
Soybean Meal	100 tons	Agricultural	674,315	653,172	8,158,445	8,569,243
Rice	200,000 lbs	Agricultural	26,684	15,962	265,234	168,165
Mini New York Silver	1,000 oz	Precious	4,197	19,155	34,804	204,255
Mini New York Gold	33.2 troy oz.	Precious	21,106	34,919	145,173	420,604
Silver	5,000 oz	Precious		5,226		12,398
Gold	100 oz	Precious		31,844		89,539
U.S.T-Bonds	$100,000	Interest	4,835,173	5,913,977	63,521,507	72,949,053
Mini U.S. T-Bonds	$50,000	Interest	909	981	15,707	11,373
Ten-Year T-Notes	$100,000	Interest	10,912,239	15,038,943	146,745,281	196,119,150
Mini Ten-Year T-Notes	$50,000	Interest	5		49	82
Five-Year T-Notes	$100,000	Interest	6,285,624	9,416,772	73,746,445	105,469,410
Two-Year T-Notes	$200,000	Interest	488,459	1,058,503	4,415,906	9,454,774
WHEN Issued Two-Year T-Notes		Interest				1
Ten-Year Agency Debt	$100,000	Interest	60		89,342	
Five-Year Agency Debt	$100,000	Interest			2,000	
Mini Eurodollars	$500,000	Interest	28	1	543	91
Ten-Year Interest Rate Swap	$100,000	Interest	101,452	87,959	1,038,777	856,968
Five-Year Interest Rate Swap	$100,000	Interest	17,889	50,605	110,275	243,353
Ten-Year Municipal Note Index	$100,000	Interest	9,075	6,248	94,541	65,026
30-Day Federal Funds	$5,000,000	Interest	509,070	780,208	8,271,726	11,940,120
Bund	EUR 100,000	Interest		22		2,303
Bobl	EUR 100,000	Interest				3,219
Schatz	EUR 100,000	Interest		653		4,306
Dow Jones Industrial Index	$10 × Index	Equity	266,032	237,528	4,416,302	2,577,138
Mini ($5) Dow Jones Industrial Index	$5 × Index	Equity	990,502	1,710,046	10,859,690	20,695,848
Dow Jones U.S. Total Market Index	$500 × Index	Equity				3,028
Dow Jones–AIGCI Index	100 × Index	Equity	7,076	2,338	43,321	40,882
Futures Total			**29,204,698**	**38,820,183**	**373,669,290**	**489,230,144**

Options on Futures

	Category	Contract Size				
Wheat	Agricultural	5,000 bu	109,604	76,387	1,788,500	1,465,760
Corn	Agricultural	5,000 bu	302,153	265,830	4,515,240	7,593,355
Oats	Agricultural	5,000 bu	1,458	1,089	36,163	36,498
Soybeans	Agricultural	5,000 bu	450,715	318,675	4,885,399	6,045,952
Soybean Oil	Agricultural	60,000 lbs	63,307	32,203	665,532	947,383
Soybean Meal	Agricultural	100 tons	60,090	32,395	546,267	971,335
Rice	Agricultural	200,000 lbs	3,648	915	34,978	22,064
U.S. T-Bonds	Interest	$100,000	951,080	930,628	15,180,025	13,788,908
Ten-Year T-Notes	Interest	$100,000	3,010,919	4,231,068	41,165,629	56,878,013
Five-Year T-Notes	Interest	$100,000	651,393	1,008,141	9,697,455	17,215,903
Two-Year T-Notes	Interest	$200,000	2	1,059	11,874	10,206
Ten-Year Interest Rate Swap	Interest	$100,000			1,787	
Five-Year Interest Rate Swap	Interest	$100,000			100	
30-Day Federal Funds	Interest	$5,000,000	126,475	309,697	1,614,319	4,707,103
Flexible U.S. T-Bonds	Interest		3,035	15,750	57,442	193,663
Flexible T-Notes (10-Year)	Interest		1,550	21,829	56,920	96,192
Flexible T-Notes (5-Year)	Interest			15,200	200	29,900
Dow Jones Industrial Index	Equity	$10 × Index	47,028	7,671	263,629	190,708
Mini ($5) Dow Jones Industrial Index	Equity	$5 × Index		55,159	55,159	571,299
Options on Futures Total			**5,782,457**	**7,323,696**	**80,521,459**	**110,764,242**
CBOT Total			**34,987,155**	**46,143,879**	**454,190,749**	**599,994,386**

CHICAGO MERCANTILE EXCHANGE

Futures

	Category	Contract Size				
Lean Hogs	Agricultural	40,000 lbs	148,117	255,488	2,164,155	3,204,186
Pork Bellies, Frozen	Agricultural	40,000 lbs	11,024	7,783	161,329	151,949
Butter	Agricultural	40,000 lbs	604	303	8,544	6,167
Nonfat Dry Milk	Agricultural	44,000 lbs		230		114
Class III Milk	Agricultural	200,000 lbs	15,856	21,277	191,351	345,973
Class IV Milk	Agricultural	200,000 lbs		2	137	690
Live Cattle	Agricultural	40,000 lbs	332,862	359,749	4,436,089	4,510,128
Feeder Cattle	Agricultural	50,000 lbs	60,198	61,586	704,852	741,265
Random Lumber	Other	80,000 bd. ft.	13,272	19,617	223,891	242,873
Diammonium Phosphate	Other	100 tons		4		62
Urea Ammonium Nitrate	Other	100 tons		25		218
Urea	Other	100 tons		65		300
90-Day T-Bills	Interest	$1,000,000			3,974	
Three-Month Eurodollar	Interest	$1,000,000	16,978,187	21,920,233	208,771,164	297,584,038

(continues)

Domestic Exchanges Futures, Options, and Options on Equities Volume, January–December 2004 (Continued)

	Commodity Group	Unit	Dec. 2003	Dec. 2004	Jan.–Dec. 2003	Jan.–Dec. 2004
Three-Month Eurodollar FRA	Interest	$1,000,000				328
Euroyen	Interest	$100,000,000 yen	14,280	23,623	179,573	224,821
Euroyen LIBOR	Interest	$100,000,000 yen	1,150		1,650	
Two-Year Swap	Interest		640	10,300	6,640	26,240
Five-Year Swap	Interest		9,551	5,880	43,616	56,438
Ten-Year Swap	Interest		4,225	6,110	40,030	65,281
Consumer Price Index	Interest	$2,500 × CPI		175		5,264
Mexican CETES	Interest	400,000 peso				2
28-Day Mexican TIIE	Interest	$1,200,000 peso			3,506	
One Month LIBOR	Interest	$3,000,000	116,616	79,562	1,138,358	2,886,987
Australian Dollar	Foreign	$100,000	249,731	377,473	1,609,289	2,672,733
British Pound	Foreign	62,500	364,543	635,180	2,595,155	4,676,512
Brazilian Real	Foreign	100,000	10	198	277	2,911
Canadian Dollar	Foreign	100,000	509,304	726,797	4,219,618	5,611,328
CME $ Index	Foreign	1,000 × Index	122		457	306
Czech Koruna	Foreign	4,000,000		31		31
Euro FX	Foreign	125,000 × Euro	1,232,569	2,591,851	11,193,922	20,456,672
E-mini Euro FX	Foreign	62,500 × Euro	3,097	48,631	16,860	190,554
Hungarian Forint	Foreign	30,000,000				10
Japanese Yen	Foreign	12,500,000	641,804	1,074,947	6,085,209	7,395,322
E-mini Japanese Yen	Foreign	6,250,000	474	373	2,740	5,466
Mexican Peso	Foreign	500,000	200,843	412,284	2,123,623	3,247,222
New Zealand Dollar	Foreign	100,000	19,115	36,111	120,235	162,370
Norwegian Krone	Foreign	227,000	190	704	388	2,122
Polish Zloty	Foreign	500,000		1,239		4,461
Russian Ruble	Foreign	2,500,000	1,979	6,816	4,420	30,620
South African Rand	Foreign	500,000	15,739	9,849	73,542	65,749
Swedish Krona	Foreign	193,600		43	4	812
Swiss Franc	Foreign	125,000	300,492	568,358	3,596,658	4,067,767
Australian Dollar/Canadian Dollar	Foreign	200,000 AD	12	395	220	676
Australian Dollar/Japanese Yen	Foreign	200,000 AD	6	24	94	1,066
Australian Dollar/New Zealand Dollar	Foreign	200,000 AD		67		639
British Pound/Japanese Yen	Foreign	125,000 BP	279	37	894	651
British Pound/Swiss Franc	Foreign	125,000 BP	12	288	103	689
Canadian Dollar/Japanese Yen	Foreign	200,000 CD	30	14	102	344

Contract	Size	Type				
Swiss Franc/Japanese Yen	250,000 SF	Foreign	24	7	247	110
Euro/Australian Dollar	125,000 Euro	Foreign	208	199	554	769
Euro/Canadian Dollar	125,000 Euro	Foreign	66	55	247	901
Euro/Norwegian Krone	125,000 Euro	Foreign		43		98
Euro/Polish Zloty	500,000	Foreign		1,111		3,859
Euro/Pound	125,000 Euro	Foreign	3,873	6,535	65,696	43,635
Euro/Yen	125,000 Euro	Foreign	5,561	11,488	161,600	118,614
Euro/Swedish Krona	125,000 Euro	Foreign		146		318
Euro/Swiss Franc	125,000 Euro	Foreign	68	324	1,794	7,290
Nikkei 225 ($)	$5 × Index	Equity	98,246	156,570	765,463	1,239,010
Nikkei 225 (Yen)	$5 × Index	Equity		44,862		260,128
S&P 500 Index	$250 × Index	Equity	2,281,453	2,101,283	20,175,462	16,175,584
E-mini S&P 500 Index	$50 × S&P Index	Equity	11,107,884	13,039,135	161,176,639	167,202,962
S&P 500 Barra Growth Index	$500 × Index	Equity	941	354	5,119	2,754
S&P 500 Barra Value Index	$500 × Index	Equity	2,798	2,167	14,131	8,852
S&P Financial Sector	$125 × Index	Equity	1,012		4,093	2,527
S&P Technology-Telecomm Sector	$125 × Index	Equity	8	6	60	197
S&P MidCap 400 Index	$500 × Index	Equity	50,797	36,971	302,817	260,764
S&P SmallCap 600	$200 × Index	Equity	499	354	1,635	2,354
E-mini S&P MidCap 400 Index	$100 × Index	Equity	182,529	298,370	1,417,513	3,282,347
X-Fund 2	$1,000 × Index	Equity				1
Fortune E-50	$20 × Index	Equity			32	
Nasdaq 100 Index	$100 × Index	Equity	447,119	356,171	4,421,221	4,011,983
E-mini Nasdaq 100	$20 × Index	Equity	5,655,230	5,674,862	67,888,938	77,168,513
E-mini Nasdaq Composite	$20 × Index	Equity	1,784		6,444	445
Russell 2000	$500 × Index	Equity	84,777	88,270	655,778	614,040
E-mini Russell 2000	$100 × Index	Equity	614,512	1,451,062	3,878,935	17,121,233
Russell 1000	$100 × Index	Equity	3,485	15,574	14,941	51,437
Long-Short TRAKRS	$1 × Index	Equity	27,435	38,395	994,756	1,070,408
Long-Short TRAKRS II	$1 × Index	Equity		472,223		5,693,223
TRAKRS Select 50	$1 × Index	Equity	72,970	38,168	2,436,069	676,801
LMC TRAKRS	$1 × Index	Equity	28,920	8,525	1,803,316	460,246
TRAKRS Commodity	$1 × Index	Equity	473,285	168,741	7,424,763	4,138,262
TRAKRS Euro Currency	$1 × Index	Equity	108,245	787,063	1,196,525	1,248,272
TRAKRS Gold	$1 × Index	Equity	6,065,013	550,151	6,065,013	4,868,842
HDD Weather	$20 × Index	Other	715	6,440	6,058	16,404
HDD Seasonal Weather	$20 × Index	Other		250	225	2,080
CDD Weather	$20 × Index	Other			8,176	23,656
CDD Seasonal Weather	$20 × Index	Other				2,395

(continues)

Domestic Exchanges Futures, Options, and Options on Equities Volume, January–December 2004 (Continued)

	Unit	Commodity Group	Dec. 2003	Dec. 2004	Jan.–Dec. 2003	Jan.–Dec. 2004
Euro HDD Weather	£ 20 × Index	Other	165	800	375	2,015
Euro CAT	£ 20 × Index	Other				535
Euro Seasonal HDD Weather	£ 20 × Index	Other				350
Goldman Sachs Commodity Index	$250 × Index	Other	30,748	40,737	371,473	450,036
Futures Total			**48,597,303**	**54,660,904**	**530,989,007**	**664,884,607**
Options on Futures						
Lean Hogs	40,000 lbs	Agricultural	10,938	17,930	129,227	179,093
Pork Bellies, Frozen	40,000 lbs	Agricultural	198	158	7,991	4,010
Butter	40,000 lbs	Agricultural	60	12	800	401
Midi BFP Milk	100,000 lbs	Agricultural	104	113	1,269	1,654
Class III Milk	200,000 lbs	Agricultural	4,863	8,202	79,901	122,014
Class IV Milk	200,000 lbs	Agricultural			41	15
Live Cattle	40,000 lbs	Agricultural	46,054	38,926	664,291	500,927
Feeder Cattle	50,000 lbs	Agricultural	15,602	10,382	179,347	142,638
Random Lumber	80,000 bd. ft.	Other	1,429	1,404	18,139	20,056
Euroyen	$100,000,000 yen	Interest			53	437
Three-Month Eurodollar	$1,000,000	Interest	6,739,258	8,790,167	100,823,779	130,598,377
Five-Year Euro $ Bundle	1–5 yr ED Bundle	Interest				52
One-Month LIBOR	$3,000,000	Interest			4,191	201
British Pound	62,500	Foreign	13,825	15,917	156,569	166,360
Canadian Dollar	100,000	Foreign	13,297	28,236	206,862	190,976
Japanese Yen	12,500,000	Foreign	37,190	70,615	489,123	465,261
Mexican Peso	500,000	Foreign	238	259	5,050	3,664
New Zealand Dollar	100,000	Foreign				
Swiss Franc	125,000	Foreign	3,294	5,174	53,766	55,596
Australian Dollar	100,000	Foreign	6,499	6,921	42,495	60,593
CME $ Index	1,000 × Index	Foreign			1,000	
EuroFX	125,000 × Euro	Foreign	106,480	235,931	1,187,819	1,492,887
Nikkei 225	$5 × Index	Equity	1,189	910	8,564	8,774
S&P 500 Index	$250 × Index	Equity	408,425	551,907	4,986,456	5,834,225
E-mini S&P 500	$50 × S&P Index	Equity	14,352	118,901	112,864	477,712
S&P 400 Index	$500 × Index	Equity		50	780	375
Nasdaq-100 Index	$100 × Index	Equity	2,848	1,116	50,439	37,612
E-mini Nasdaq 100 Index	$20 × Index	Equity		8,031		10,015
Russell 2000	$500 × Index	Equity	274	280	4,048	6,205

Contract	Type	Contract Size				
CDD Weather	Other	$20 × Index			230	3,475
HDD Weather	Other	$20 × Index	81	6,500	501	11,527
HDD Seasonal Weather	Other	$20 × Index	550	17,000	3,390	39,650
CDD Seasonal Weather	Other	$20 × Index			150	5,650
Euro HDD Weather	Other	£ 20 × Index			200	850
Euro CAT Weather	Other	£ 20 × Index				450
Euro HDD Seasonal Weather	Other	£ 20 × Index		5,000		13,950
Goldman Sachs Commodity Index	Other	$250 × Index	90	125	1,492	1,392
Options on Futures Total			7,427,138	9,940,367	109,220,627	140,457,074
CME Total			56,024,441	64,601,271	640,209,634	805,341,681
EUREX US						
Two-Year T-Note	Interest	$200,000		12,822		53,663
Five-Year T-Note	Interest	$100,000		548,475		2,332,942
Ten-Year T-Note	Interest	$100,000		240,705		2,818,977
U.S. Treasury Bonds	Interest	$100,000		98,012		980,426
Futures Total				900,014		6,186,008
Ten-Year T-Note	Interest Opt.	$100,000				800
Options on Futures Total						800
EUREX U.S. Total				900,014		6,186,808
INTERNATIONAL SECURITIES EXCHANGE						
Morgan Stanley Technology Index (MSH)	Equity			3,232		49,873
S&P MidCap 400 Index (MID)	Equity			3,330		15,658
S&P SmallCap 600 Index (SML)	Equity			302		17,827
All Options on Individual Equities	Indiv. Equity		24,890,751	32,314,987	244,968,190	360,769,161
ISE Total			24,890,751	32,321,851	244,968,190	360,852,519
KANSAS CITY BOARD OF TRADE						
Wheat	Agricultural	5,000 bu	186,052	170,965	2,632,033	2,833,370
Value Line Index	Equity	$100 × Index	204	174	2,391	1,429
Futures Total			186,256	171,139	2,634,424	2,834,799
Wheat	Agric. Opt.	5,000 bu	17,324	11,218	465,381	254,304
Options on Futures Total			17,324	11,218	465,381	254,304
KCBOT Total			203,580	182,357	3,099,805	3,089,103
MIDAMERICA COMMODITY EXCHANGE						
Wheat	Agricultural	1,000 bu			5,580	
Corn	Agricultural	1,000 bu			39,555	

(continues)

Domestic Exchanges Futures, Options, and Options on Equities Volume, January–December 2004 (Continued)

	Unit	Commodity Group	Dec. 2003	Dec. 2004	Jan.–Dec. 2003	Jan.–Dec. 2004
Soybeans	1,000 bu	Agricultural			97,163	
MIDAM TOTAL					**142,298**	
MINNEAPOLIS GRAIN EXCHANGE						
Spring Wheat	5,000 bu	Agricultural	71,243	74,637	1,066,489	1,378,694
Hard Red Spring Wheat Index	5,000 bu	Agricultural		56		56
Hard Red Winter Wheat Index	5,000 bu	Agricultural	3,323	14	16,535	2,521
Soft Red Winter Wheat Index	5,000 bu	Agricultural		69		69
National Corn Index	5,000 bu	Agricultural	123	98	3,996	116
Futures Total			**74,689**	**74,874**	**1,087,020**	**1,381,456**
Spring Wheat	5,000 bu	Agric. Opt.	1,298	1,739	39,764	34,260
Hard Red Spring Wheat Index	5,000 bu	Agric. Opt.		30		30
Hard Red Winter Wheat Index	5,000 bu	Agric. Opt.	534	1	5,773	416
Soft Red Winter Wheat Index	5,000 bu	Agric. Opt.		120		120
National Corn Index	5,000 bu	Agric. Opt.	2		1,174	
Options on Futures Total			**1,834**	**1,890**	**46,711**	**34,826**
MGE TOTAL			**76,523**	**76,764**	**1,133,731**	**1,416,282**
NEW YORK BOARD OF TRADE						
Coffee "C"	37,500 lbs	Agricultural	219,595	292,540	3,211,031	4,193,303
Mini Coffee	12,500 lbs	Agricultural	30	8	332	276
Sugar #11	112,000 lbs	Agricultural	674,355	632,736	7,140,724	9,766,550
Sugar #14	112,000 lbs	Agricultural	11,150	6,991	133,811	114,619
Cocoa	10 M tons	Agricultural	135,857	128,604	2,128,206	2,389,050
Cotton #2	50,000 lbs	Agricultural	148,310	185,370	3,035,992	3,156,018
Ethanol	7,750 U.S. gallons	Agricultural				1,371
Orange Juice, Frozen Concentrate	15,000 lbs	Agricultural	78,005	85,438	652,715	970,437
Frozen Concentrate, Orange Juice—Diff.		Agricultural				10
U.S. Dollar/Canadian	$200,000 US	Foreign	149	648	2,458	2,949
U.S. Dollar/Swedish Krona	$200,000 US	Foreign	3,631	2,821	12,377	11,654
U.S. Dollar/Norwegian Krone	$200,000 US	Foreign	1,209	1,316	11,350	17,016
U.S. Dollar/Swiss Franc	$200,000 US	Foreign	1,804	609	26,119	8,513
U.S. Dollar/Japanese Yen	$200,000 US	Foreign	2,786	3,609	43,351	46,433
U.S. Dollar/British Pound	$125,000 BP	Foreign	3,836	3,172	40,467	49,150
U.S. Dollar/Czech Koruna	$200,000 US	Foreign	336	3,265	527	9,852
U.S. Dollar/Hungarian Forint	$200,000 US	Foreign	599	2,541	1,120	9,283

U.S. Dollar/Rand	$100,000 US	Foreign	11,307	17,675	31,272	71,332
Canadian Dollar/Japanese Yen	$200,000 CAN	Foreign	1,344	2,021	16,440	16,604
Australian Dollar/U.S. Dollar	$200,000 AUS	Foreign	1,493	1,462	6,061	13,141
Australian Dollar/Canadian Dollar	$200,000 AUS	Foreign	4,806	438	15,104	9,178
Australian Dollar/New Zealand	$200,000 AUS	Foreign	4,603	1,754	16,357	34,904
New Zealand Dollar/U.S. Dollar	$200,000 NZ	Foreign	7,486	8,676	26,395	37,899
Australian Dollar/Japanese Yen	$200,000 AUS	Foreign	7,773	12,152	41,468	66,006
Norwegian Krone/Swedish Koruna	$500,000 NK	Foreign	3,408	2,693	20,503	10,192
Pound/Swiss	$125,000 BP	Foreign	8,160	5,321	52,145	31,151
Pound/Yen	$125,000 BP	Foreign	5,045	12,395	22,193	68,519
Swiss/Yen	200,000 S. Francs	Foreign	4,210	5,930	60,926	41,614
Euro	200,000 Euros	Foreign	1,635	5,288	5,365	65,808
Euro/U.S. Dollar	100,000 Euros	Foreign	6,933	1,493	30,466	12,409
Euro/Australian Dollar	100,000 Euros	Foreign	9,571	4,171	49,890	44,000
Euro/Canadian	100,000 Euros	Foreign	2,768	2,617		52,496
Euro/Czech Koruna	100,000 Euros	Foreign		4,105	2,774	28,093
Euro/Hungarian Forint	100,000 Euros	Foreign		3,413	24	17,640
Euro/Yen	100,000 Euros	Foreign	19,639	52,325	346,751	363,069
Euro/Krona	100,000 Euros	Foreign	5,666	10,962	49,977	64,334
Euro/Pound	100,000 Euros	Foreign	8,957	35,565	117,989	226,404
Euro/Norwegian	100,000 Euros	Foreign	9,279	5,577	29,815	29,536
Euro/Swiss	100,000 Euros	Foreign	12,284	10,068	133,218	143,274
Small British Pound/U.S. Dollar	$62,500 BP	Foreign		679	679	6,006
Small U.S. Dollar/Canadian Dollar	$100,000 US	Foreign		40	40	247
Small U.S. Dollar/Japanese Yen	$100,000 US	Foreign		428	428	5,664
Small U.S. Dollar/Swiss Franc	$100,000 US	Foreign		14	14	41
U.S. Dollar Index	$1,000 × Index	Foreign	75,358	116,853	563,032	748,204
NYSE Composite Index	$500 × Index	Equity			34,021	14,678
Revised NYSE Composite Index	$50 × Index	Equity	3,282	2,457	7,143	961,771
Russell 1000	$500 × Index	Equity	149,054	151,555	677,626	2,442
Russell 1000 Growth Index	$500 × Index	Equity	292	563	836	2,392
Russell 1000 Value Index	$500 × Index	Equity	360	480	415	424
Russell 2000 Index	$500 × Index	Equity	46	4	10	4
Russell 2000 Growth Index	$500 × Index	Equity				
Russell 2000 Value Index	$500 × Index	Equity				
Russell 3000 Index	$500 × Index	Equity			96	2
CRB Index	$500 × Index	Other	2,314	979	23,156	20
Futures Total			**1,648,725**	**1,829,821**	**18,822,048**	**23,955,212**

(continues)

Domestic Exchanges Futures, Options, and Options on Equities Volume, January–December 2004 (Continued)

	Unit	Commodity Group	Dec. 2003	Dec. 2004	Jan.-Dec. 2003	Jan.-Dec. 2004
Coffee "C"	37,500 lbs	Agricultural	109,272	197,331	1,328,081	1,970,068
Sugar #11	112,000 lbs	Agricultural	213,780	213,209	1,690,190	2,854,683
Cocoa	10 M tons	Agricultural	26,302	27,419	497,188	429,769
Cotton #2	50,000 lbs	Agricultural	187,169	72,167	2,157,441	1,725,982
Ethanol	7,750 U.S. gallons	Agricultural			10	10
Orange Juice, Frozen Concentrate	15,000 lbs	Agricultural	31,278	81,900	195,541	554,432
U.S. Dollar Index	$1,000 × Index	Foreign	5,056	6,472	29,532	57,189
Euro	200,000 Euros	Foreign	30	17	578	352
Australian Dollar/Canadian Dollar	$200,000 AUS	Foreign		2	3	2
Australian Dollar/Japanese Yen	$200,000 AUS	Foreign			3	
Australian Dollar/New Zealand	$200,000 AUS	Foreign			1	
Australian Dollar/U.S. Dollar	$200,000 AUS	Foreign			10	
Euro/Krona	100,000 Euros	Foreign			2	
Euro/Pound	100,000 Euros	Foreign	15	13	253	67
Euro/Swiss	100,000 Euros	Foreign				300
Euro/Yen	100,000 Euros	Foreign			776	40
Pound/Yen	$125,000 BP	Foreign	3	3	209	17
New Zealand Dollar/U.S. Dollar	200,000 NZ	Foreign			13	
U.S. Dollar/Canadian	$200,000 US	Foreign	10		60	45
U.S. Dollar/Rand	$100,000 US	Foreign			1	170
U.S. Dollar/Japanese Yen	$12,500,000 Y	Foreign			112	12
U.S. Dollar/Norwegian Krone	$200,000 US	Foreign			3	
U.S. Dollar/British Pound	$125,000 BP	Foreign	4	4	31	25
U.S. Dollar/Swiss Franc	$200,000 US	Foreign				1
U.S. Dollar/Swedish Krona	$200,000 US	Foreign			3	
NYSE Composite Index	$500 × Index	Equity			25,320	
Revised NYSE Composite Index	$50 × Index	Equity	8,100	4	18,912	32,525
Russell 1000 Growth Index	$500 × Index	Equity	12		358	273
Russell 1000 Value Index	$500 × Index	Equity	32	4	1,578	6
Russell 1000 Index	$500 × Index	Equity	7,976	8,115	61,264	103,944
Russell 2000 Index	$500 × Index	Equity	320	10,102	734	36,305
Russell 3000 Index	$500 × Index	Equity		550		4,647
CRB Index	$500 × Index	Other	275	87	1,913	3,515
Options on Futures Total			**589,634**	**617,399**	**6,010,110**	**7,774,379**
NYBOT TOTAL			**2,238,359**	**2,447,220**	**24,832,158**	**31,729,591**

NEW YORK MERCANTILE EXCHANGE

COMEX Division

Gold	100 oz	Precious	776,278	1,053,245	12,235,689	14,959,617
Silver	5,000 oz	Precious	250,835	360,775	4,111,190	5,006,125
High Grade Copper	25,000 lbs	Nonprecious	172,438	207,878	3,089,270	3,190,625
Aluminum	44,000 lbs	Nonprecious	11,542	2,691	107,490	72,169
Futures Total			**1,211,093**	**1,624,589**	**19,543,639**	**23,228,536**
Gold	100 oz	Precious	308,690	274,785	4,310,318	4,667,523
Silver	5,000 oz	Precious	56,537	77,417	560,018	1,022,348
High-Grade Copper	25,000 lbs	Nonprecious	10,198	8,968	47,326	216,350
Aluminum	44,000 lbs	Nonprecious			2,679	
Options on Futures Total			**375,425**	**361,170**	**4,920,341**	**5,906,221**
COMEX Division Total			**1,586,518**	**1,985,759**	**24,463,980**	**29,134,757**

NYMEX Division

Palladium	100 oz	Precious	11,142	16,429	95,613	267,552
Platinum	50 oz	Precious	42,301	39,834	268,305	295,695
No. 2 Heating Oil, NY	1,000 bbl	Energy	971,848	1,164,381	11,581,670	12,884,511
Unleaded Reg. Gas., NY	1,000 bbl	Energy	761,626	995,938	11,172,050	12,777,442
Crude Oil	1,000 bbl	Energy	3,646,046	4,108,288	45,436,931	52,883,200
e-miNY Crude Oil	400 bbl	Energy	14,930	116,968	277,411	720,421
Brent Crude Oil	1,000 bbl	Energy		39,950	30	135,385
Propane	42,000 gal	Energy	3,826	580	14,710	14,764
Natural Gas	10,000 MMBTU	Energy	1,515,200	1,218,577	19,037,118	17,441,942
e-miNY Natural Gas	4,000 MMBTU	Energy	11,115	14,618	115,502	136,123
PJM Monthly		Energy	20,666	16,843	142,859	234,207
Coal		Energy	353	700	5,235	7,490
NYISO A		Energy	9,560	9,030	88,826	91,067
NYISO G		Energy	3,286	1,886	52,996	26,018
NYISO J		Energy	870	2,754	10,245	13,214
PJM Electricity		Energy				
PJM Daily		Energy	6,859	17,911	30,221	190,591
PJM Weekly		Energy	360	1,440	3,963	18,725
Dow Jones Mid-Columbia		Energy		130		3,310
Dow Jones NP15		Energy				3,770
Dow Jones SP15		Energy	114			6,594
Dow Jones Palo Verde		Energy	90			1,510
ISO New England Peak LMP Swap		Energy	3,090			4,030
WTI Midland Crude		Energy				200

(continues)

223

Domestic Exchanges Futures, Options, and Options on Equities Volume, January–December 2004 (Continued)

Unit	Commodity Group	Dec. 2003	Dec. 2004	Jan.–Dec. 2003	Jan.–Dec. 2004
WTI Crude Oil Calendar Swap	Energy	3,774	6,248	33,785	152,680
NY Harbor Residual Fuel 1.0% Sulfur Swap	Energy	150		375	625
US Gulf Coast No. 2 Crack Spread Calendar	Energy				1,375
NY Harbor No. 2 Crack Spread Calendar Swap	Energy		4,820		120,780
Gulf Coast Gas vs. Heating Oil Spread Swap	Energy				3,650
Gulf Coast Jet vs. NYMEX HO Spread Swap	Energy				1,750
Gulf Coast No. 6 Fuel Oil 3/0% Swap	Energy		200		200
NY Harbor Conventional Gasoline vs. NYH Gasoline Spread Swap	Energy				900
NY Harbor Heating Oil Calendar Swap	Energy	450	2,642	2,355	51,347
NYMEX Gasoline vs. NYMEX Heating Oil Swap	Energy		3,940	150	20,795
NYMEX Gasoline Calendar Swap	Energy		841		20,279
US Gulf Coast Unleaded 87 Crack Spread Calendar	Energy		575		45,775
NY Harbor Unleaded Crack Spread Calendar	Energy		4,971		45,336
Unleaded 87 Up-Down Calendar Swap	Energy		775		6,675
Henry Hub Basis Swap	Energy		19,190		98,408
AECO-C/NIT Basis Swap	Energy		38,551		488,699
Chicago Basis Swap	Energy		17,747		174,498
ANR-Oklahoma Basis	Energy	1,166	9,493	8,235	52,967
Columbia Gulf Onshore Basis	Energy	1,518	1,042	3,526	24,272
Tetco Ela Basis	Energy		612	4,872	24,755
Michigan Basis	Energy	1,929	7,021	81,074	94,137
Tetco Stx Basis	Energy		2,154	13,132	19,790
Transco Zone 3 Basis Swap	Energy	186	1,736	2,750	56,993
Houston Ship Channel Basis Swap	Energy		53,745		429,266
San Juan Basis Swap	Energy		6,052		62,048
Sumas Basis Swap	Energy	11,850	15,079	172,313	320,144
NGPL Mid-Continent	Energy	1,081	10,658	32,580	69,854
WAHA Basis Swap	Energy	6,168	13,026	134,632	184,909
CIG Rockies Swap	Energy	924	6,897	7,026	69,555
Henry Hub Swap	Energy	230,652	682,085	2,356,600	5,353,792
Northwest Rockies Basis Swap	Energy		40,188		652,511
Natural Gas Penultimate Swap	Energy		121,208		294,011
Social Basis Swap	Energy		52,059		569,540

Instrument	Category	Unit				
Texas Eastern Zone M-3 Basis	Energy		14,418	23,324	178,591	278,235
NGPL LA	Energy		306	1,886	2,260	3,724
TRANSCO Zone 6 Basis Swap	Energy			32,653		481,097
Malin Basis	Energy		17,692	16,315	241,769	334,230
PG&E Citygate Basis	Energy		10,466	28,167	110,812	209,906
NGPL TEX/OK Basis	Energy		1,075	8,334	13,418	60,266
Northern Natural Gas Demarcation Basis	Energy		1,811	529	35,901	17,651
Northern Natural Gas Ventura Iowa	Energy		4,821	155	65,843	21,771
Dominion Transmission—Appalachian Basis	Energy		5,984	12,514	95,595	247,191
Panhandle Basis Swap	Energy			44,115		224,329
Permian Basis	Energy		4,974	5,734	211,397	128,814
TCO Basis	Energy		3,759	40,750	103,343	244,049
Chicago Swing Future	Energy			31		102
Henry Hub Swing	Energy			9,286		40,102
Panhandle Swing	Energy			28		599
Houston Ship Channel Swing Swap	Energy			494		1,078
WAHA Swing	Energy			770		1,310
El Paso, Permian Index Swap	Energy			1,266		2,250
Henry Hub Index Swap	Energy			26,104		65,860
Houston Ship Channel Index Swap	Energy			4,230		12,791
Panhandle Index Swap Future	Energy			1,426		1,798
WAHA Index Swap	Energy			1,240		4,549
Chicago Index Swap	Energy			1,333		1,581
No. 2 Up-Down Spread Cal Swap	Energy			52		2,352
Futures Total			**7,345,142**	**9,153,842**	**92,246,019**	**110,055,712**
Platinum	Precious	50 oz	64	18	633	637
No. 2 Heating Oil, NY	Energy	1,000 bbl	72,981	135,664	668,859	800,277
Heating Oil 1 Month CSO	Energy		250	2,430		1,880
Heating Oil 2 Month CSO	Energy			100		
Heating Oil APO	Energy			1,124		1,134
Unleaded Reg. Gas., NY	Energy	1,000 bbl	28,580	42,274	616,245	904,466
Unleaded Gas 1 Month CSO	Energy			350	3,465	3,175
Unleaded Gas 2 Month CSO	Energy				25	
Unleaded Gasoline APO	Energy					300
Crude Oil	Energy	1,000 bbl	754,331	1,132,814	10,237,121	11,512,918
Crude Oil 1 Month CSO	Energy		23,790	23,470	164,928	357,156
Crude Oil 2 Month CSO	Energy					
Crude Oil 6 Month CSO	Energy			300		

(continues)

Domestic Exchanges Futures, Options, and Options on Equities Volume, January–December 2004 (Continued)

	Unit	Commodity Group	Dec. 2003	Dec. 2004	Jan.–Dec. 2003	Jan.–Dec. 2004
Crude Oil 12 Month CSO		Energy			825	9,600
Crude Oil APO		Energy		162	131	23,622
Natural Gas	10,000 MMBTU	Energy	833,000	747,803	8,742,277	8,071,967
Natural Gas 1 Month CSO		Energy	355	6,597	13,557	47,328
Natural Gas 2 Month CSO		Energy		500		500
Natural Gas 3 Month CSO		Energy		50		50
Natural Gas 6 Month CSO		Energy		50		
Natural Gas 12 Month CSO		Energy		50		100
Gas-Crude Oil Spread	1,000 bbl	Energy	3,060	2,259	35,797	79,664
Heating Oil-Crude Oil Spread	1,000 bbl	Energy	3,525	12,629	28,747	98,503
PJM Monthly		Energy		1,960		3,985
European Style Natural Gas		Energy		413,105		2,012,703
European Style Crude Oil		Energy		5,075		17,080
European Style Heating Oil		Energy		1,579		8,023
European Style Unleaded Gasoline		Energy		822		12,270
Options on Futures Total			**1,719,936**	**2,105,764**	**20,515,440**	**21,913,277**
NYMEX Division Total			**9,065,078**	**11,259,606**	**112,761,459**	**131,968,989**
New York Mercantile Exchange Total			**10,651,596**	**13,245,365**	**137,225,439**	**161,103,746**
NQLX						
Single-Stock Futures		Indiv. Equity	69,097	922	576,765	234,392
Exchange Traded Funds Futures		Indiv. Equity	3,796	507	282,135	22,608
NQLX Total			**72,893**	**1,429**	**858,900**	**257,000**
ONECHICAGO						
Single-Stock Futures		Indiv. Equity	337,448	146,783	1,488,573	1,890,097
Exchange Traded Funds Futures		Indiv. Equity	4,504	5,199	127,424	29,585
Dow Jones MicroSector Index SM Futures		Equity	275	246	3,197	3,044
ONECHICAGO Total			**342,227**	**152,228**	**1,619,194**	**1,922,726**
PACIFIC EXCHANGE						
All Options on Individual Equities		Indiv. Equity	8,692,470	11,774,411	86,152,637	103,262,458
PCX Total			**8,692,470**	**11,774,411**	**86,152,637**	**103,262,458**
PHILADELPHIA STOCK EXCHANGE						
Utility Index (UTY)	$100 × Index	Equity	2,168	1,655	10,813	74,005
Oil Service Sector (OSX)	$100 × Index	Equity	91,215	99,556	1,006,718	1,472,900

Product	Type	Multiplier				
Europe Sector (XEX)	Equity	$100 × Index		106	22	606
Forest & Paper Products Index (FPP)	Equity	$100 × Index			43	
Semiconductor Index (SOX)	Equity	$100 × Index	101,871	76,808	811,558	1,220,505
OTC Prime Sector Index (OTX)	Equity	$100 × Index		170	6,521	2,953
Computer Box Maker (BMX)	Equity	$100 × Index		25	1,449	3,010
Gold/Silver Index (XAU)	Equity	$100 × Index	128,684	125,754	1,130,430	1,760,404
Bank Index (BKX)	Equity	$100 × Index	33,994	32,849	194,366	637,745
Defense Index (DFX)	Equity	$100 × Index	3,102	203	10,381	14,150
Drug Index (RXS)	Equity	$100 × Index	356	709	4,662	9,813
Housing Sector Index (HGX)	Equity	$100 × Index	1,906	4,981	20,729	46,409
KBW Capital Market Index (KSX)	Equity	$100 × Index		210		210
KBW Insurance Index (KIX)	Equity	$100 × Index		289		9,890
SIG Cable, Media & Entertainment Index (SCQ)	Equity	$100 × Index	3,417	2,025	6,615	5,501
SIG Casino Gaming Index (SGV)	Equity	$100 × Index		643		694
SIG Investment Managers Index (SMQ)	Equity	$100 × Index	411	1	4,999	1,232
SIG Semiconductor Capital Equipment Index (SEZ)	Equity	$100 × Index		95		480
SIG Semiconductor Device Index (SDL)	Equity	$100 × Index		40		985
SIG Steel Producers Index (STQ)	Equity	$100 × Index	1,056	1,056		1,056
TheStreet.com Internet Index (DOT)	Equity	$100 × Index	430	225	12,477	8,294
Wireless Telecom Sector (YLS)	Equity					
Nasdaq Composite Index (QCX)	Equity			1	1	574
Nasdaq Composite Index—Mini (QCE)	Equity			11		720
All Currency Options	Foreign		33,603	14,132	278,649	230,779
All Options on Individual Equities	Indiv. Equity		13,578,288	9,799,726	109,205,164	127,898,363
PHLX Total			**13,979,619**	**10,161,100**	**112,705,597**	**133,401,278**
TOTAL FUTURES			88,683,026	107,394,099	1,042,968,664	1,324,027,532
Percent Change				21.10%		26.95%
TOTAL OPTIONS ON FUTURES			15,913,748	20,361,504	221,700,069	287,105,123
Percent Change				27.95%		29.50%
TOTAL OPTIONS ON SECURITIES			89,508,222	105,118,214	907,847,697	1,182,025,229
Percent Change				17.44%		30.20%
GRAND TOTAL			194,104,996	232,873,817	2,172,516,430	2,793,157,884
Percent Change				19.97%		28.57%

(continues)

Domestic Exchanges Futures, Options, and Options on Equities Volume, January–December 2004 (Continued)

Unit	Commodity Group	Dec. 2003	Dec. 2004	Jan.-Dec. 2003	Jan.-Dec. 2004
COMMODITY GROUPS					
Futures					
	Interest Rate	40,284,632	55,300,769	509,597,435	704,154,636
	Agricultural Commodities	6,852,506	6,707,969	87,948,750	101,834,155
	Energy Products	7,291,699	9,097,579	91,882,101	109,492,465
	Foreign Currency/Index	3,776,226	6,853,714	33,649,882	51,135,242
	Equity Indexes	28,726,065	27,439,744	296,694,711	329,955,619
	Individual Equities	414,845	153,411	2,474,897	2,176,682
	Precious Metals	1,105,859	1,561,427	16,890,774	21,255,785
	Nonprecious Metals	183,980	210,569	3,196,760	3,262,794
	Other	47,214	68,917	633,354	760,154
	Total	**88,683,026**	**107,394,099**	**1,042,968,664**	**1,324,027,532**
Percentages					
	Interest Rate	45.43%	51.49%	48.86%	53.18%
	Agricultural Commodities	7.73%	6.25%	8.43%	7.69%
	Energy Products	8.22%	8.47%	8.81%	8.27%
	Foreign Currency/Index	4.26%	6.38%	3.23%	3.86%
	Equity Indexes	32.39%	25.55%	28.45%	24.92%
	Individual Equities	0.47%	0.14%	0.24%	0.16%
	Precious Metals	1.25%	1.45%	1.62%	1.61%
	Nonprecious Metals	0.21%	0.20%	0.31%	0.25%
	Other	0.05%	0.06%	0.06%	0.06%
	Total	**100.00%**	**100.00%**	**100.00%**	**100.00%**
Options on Futures					
	Interest Rate	11,483,712	15,323,539	168,613,774	223,519,755
	Agricultural Commodities	1,655,753	1,408,351	19,915,479	25,857,173
	Energy Products	1,719,872	2,528,287	20,514,807	23,966,701
	Foreign Currency/Index	185,941	369,564	2,174,274	2,493,557
	Equity Indexes	490,556	762,800	5,534,946	7,314,625
	Precious Metals	365,291	352,220	4,870,969	5,690,508
	Nonprecious Metals	10,198	8,968	50,005	216,350
	Other	2,425	30,316	25,815	100,515
	Total	**15,913,748**	**20,784,045**	**221,700,069**	**289,159,184**

Percentages

Interest Rate	72.16%	73.73%	76.05%	77.30%
Agricultural Commodities	10.40%	6.78%	8.98%	8.94%
Energy Products	10.81%	12.16%	9.25%	8.29%
Foreign Currency/Index	1.17%	1.78%	0.98%	0.86%
Equity Indexes	3.08%	3.67%	2.50%	2.53%
Precious Metals	2.30%	1.69%	2.20%	1.97%
Nonprecious Metals	0.06%	0.04%	0.02%	0.07%
Other	0.02%	0.15%	0.01%	0.03%
Total	**100.00%**	**100.00%**	**100.00%**	**100.00%**

Options on Securities

Interest Rate	7,150	8,325	90,438	90,608
Foreign Currency/Index	33,603	14,132	278,649	230,779
Equity Indexes	11,212,458	12,777,688	118,316,616	149,313,094
Individual Equities	78,255,011	92,318,069	789,161,994	1,032,390,748
Total	**89,508,222**	**105,118,214**	**907,847,697**	**1,182,025,229**

Percentages

Interest Rate	0.01%	0.01%	0.01%	0.01%
Foreign Currency/Index	0.04%	0.01%	0.03%	0.02%
Equity Indexes	12.53%	12.16%	13.03%	12.63%
Individual Equities	87.43%	87.82%	86.93%	87.34%
Total	**100.00%**	**100.00%**	**100.00%**	**100.00%**

GRAND TOTAL	**194,104,996**	**233,296,358**	**2,172,516,430**	**2,795,211,945**

Source: Futures Industry Association.

International Exchanges Futures, Options, and Options on Equities Volume, January–December 2004

	Commodity Group	Dec. 2003	Dec. 2004	Jan.–Dec. 2003	Jan.–Dec. 2004
AUSTRALIAN STOCK EXCHANGE					
S&P/ASX Index	Equity	6,598	20,191	67,769	66,256
All Futures on Individual Equities	Indiv. Equity	28,630	57,314	267,630	460,501
Futures Total		**35,228**	**77,505**	**335,399**	**526,757**
S&P/ASX Index Options	Equity Opt.	47,847	103,733	578,066	794,121
All Options on Individual Equities	Ind. Equity Opt.	1,142,695	1,406,185	15,988,740	19,164,851
Options Total		**1,190,542**	**1,509,918**	**16,566,806**	**19,958,972**
ASX Total		**1,225,770**	**1,587,423**	**16,902,205**	**20,485,729**
BM&F, BRAZIL					
Arabica Coffee	Agricultural	47,548	55,301	478,544	620,997
Robusta Conillon Coffee	Agricultural			405	20
Live Cattle	Agricultural	9,769	24,096	113,473	225,200
Live Cattle (WTr)	Agricultural		6		6
Feeder Cattle	Agricultural	275	77	9,475	1,024
Sugar Crystal	Agricultural	3,668	4,805	40,257	47,347
Cotton	Agricultural			172	60
Corn	Agricultural	2,548	3,883	43,902	52,600
Soybeans	Agricultural	248	904	2,917	7,225
Gold Forward	Precious	20		483	15
Gold	Precious				2,742
Gold Spot	Precious	6,082	4,657	98,386	57,609
Anhydrous Fuel Alcohol Futures	Energy	2,114	5,444	49,158	40,453
Bovespa Stock Index Futures	Equity	545,127	443,885	6,630,407	7,063,923
IBrX-50	Equity		1,470	85	6,265
Bovespa Mini Index	Equity	78,167	179,709	1,158,155	2,892,016
IGP-M	Other			780	
IGP-M Mini	Other				
Interest Rate	Interest	5,822,452	8,136,243	57,641,625	100,290,263
Interest Rate Swap	Interest	9,552	6,728	888,957	1,005,212
Interest Rate × Exchange Rate Swap	Interest	166,623	30,634	3,520,170	1,189,805
Interest Rate × Reference Rate Swap	Interest			5,052	9,762
Interest Rate × Price Index Swap	Interest	31,519	30,983	666,988	775,591
Interest Rate × Ibovespa Index Swap	Interest	128	241	435	1,175
Exchange Rate Swap	Interest	1,051	1,685	9,778	27,069
Price Index	Interest	1,200		13,200	14,255
ID × U.S. Dollar Spread Futures	Interest	38,658	67,227	731,544	536,358
ID × U.S. Dollar FRA	Interest	1,936,365	2,043,525	22,823,905	33,326,518
ID × U.S. Dollar Swap with reset	Interest	7,291	10,130	234,958	126,525
ID × U.S. Dollar Mini Swap with reset	Interest			1,057,259	189,441
ID × U.S. Dollar Swap without reset	Interest				
ID × IGP-M Spread Futures	Interest			760	
ID × IGP-M Spread Forward	Interest				
ID Forward with reset	Interest			50	5
Global 2040	Interest	160	10,315	160	79,645
C-Bond	Interest	4,314	1,382	35,903	25,919
EI-Bond	Interest				

International Exchanges Futures, Options, and Options on Equities Volume *(Continued)*

	Commodity Group	Dec. 2003	Dec. 2004	Jan.–Dec. 2003	Jan.–Dec. 2004
U.S. Dollar	Foreign	1,308,377	2,209,096	16,784,939	23,943,757
Mini U.S. Dollar	Foreign	28,271	65,664	625,382	608,772
U.S. Dollar Forward Points	Foreign	19,526	39,479	227,097	365,914
Euro	Foreign			300	20
Futures Total		**10,071,053**	**13,377,569**	**113,895,061**	**173,533,508**
Gold Options on Actuals	Precious Opt.	6,110	46,628	173,142	236,058
Gold Options Exercise	Precious Opt.			82,728	62,378
US$ d. Arabica Coffee Options	Agric. Opt.	1,282	5,532	37,423	50,148
US$ d. Arabica Coffee Options Exercise	Agric. Opt.	1	210	1,143	3,206
Live Cattle Options on Futures	Agric. Opt.			764	550
Live Cattle Options Exercise	Agric. Opt.			42	2
Anhydrous Fuel Alcohol Options	Energy Opt.				100
Anhydrous Fuel Alcohol Options Exercise	Energy Opt.				50
Bovespa Stock Options	Interest Opt.		9,475		21,730
Bovespa Stock Options Exercise	Interest Opt.		3,245		11,350
Bovespa Stock Options Volatility	Interest Opt.		16,770		56,885
Interest Rate Options	Interest Opt.	46,693	57,516	182,183	1,253,545
IDI Index	Interest Opt.	92,116	161,982	1,772,583	2,224,832
Interest Rate Options Exercise	Interest Opt.			155,263	154,100
Interest Rate Options (volatility)	Interest Opt.	9,810	111,955	9,810	879,575
IDI Index (exercise)	Interest Opt.				131,099
IDI Index (volatility)	Interest Opt.	1,185	11,915	1,185	143,180
Flexible Bovespa Stock Index Options	Equity Opt.	161,852	12,043	1,216,418	687,412
U.S. Dollar Options	Foreign Opt.	200,396	404,315	2,148,440	2,708,961
U.S. Dollar Options Exercise	Foreign Opt.	8,520	14,020	130,187	147,645
U.S. Dollar Option Volatility	Foreign Opt.	15,800	15,860	30,030	255,150
Flexible U.S. Dollar Options	Foreign Opt.	76,838	10,316	949,200	866,474
Options Total		**620,603**	**881,782**	**6,890,541**	**9,894,430**
BM&F, Brazil, Total		**10,691,656**	**14,259,351**	**120,785,602**	**183,427,938**
BOVESPA, BRAZIL					
Ibovespa Index Options	Equity Opt.	172,655	174,397	1,600,261	1,586,762
Mini Ibovespa Index Options	Equity Opt.				3,003
Exchange Traded Funds Options	Equity Opt.				36
IbrX-50 Index Options	Equity Opt.			200	
All Options on Individual Equities	Ind. Equity Opt.	14,623,235	16,978,671	175,622,679	233,759,713
BOVESPA, Brazil, Total		**14,795,890**	**17,153,068**	**177,223,140**	**235,349,514**
DALIAN COMMODITY EXCHANGE, CHINA					
Soybeans	Agricultural			19,287	
Corn	Agricultural		2,876,898		5,828,045
No. 1 Soybeans	Agricultural	6,151,181	3,123,307	60,000,808	57,340,803
No. 2 Soybeans	Agricultural		114,347		114,347
Soy Meal	Agricultural	742,395	1,300,025	14,953,398	24,750,958
Dalian Commodity Exchange, China, Total		**6,893,576**	**7,414,577**	**74,973,493**	**88,034,153**

(continues)

International Exchanges Futures, Options, and Options on Equities Volume *(Continued)*

	Commodity Group	Dec. 2003	Dec. 2004	Jan.–Dec. 2003	Jan.–Dec. 2004
BUDAPEST COMMODITY EXCHANGE					
Corn	Agricultural	528	351	12,513	9,617
CE Corn	Agricultural		6		6
Feed Wheat	Agricultural	16	151	711	1,351
CE Feed Wheat	Agricultural		1		1
Feed Barley	Agricultural	4	70	354	366
CE Feed Barley	Agricultural		1		1
Wheat	Agricultural	311	150	6,883	4,246
CE Wheat	Agricultural		1		1
Extra Wheat	Agricultural				
Sunflower Seed	Agricultural	117	326	1,031	1,909
CE Sunflower	Agricultural		1		1
Rapeseed	Agricultural			24	270
Soybean	Agricultural				
GAX	Agricultural				
Ammonium Nitrate	Agricultural			3	1
U.S. Dollar	Foreign	164,997	90,280	1,153,307	401,800
Japanese Yen	Foreign	18,180		197,763	57,980
Euro	Foreign	270,827	27,810	1,602,075	615,144
British Pound	Foreign			62,270	26,134
Czech Koruna	Foreign	160		3,370	310
Polish Zloty	Foreign	40	360	3,565	1,258
Swiss Franc	Foreign	34,802	100	188,786	44,930
EUR/CHF	Foreign	5	3	111	215
EUR/USD	Foreign	122	355	937	5,255
EUR/JPY	Foreign	10		373	578
EUR/PLN	Foreign	83	80	433	2,441
GBP/CHF	Foreign	22	93	27	551
GBP/JPY	Foreign		180		1,825
GBP/USD	Foreign		1,462	68	2,896
USD/CHF	Foreign	70	1	86	231
USD/JPY	Foreign	4	33	139	620
USD/PLN	Foreign	247	391	719	1,249
Three-Month BUBOR	Interest			1,540	4,320
Futures Total		**490,545**	**122,206**	**3,237,088**	**1,185,507**
Corn	Agric. Opt.			888	432
Wheat	Agric. Opt.			242	90
U.S. Dollar	Foreign Opt.			21,650	
EUR	Foreign Opt.	34,620	1,500	414,095	113,970
EUR/PLN	Foreign Opt.		20		225
EUR/USD	Foreign Opt.	15	15	15	44
GBP/JPY	Foreign Opt.		10		10
USD/PLN	Foreign Opt.		110		448
Options Total		**34,635**	**1,655**	**436,890**	**115,219**
Budapest Commodity Exchange Total		**525,180**	**123,861**	**3,673,978**	**1,300,726**

International Exchanges Futures, Options, and Options on Equities Volume *(Continued)*

	Commodity Group	Dec. 2003	Dec. 2004	Jan.–Dec. 2003	Jan.–Dec. 2004
BUDAPEST STOCK EXCHANGE					
Budapest Stock Index (BUX) Futures	Equity	35,564	36,150	400,003	376,679
Budapest Stock Mid & SmallCap Index (BUMIX)	Equity		5		51
Three-Month BUBOR	Interest	50	300	150	3,445
EUR/HUF	Foreign		50,729	178,460	68,069
JPY/HUF	Foreign	100	2,250	67,390	41,350
CHF/HUF	Foreign	42,670	596	326,090	71,800
CZK/HUF	Foreign	300	4,850	3,770	26,410
EUR/HUF	Foreign	105,590		514,451	512,991
GBP/HUF	Foreign		3,000	1,000	28,000
PLN/HUF	Foreign			1,800	42,092
USD/HUF	Foreign	4,120	34,801	36,586	227,235
GBP/USD	Foreign	5,400	24,330	72,350	197,560
GBP/CHF	Foreign	3,500	25,310	33,000	100,630
GBP/JPY	Foreign		9,350	4,800	311,030
GBP/SEK	Foreign	6,200	4,900	23,300	33,800
EUR/CHF	Foreign	1,200	300	43,575	38,700
EUR/CZK	Foreign				2,200
EUR/GBP	Foreign	1,500		25,100	17,500
EUR/NOK	Foreign	2,400	9,100	23,900	18,600
EUR/JPY	Foreign	600	5,100	8,200	46,200
EUR/PLN	Foreign	3,900	400	24,200	28,300
EUR/ROL	Foreign		5,000		5,000
EUR/SEK	Foreign	1,000	5,700	2,039,000	51,200
EUR/TRL	Foreign		1,500		1,500
EUR/USD	Foreign	41,600	29,618	249,750	501,448
USD/CHF	Foreign	1,200	4,500	16,440	117,700
USD/JPY	Foreign	22,000	126,350	146,525	666,030
USD/NOK	Foreign			5,000	
USD/PLN	Foreign		1,100		5,400
USD/TRL	Foreign		3,800		3,800
USD/SEK	Foreign	100		300	
CHF/JPY	Foreign			200	
All Futures on Individual Equities	Indiv. Equity	80,135	76,232	694,553	707,875
Budapest Stock Exchange Total		**359,129**	**465,271**	**4,939,893**	**4,252,595**
EUREX					
DAX	Equity	2,286,961	2,361,161	27,181,218	29,229,847
OMXH25	Equity	7,888	4,145	32,589	24,934
NEMAX 50	Equity	53,902	5,383	750,125	124,411
TecDAX	Equity	49,887	55,514	181,954	456,346
Dow Jones Global Titans 50	Equity	1,730	103	2,017	333
Dow Jones Italy Titans 50	Equity		16,459		70,403
DJ Euro STOXX 50	Equity	9,402,025	10,504,642	116,035,326	121,661,944
DJ Euro STOXX Automobiles & Parts	Equity	29,561	10,211	152,714	99,776
DJ Euro STOXX Banks	Equity	58,503	32,111	483,451	243,541
DJ Euro STOXX Basic Resources	Equity	1,520	1,869	10,185	18,018

(continues)

International Exchanges Futures, Options, and Options on Equities Volume *(Continued)*

	Commodity Group	Dec. 2003	Dec. 2004	Jan.–Dec. 2003	Jan.–Dec. 2004
DJ Euro STOXX Chemicals	Equity	14	994	54	5,254
DJ Euro STOXX Construction & Materials	Equity	1	89	481	573
DJ Euro STOXX Travel & Leisure	Equity	40	664	40	5,358
DJ Euro STOXX Oil & Gas	Equity	14,192	18,070	105,614	118,457
DJ Euro STOXX Financial Services	Equity	1	122	995	1,050
DJ Euro STOXX Food and Beverage	Equity	3,348	3,584	8,538	16,382
DJ Euro STOXX Healthcare	Equity	488	1,049	3,281	4,288
DJ Euro STOXX Industry Goods & Services	Equity	10	224	230	844
DJ Euro STOXX Insurance	Equity	48,321	30,913	323,207	236,325
DJ Euro STOXX Media	Equity	1,898	2,405	8,339	8,863
DJ Euro STOXX Personal & Household Goods	Equity		206	444	2,035
DJ Euro STOXX Retail	Equity	2	609	42	1,983
DJ Euro STOXX Technology	Equity	32,258	33,894	281,967	160,160
DJ Euro STOXX Telecom	Equity	23,657	38,720	192,907	182,949
DJ Euro STOXX Utilities	Equity	3,779	3,709	16,927	12,705
DJ STOXX 50	Equity	132,163	129,411	970,107	798,106
DJ STOXX 600 Banks	Equity	1,414	8,851	8,595	32,222
DJ STOXX 600 Basic Resources	Equity		70		647
DJ STOXX 600 Oil & Gas	Equity		192		3,261
DJ STOXX 600 Financial Services	Equity		24		166
DJ STOXX 600 Food & Beverage	Equity		71		347
DJ STOXX 600 Healthcare	Equity	7,155	16,225	41,394	70,931
DJ STOXX 600 Industrial G&S	Equity		1,405		1,527
DJ STOXX 600 Insurance	Equity	60	1,586	170	18,803
DJ STOXX 600 Media	Equity		170		305
DJ STOXX 600 Technology	Equity	2,365	1,609	8,331	15,887
DJ STOXX 600 Telecom	Equity	4,001	997	20,537	19,596
DJ STOXX 600 Utilities	Equity	2,920	5,997	9,651	29,622
Swiss Market Index (SMI)	Equity	815,548	968,675	8,969,235	8,098,575
Exchange Traded Funds	Indiv. Equity	2,196	226	187,996	78,393
Swiss Government Bond (CONF)	Interest	32,892	47,909	284,809	308,206
Euro-BUND	Interest	13,434,122	20,182,331	244,414,274	239,787,517
Euro-BOBL	Interest	9,227,155	12,495,287	150,087,139	159,166,394
Three-Month Euribor	Interest	49,238	70,552	503,951	585,142
One-Month EONIA	Interest			666	
Euro-BUXL	Interest				
Euro-SCHATZ	Interest	7,202,705	9,187,853	117,370,528	122,928,076
Futures Total		**42,933,920**	**56,246,291**	**668,650,028**	**684,630,502**
DAX Options	Equity Opt.	2,509,078	2,799,993	41,521,920	42,184,611
OMXH25 Options	Equity Opt.	1,510	30	7,128	1,050
NEMAX 50	Equity Opt.	575		48,969	210
TecDAX Options	Equity Opt.	1,638	2,988	13,477	27,370
Dow Jones Global Titans 50	Equity Opt.			48	29
DJ Euro STOXX 50	Equity Opt.	4,173,179	4,284,742	61,794,673	71,406,377
DJ Euro STOXX Automobiles & Parts	Equity Opt.			50,673	24,536

International Exchanges Futures, Options, and Options on Equities Volume *(Continued)*

	Commodity Group	Dec. 2003	Dec. 2004	Jan.–Dec. 2003	Jan.–Dec. 2004
DJ Euro STOXX Banks	Equity Opt.	25,981	4,746	413,834	150,913
DJ Euro STOXX Chemicals	Equity Opt.	2		2	2
DJ Euro STOXX Gas & Oil	Equity Opt.	2,601	40	63,427	46,243
DJ Euro STOXX Financial Services	Equity Opt.			307	160
DJ Euro STOXX Food and Beverage	Equity Opt.				300
DJ Euro STOXX Healthcare	Equity Opt.			19	600
DJ Euro STOXX Insurance	Equity Opt.	14,945	1,445	269,736	91,371
DJ Euro STOXX Media	Equity Opt.				799
DJ Euro STOXX Technology	Equity Opt.	10,477	20	86,830	28,102
DJ Euro STOXX Telecom	Equity Opt.	3,329	4,500	110,664	39,396
DJ STOXX 50	Equity Opt.	595	1,734	55,417	14,952
DJ STOXX 600 Banks	Equity Opt.		1,000		1,865
DJ STOXX 600 Basic Resources	Equity Opt.		3,850		3,850
DJ STOXX 600 Healthcare	Equity Opt.		2,750	11,270	20,017
DJ STOXX 600 Technology	Equity Opt.			4	1,000
DJ STOXX 600 Telecom	Equity Opt.	2		2	3,405
DJ STOXX 600 Utilities	Equity Opt.		1,000	1,633	1,000
Swiss Market Index (SMI) Option	Equity Opt.	214,965	276,955	3,983,918	3,645,596
Options on Euro-BUND	Interest Opt.	1,188,660	2,812,952	27,316,536	30,896,920
Options on Euro-SCHATZ	Interest Opt.	465,879	402,681	11,723,090	9,782,863
Options on Euro-BOBL	Interest Opt.	560,764	572,331	10,498,534	10,829,250
All Options on Swiss Equities	Ind. Equity Opt.	2,981,560	3,768,045	46,302,221	47,714,268
All Options on Finnish Equities	Ind. Equity Opt.	842,818	1,049,547	13,265,471	17,836,215
All Options on Dutch Equities	Ind. Equity Opt.	392,066	547,801	6,862,703	8,364,977
All Options on Exchange Traded Funds	Ind. Equity Opt.	4,526	3,853	70,350	85,478
All Options on French Equities	Ind. Equity Opt.	163,435	153,315	1,487,428	2,743,950
All Options on German Equities	Ind. Equity Opt.	9,477,837	7,417,639	120,211,761	134,857,678
All Options on Italian Equities	Ind. Equity Opt.	15,328	42,185	80,041	187,948
All Options on U.S. Equities	Ind. Equity Opt.	1,909	962	30,198	15,207
Options Total		**23,053,659**	**24,157,104**	**346,282,284**	**381,008,508**
EUREX Total		**65,987,579**	**80,403,395**	**1,014,932,312**	**1,065,639,010**
EURONEXT—AMSTERDAM					
Live Hogs (AVC)	Agricultural	12		1,257	33
Potatoes (APC)	Agricultural	1,756		40,265	14,397
Potatoes (FAP)	Agricultural		845		11,876
AEX Stock Index (FTI)	Equity	344,604	458,553	5,215,465	5,651,747
Light AEX Stock Index (FTIL)	Equity	288	454	6,639	5,827
FTSE Eurotop 100 Index (FET1)	Equity			313	
Euro/U.S. Dollar (FED)	Foreign	136	166	1,405	2,026

(continues)

International Exchanges Futures, Options, and Options on Equities Volume *(Continued)*

	Commodity Group	Dec. 2003	Dec. 2004	Jan.–Dec. 2003	Jan.–Dec. 2004
U.S. Dollar/Euro (FDE)	Foreign	396	50	1,088	1,959
All Futures on Individual Equities	Indiv. Equity	3,892		32,429	13,257
Futures Total		**351,084**	**460,068**	**5,298,861**	**5,701,122**
Potato Options (OPA)	Agric. Opt.		155		2,426
Euro/U.S. Dollar (EDX)	Foreign Opt.	16,241	19,100	74,279	139,758
U.S. Dollar/Euro Options (DEX)	Foreign Opt.	15,683	13,870	64,045	99,322
AEX Stock Index Options (AEX)	Equity Opt.	819,502	1,034,668	14,120,099	17,093,573
Light AEX Stock Index Options (AEXL)	Equity Opt.	1,694	1,309	131,209	34,539
FTSE Eurotop 100 Options (ET1)	Equity Opt.			1,560	
All Options on Individual Equities	Ind. Equity Opt.	3,422,869	3,982,097	59,754,703	60,196,898
Options Total		**4,275,989**	**5,051,199**	**74,145,895**	**77,566,516**
Euronext—Amsterdam Total		**4,627,073**	**5,511,267**	**79,444,756**	**83,267,638**
EURONEXT—BRUSSELS					
Bel 20 Index (BXF)	Equity	30,481	30,887	328,673	379,855
Futures Total		**30,481**	**30,887**	**328,673**	**379,855**
Bel 20 Index Options (BXO)	Equity Opt.	20,245	15,940	320,540	271,717
All Options on Individual Equities	Ind. Equity Opt.	12,920	26,527	319,850	326,844
Options Total		**33,165**	**42,467**	**640,390**	**598,561**
Euronext—Brussels Total		**63,646**	**73,354**	**969,063**	**978,416**
EURONEXT.LIFFE, U.K.					
Three-Month Sterling	Interest	2,316,635	3,794,833	42,323,094	51,324,125
Three-Month Euroswiss	Interest	415,585	502,309	5,009,460	7,296,932
Three-Month Euroyen Tibor	Interest				736
One-Month Eonia	Interest	135		58,341	35,152
Three-Month Euribor	Interest	7,997,524	10,514,817	137,692,190	157,746,684
Three-Month Eurodollar	Interest		544,239		4,666,508
Long Gilt	Interest	640,572	1,111,223	10,150,267	14,045,404
Schatz	Interest			2,543	
Swapnote €—Two-Year	Interest	78,923	42,192	580,516	458,492
Swapnote €—Five-Year	Interest	146,975	117,550	1,022,358	688,952
Swapnote €—10-Year	Interest	124,335	104,988	1,031,016	653,046
Swapnote US$—Two-Year	Interest	120		1,120	1
Swapnote US$—Five-Year	Interest	633	25	17,660	430
Swapnote US$—10-Year	Interest	872	10	28,595	2,968
Japanese Government Bond	Interest	3,972	6,933	44,613	80,569
FTSE 100 Index	Equity	2,196,246	2,214,487	20,252,114	20,772,878
FTSE Eurotop 100 Index	Equity	28,047	16,299	109,846	88,475
FTSEurofirst 80 Index	Equity	58,905	39,197	344,100	814,030
FTSEurofirst 100 Index	Equity	38,195	5,196	210,171	277,661
MSCI Euro Index	Equity	7,668	8,228	107,207	60,414
MSCI Pan-Euro Index	Equity	88,529	92,596	563,944	474,949
FTSE Mid 250 Index	Equity	3,081	2,907	5,422	32,896
Barley	Agricultural			1,058	

International Exchanges Futures, Options, and Options on Equities Volume *(Continued)*

	Commodity Group	Dec. 2003	Dec. 2004	Jan.–Dec. 2003	Jan.–Dec. 2004
No. 7 Cocoa	Agricultural	218,776	236,439	2,328,609	2,643,199
Robusta Coffee	Agricultural	264,167	264,652	2,320,831	3,054,386
Wheat	Agricultural	6,731	3,732	91,387	75,455
White Sugar	Agricultural	72,540	93,719	1,062,494	1,251,233
All Futures on Individual Equities	Indiv. Equity	624,833	598,870	6,349,198	12,929,406
Futures Total		**15,333,999**	**20,315,441**	**231,708,154**	**279,474,981**
Three-Month Sterling Option	Interest Opt.	453,016	947,731	14,162,149	16,139,006
Three-Month Sterling Mid Curve Option	Interest Opt.	22,780	78,326	967,384	1,461,723
Three-Month Euroswiss Option	Interest Opt.	12,500	200	65,925	49,251
Three-Month Euribor Option	Interest Opt.	3,875,860	1,592,158	57,733,239	52,245,463
Three-Month Euribor Mid Curve Option	Interest Opt.	220,901	287,535	4,907,879	6,433,100
Three-Month Eurodollar Option	Interest Opt.				376
Euro Bund	Interest Opt.				72
Swapnote €—Two-Year	Interest Opt.	2,490		15,904	1,400
Swapnote €—Five-Year	Interest Opt.	206		2,452	2,516
Swapnote €—10-Year	Interest Opt.	1,784		7,888	540
FTSE 100 Option (ESX)	Equity Opt.	800,534	834,195	14,619,893	17,866,310
FTSE 100 Option (SEI)	Equity Opt.	2,363	10	55,215	10,766
FTSEurofirst 80 Index	Equity Opt.	112	43	1,841	521
FTSEurofirst 100 Index	Equity Opt.	15		1,166	20
FTSE 100 FLEX Options	Equity Opt.	30,231	68,518	1,066,997	1,178,067
No. 7 Cocoa Options	Agric. Opt.	7,048	15,332	188,822	170,079
Robusta Coffee Options	Agric. Opt.	15,752	14,868	143,148	248,990
Wheat Options	Agric. Opt.	105	92	3,262	2,387
White Sugar Options	Agric. Opt.	4,750	7,501	66,561	94,705
All Options on Individual Equities	Ind. Equity Opt.	621,988	670,914	10,108,068	11,578,961
Options Total		**6,072,435**	**4,517,423**	**104,117,793**	**107,484,253**
Euronext.liffe, U.K., Total		**21,406,434**	**24,832,864**	**335,825,947**	**386,959,234**
EURONEXT—LISBON					
PSI-20 Index	Equity	15,128	18,076	214,415	114,955
All Futures on Individual Equities	Indiv. Equity	61,241	33,775	560,224	520,966
Futures Total		**76,369**	**51,851**	**774,639**	**635,921**
All Options on Individual Equities	Ind. Equity Opt.	640		74,664	28,152
Options Total		**640**	**0**	**74,664**	**28,152**
Euronext—Lisbon Total		**77,009**	**51,851**	**849,303**	**664,073**
EURONEXT—PARIS					
EURIBOR	Interest			51	
Wheat	Agricultural	8,059	12,367	114,758	160,200
Corn	Agricultural	4,948	8,324	90,973	71,124
Rapeseed	Agricultural	9,897	12,685	174,538	191,644
CAC 40 10 Euro	Equity	1,987,099	1,935,232	29,319,624	24,058,528
DJ EURO STOXX SM 50	Equity			11,866	

(continues)

International Exchanges Futures, Options, and Options on Equities Volume *(Continued)*

	Commodity Group	Dec. 2003	Dec. 2004	Jan.–Dec. 2003	Jan.–Dec. 2004
DJ STOXX SM 50	Equity			6	
Futures Total		**2,010,003**	**1,968,608**	**29,711,816**	**24,481,496**
Options on Rapeseed	Agric. Opt.	420	754	7,003	8,075
Options on Wheat	Agric. Opt.	642	273	7,643	7,109
CAC 40 Index Options	Equity Opt.	4,779,861	3,173,120	73,668,131	63,152,339
All Options on Individual Equities	Ind. Equity Opt.	12,693,995	11,743,384	174,487,319	230,863,609
Options Total		**17,474,918**	**14,917,531**	**248,170,096**	**294,031,132**
Euronext—Paris Total		**19,484,921**	**16,886,139**	**277,881,912**	**318,512,628**
Euronext Total		**45,659,083**	**47,355,475**	**694,970,981**	**790,381,989**
COPENHAGEN STOCK EXCHANGE, THE FUTOP MARKET, DENMARK					
KFX Stock Index	Equity	48,606	61,189	610,908	555,052
Futures Total		**48,606**	**61,189**	**610,908**	**555,052**
KFX Stock Index Options	Equity Opt.		120	8,440	1,299
All Options on Individual Equities	Ind. Equity Opt.	9,086	12,686	142,702	147,655
Options Total		**9,086**	**12,806**	**151,142**	**148,954**
Copenhagen Stock Exchange Total		**57,692**	**73,995**	**762,050**	**704,006**
INTERNATIONAL PETROLEUM EXCHANGE, U.K.					
Brent Crude Oil	Energy	1,729,030	1,805,069	24,012,969	25,458,259
Gas Oil	Energy	572,190	675,081	8,429,981	9,355,767
Natural Gas—Seasons	Energy		1,080	600	15,090
Natural Gas—Quarters	Energy	90	390	1,590	24,045
Natural Gas BOM	Energy			1,455	90
Natural Gas Daily (NBP)	Energy			74,180	90
Natural Gas Monthly (NBP)	Energy	33,235	40,365	737,610	609,350
Electricity Baseload—Monthly	Energy		280		1,070
Electricity Baseload—Quarters	Energy				900
Electricity Baseload—Seasons	Energy		480		2,280
Futures Total		**2,334,545**	**2,522,745**	**33,258,385**	**35,466,941**
Brent Crude Oil Options	Energy Opt.	1,502	1,702	49,520	28,688
Gasoil Options	Energy Opt.	1,515	5,568	33,339	45,154
Options Total		**3,017**	**7,270**	**82,859**	**73,842**
International Petroleum Exchange, U.K., Total		**2,337,562**	**2,530,015**	**33,341,244**	**35,540,783**
ITALIAN DERIVATIVES MARKET OF THE ITALIAN STOCK EXCHANGE					
MIB 30 Index	Equity	282,296	268,859	4,263,886	3,331,843
Mini FIB 30 Index	Equity	132,719	83,325	2,570,238	1,485,112
MIDEX	Equity			358	
All Futures on Individual Equities	Indiv. Equity	18,084	176,428	468,083	1,734,256
Futures Total		**433,099**	**528,612**	**7,302,565**	**6,551,211**

International Exchanges Futures, Options, and Options on Equities Volume *(Continued)*

	Commodity Group	Dec. 2003	Dec. 2004	Jan.–Dec. 2003	Jan.–Dec. 2004
MIB 30 Index Options	Equity Opt.	161,464	157,277	2,505,351	2,220,807
All Options on Individual Equities	Ind. Equity Opt.	514,303	894,403	7,924,078	9,500,498
Options Total		**675,767**	**1,051,680**	**10,429,429**	**11,721,305**
Italian Derivatives Market Total		**1,108,866**	**1,580,292**	**17,731,994**	**18,272,516**
KOREA FUTURES EXCHANGE					
Korea Treasury Bonds	Interest	604,880	477,172	10,285,042	7,352,307
Five-Year Treasury Bond	Interest	43,737		171,538	61
Monetary Stabilization Bond	Interest	11,212		207,209	2,621
KOSPI 200*	Equity	4,492,804	4,252,688	62,204,783	55,608,856
KOSDAQ50 Index	Equity	44,177	4,612	727,997	206,221
Gold	Precious	9,164		56,998	969
U.S. Dollar	Foreign	127,257	212,294	1,506,123	2,090,291
Futures Total		**5,333,231**	**4,946,766**	**75,159,690**	**65,261,326**
Korea Treasury Bond Options	Interest Opt.			1,229	
KOSPI 200 Options*	Equity Opt.	230,836,792	173,874,552	2,837,724,953	2,521,557,274
KOSDAQ50 Index	Equity Opt.			3	1
All Options on Individual Equities*	Ind. Equity Opt.			8,159	1
Options Total		**230,836,792**	**173,874,552**	**2,837,734,344**	**2,521,557,276**
Korea Futures Exchange Total		**236,170,023**	**178,821,318**	**2,912,894,034**	**2,586,818,602**
LONDON METAL EXCHANGE					
High Grade Primary Aluminum	Nonprecious	2,300,444	2,648,873	26,953,102	29,232,921
Aluminium Alloy	Nonprecious	70,318	30,177	703,356	429,459
North American Special Aluminum Alloy	Nonprecious	91,598	106,070	833,022	1,192,100
Copper—Grade A	Nonprecious	1,652,200	1,370,823	19,437,740	18,171,204
Standard Lead	Nonprecious	355,474	281,725	4,504,246	3,786,375
Primary Nickel	Nonprecious	338,580	246,522	4,220,434	3,177,206
Special High Grade Zinc	Nonprecious	859,600	834,352	10,470,171	10,211,096
Tin	Nonprecious	117,971	85,289	1,448,083	971,612
LMEX	Nonprecious				
Futures Total		**5,786,185**	**5,603,831**	**68,570,154**	**67,171,973**
High Grade Primary Aluminum Options	Nonprec. Opt.	199,330	183,309	1,618,895	2,217,021
Aluminium Alloy Options	Nonprec. Opt.			541	288
North American Special Aluminum Alloy Options	Nonprec. Opt.		75	50	2,385
Copper—Grade A Options	Nonprec. Opt.	100,582	99,593	1,239,523	1,721,914
Standard Lead Options	Nonprec. Opt.	3,327	5,040	95,967	76,342
Primary Nickel Options	Nonprec. Opt.	8,371	7,553	144,489	119,942
Special High Grade Zinc Options	Nonprec. Opt.	20,276	67,255	386,652	471,097
Tin Options	Nonprec. Opt.	1,100	170	8,070	3,227
Primary Aluminium TAPOs	Nonprec. Opt.	6,050	1,404	137,598	55,539

*These contracts were transferred from the Korea Stock Exchange as of January 2, 2004, and now trade on KFE.

(continues)

International Exchanges Futures, Options, and Options on Equities Volume *(Continued)*

	Commodity Group	Dec. 2003	Dec. 2004	Jan.–Dec. 2003	Jan.–Dec. 2004
Aluminium Alloy TAPOs					390
Copper Grade A TAPOs	Nonprec. Opt.	48,872	7,960	90,381	37,438
Lead TAPOs	Nonprec. Opt.	80	1,762	1,551	10,653
Nickel TAPOs	Nonprec. Opt.			4,950	4,014
Tin TAPOs	Nonprec. Opt.				475
North American Special Aluminum Alloy TAPOs	Nonprec. Opt.			768	1,632
Special High Grade Zinc TAPOs	Nonprec. Opt.	816	3,120	8,738	12,571
Options Total		**388,804**	**377,241**	**3,738,173**	**4,734,928**
London Metal Exchange Total		**6,174,989**	**5,981,072**	**72,308,327**	**71,906,901**
MALAYSIA DERIVATIVES EXCHANGE BERHAD					
Crude Palm Oil (FCPO)	Agricultural	96,764	94,361	1,434,713	1,378,334
Three-Month KLIBOR (FKB3)	Interest	9,488	6,723	126,289	141,969
Three-Year Malaysian Government Securities (FMG3)	Interest	50		781	4,327
Five-Year Malaysian Government Securities (FMG5)	Interest	52	50	116,221	19,494
Ten-Year Malaysian Government Securities (FMG10)	Interest			11	
KLSE Composite Index (FKLI)	Equity	55,219	77,846	331,445	1,088,419
Futures Total		**161,573**	**178,980**	**2,009,460**	**2,632,543**
KLSE Composite Index Options (FPKO)	Equity Opt.				
Options Total		**0**	**0**	**0**	**0**
Malaysia Derivatives Exchange Berhad Total		**161,573**	**178,980**	**2,009,460**	**2,632,543**
MEFF RENTA FIJA, SPAIN					
Ten-Year Notional Bond	Interest	53	16	1,382	95
Meff Renta Fija, Spain, Total		**53**	**16**	**1,382**	**95**
MEFF RENTA VARIABLE, SPAIN					
IBEX 35	Equity	306,060	350,012	3,545,942	4,354,868
Mini IBEX 35	Equity	59,883	78,769	1,070,853	1,182,497
All Futures on Individual Equities	Indiv. Equity	3,133,676	2,719,024	12,492,568	12,054,799
Futures Total		**3,499,619**	**3,147,805**	**17,109,363**	**17,592,164**
Mini IBEX 35 Options	Equity Opt.	311,323	305,891	2,981,593	2,947,529
All Options on Individual Equities	Ind. Equity Opt.	1,029,686	1,070,874	11,378,992	8,200,314
Options Total		**1,341,009**	**1,376,765**	**14,360,585**	**11,147,843**
Meff Renta Variable, Spain Total		**4,840,628**	**4,524,570**	**31,469,948**	**28,740,007**
MERCADO A TERMINO DE BUENOS AIRES					
Wheat	Agricultural	1,503	4,093	9,014	17,348
Corn	Agricultural	285	744	2,694	8,000
Sunflower	Agricultural	11	170	161	495
Soybean	Agricultural	2,175	2,482	17,569	42,701
Futures Total		**3,974**	**7,489**	**29,437**	**68,544**

International Exchanges Futures, Options, and Options on Equities Volume *(Continued)*

	Commodity Group	Dec. 2003	Dec. 2004	Jan.–Dec. 2003	Jan.–Dec. 2004
Wheat Options	Agric. Opt.	222	458	1,960	3,302
Corn Options	Agric. Opt.	312	6	538	811
Sunflower Options	Agric. Opt.		107		703
Soybean Options	Agric. Opt.	1,844	838	7,675	12,233
Options Total		**2,378**	**1,409**	**10,173**	**17,049**
MATBA Total		**6,352**	**8,898**	**39,610**	**85,593**
MERCADO A TERMINO DE ROSARIO					
Wheat	Agricultural	129		859	36
Corn	Agricultural	4		4	
Rosafe Soybean Index (ISR)	Agricultural	616	11,637	11,912	56,468
Rosafe Corn Index (IMR)	Agricultural	49	21	615	309
U.S. Dollar (DLR)	Foreign	269,862	701,168	2,694,348	7,679,077
Euro (EC)	Foreign			575	
Futures Total		**270,660**	**712,826**	**2,708,313**	**7,735,890**
Wheat Options	Agric. Opt.	8		128	24
Rosafe Soybean Index (ISR)	Agric. Opt.	26	7,046	1,134	59,449
Rosafe Corn Index (IMR)	Agric. Opt.	8		50	
U.S. Dollar (DLR)	Foreign Opt.	15,602	19,225	132,871	368,182
Options Total		**15,644**	**26,271**	**134,183**	**427,655**
ROFEX Total		**286,304**	**739,097**	**2,842,496**	**8,163,545**
MEXICAN DERIVATIVES EXCHANGE					
U.S. Dollar	Foreign	2,920	336,517	81,395	1,289,386
IPC Stock Index	Equity	19,862	23,836	220,731	327,942
CETE 91	Interest	157,500	455,087	11,398,544	2,418,381
TIIE 28	Interest	16,126,354	10,224,830	162,077,312	206,027,203
M3 Bond	Interest			4,683	
M10 Bond	Interest	2,718	45,520	38,279	278,644
UDI Inflation Index	Foreign				20
All Futures on Individual Equities	Indiv. Equity		7,719		13,455
Futures Total		**16,309,354**	**11,093,509**	**173,820,944**	**210,355,031**
IPC Stock Index Options	Equity Opt.		5,356		35,943
All Options on Individual Equities	Ind. Equity Opt.		60		4,290
Options Total			**5,416**		**40,233**
MEXDER Total		**16,309,354**	**11,098,925**	**173,820,944**	**210,395,264**
BOURSE DE MONTREAL					
Bankers Acceptance Futures 3 Months (BAX)	Interest	478,049	727,109	6,578,451	7,765,060
30-Day Overnight Repo Rate Futures (ONX)	Interest			6,055	1,480
Canadian Government Bonds (OBA)	Interest	43		3,754	605
Two-Year Canadian Gov't Bond (CGZ)	Interest		26,695		218,069
Ten-Year Canadian Gov't Bond (CGB)	Interest	147,783	189,028	2,397,119	3,005,359
S&P Canada 60 Index (SXF)	Equity	327,596	302,033	1,681,994	1,906,038
Gold Index (SXA)	Equity	221	378	1,454	774

(continues)

International Exchanges Futures, Options, and Options on Equities Volume *(Continued)*

	Commodity Group	Dec. 2003	Dec. 2004	Jan.–Dec. 2003	Jan.–Dec. 2004
Banking Index (SXB)	Equity			110	186
Information Technology Index (SXH)	Equity	1,000	50	6,890	726
Energy Index (SXY)	Equity		1,980	452	2,524
Futures Total		**954,692**	**1,247,273**	**10,676,279**	**12,900,821**
Options on Bankers Acceptance Futures 3 Months (OBX)	Interest Opt.	15,450	22,979	341,245	265,937
Canadian Gov't Bond Options (OBK,OBV,OBZ)	Interest Opt.		8	744	8
S&P Canada 60 Index (SXO) (incl. LEAPS)	Equity Opt.	2,043	2,238	38,221	38,892
i60 Index (XIU)	Equity Opt.	16,221	8,697	130,508	120,502
Barclays iUnits S&P/TSX Capped Gold Index Fund (XGD)	Equity Opt.	5,488	7,370	18,199	54,561
Barclays iUnits S&P/TSX Capped Financials Index Fund (XFN)	Equity Opt.	3,461	23,038	101,914	73,006
Barclays iUnits S&P/TSX Capped IT Index Fund (XIT)	Equity Opt.	383	1,426	9,721	11,800
Barclays iUnits S&P/TSX Capped Energy Index Fund (XEG)	Equity Opt.	8,319	6,547	10,917	37,783
All Options on Individual Equities	Ind. Equity Opt.	528,262	648,418	6,355,251	8,311,818
Options Total		**579,627**	**720,721**	**7,006,720**	**8,914,307**
Bourse de Montreal Total		**1,534,319**	**1,967,994**	**17,682,999**	**21,815,128**
NATIONAL STOCK EXCHANGE OF INDIA					
Interest Rate	Interest			10,781	
S&P CNX Nifty Index	Equity	1,875,468	1,447,464	10,557,024	23,354,782
All Futures on Individual Equities	Indiv. Equity	3,334,468	5,238,498	25,573,756	44,051,780
Futures Total		**5,209,936**	**6,685,962**	**36,141,561**	**67,406,562**
Options on S&P CNX Nifty Index	Equity Opt.	156,077	239,207	1,332,417	2,812,109
All Options on Individual Equities	Ind. Equity Opt.	358,022	590,300	5,607,990	4,874,958
Options Total		**514,099**	**829,507**	**6,940,407**	**7,687,067**
National Stock Exchange of India Total		**5,724,035**	**7,515,469**	**43,081,968**	**75,093,629**
NEW ZEALAND FUTURES EXCHANGE		**52,015**	**45,557**	**493,250**	**497,181**
NZ Broad Wool	Agricultural		4		104
Three-Year Government Stock	Interest			1,101	
Ten-Year Government Stock	Interest	212	94	735	788
90-Day Bank Bill	Interest	51,403	45,457	484,263	491,706
FoX15 Gross Share Price Index	Equity		2		68
NZSE-10 Capital Share Price Index	Equity			21	
Futures Total		**51,615**	**45,557**	**486,120**	**492,666**
90-Day Bank Bill Options	Interest Opt.	400		7,130	4,515
Options Total		**400**		**7,130**	**4,515**
New Zealand Futures Exchange Total		**52,015**	**45,557**	**493,250**	**497,181**

International Exchanges Futures, Options, and Options on Equities Volume *(Continued)*

	Commodity Group	Dec. 2003	Dec. 2004	Jan.–Dec. 2003	Jan.–Dec. 2004
OMX EXCHANGES					
Interest Rate	Interest	587,808	705,337	6,674,408	6,546,035
OMX (Index)	Equity	1,094,490	1,297,359	14,567,900	16,460,920
HEXTech Index	Equity	2		79	
All Futures on Individual Equities	Indiv. Equity	412,880	469,859	3,072,899	4,257,168
Futures Total		**2,095,180**	**2,472,555**	**24,315,286**	**27,264,123**
OMX (Index) Options	Equity Opt.	516,660	604,182	6,371,381	8,946,939
All Options on Individual Equities	Ind. Equity Opt.	2,275,834	3,354,230	43,419,023	58,171,571
Options Total		**2,792,494**	**3,958,412**	**49,790,404**	**67,118,510**
OMX Exchanges—Stockholm and Helsinki Stock Exchanges Total*		**4,887,674**	**6,430,967**	**74,105,690**	**94,382,633**
OSLO STOCK EXCHANGE					
Forwards	Interest	46,100	114,352	436,943	1,071,127
OBX	Equity	69,087	33,494	764,376	677,615
Futures Total		**115,187**	**147,846**	**1,201,319**	**1,748,742**
OBX Options	Equity Opt.	26,020	35,532	543,090	681,783
All Options on Individual Equities	Ind. Equity Opt.	152,665	303,128	2,079,405	2,921,209
Options Total		**178,685**	**338,660**	**2,622,495**	**3,602,992**
Oslo Stock Exchange Total		**293,872**	**486,506**	**3,823,814**	**5,351,734**
SHANGHAI FUTURES EXCHANGE					
Copper	Nonprecious	1,972,138	2,109,442	11,166,288	21,248,370
Aluminum	Nonprecious	204,968	378,791	2,155,498	6,829,499
Rubber	Agricultural	2,281,714	38,483	26,757,964	9,680,649
Fuel Oil	Energy		204,326		2,818,855
Shanghai Futures Exchange Total		**4,458,820**	**2,731,042**	**40,079,750**	**40,577,373**
SIMEX, SINGAPORE					
Eurodollar	Interest	945,886	23,442	18,802,104	8,241,545
Singapore Dollar Interest Rate	Interest	3,732	1,315	58,353	42,486
Nikkei 225	Equity	728,720	861,514	7,098,920	7,769,675
Straits Times Index	Equity	415	47	6,601	1,830
S&P CNX Nifty Index	Equity				38
MSCI Singapore Index	Equity	91,450	137,007	1,046,326	1,658,600
MSCI Taiwan Index	Equity	455,541	569,116	5,455,812	6,998,626
Middle East Crude Oil	Energy	5		2,590	
Euroyen Tibor	Interest	153,541	136,597	2,015,211	2,490,390
Euroyen Libor	Interest	6,090	1,166	110,529	34,547
Five-Year Singapore Government Bond	Interest	177		14,598	446
Ten-Year Japanese Government Bond	Interest	3	2	92	86

*Effective July 2004 Helsinki and Stockholm Stock Exchanges are now reporting volume as OMX Exchanges. The 2003 and 2004 volumes have been adjusted to reflect this change.

(continues)

International Exchanges Futures, Options, and Options on Equities Volume *(Continued)*

	Commodity Group	Dec. 2003	Dec. 2004	Jan.–Dec. 2003	Jan.–Dec. 2004
Mini Japanese Government Bond	Interest	61,660	136,664	745,091	931,110
All Futures on Individual Equities	Indiv. Equity	2		549	
Futures Total		**2,447,222**	**1,866,870**	**35,356,776**	**28,169,379**
Euroyen Tibor Options	Interest Opt.	1		13	
Mini Japanese Government Bond Options	Interest Opt.	50	40	2,074	1,990
MSCI Taiwan Index Options	Equity Opt.	6,672	914	40,274	41,971
Nikkei 225 Option	Equity Opt.	6,058	12,132	249,087	205,417
Options Total		**12,781**	**13,086**	**291,448**	**249,378**
SIMEX, Singapore, Total		**2,460,003**	**1,879,956**	**35,648,224**	**28,418,757**
JSE SECURITIES EXCHANGE, SOUTH AFRICA					
White Maize (WMAZ)	Agricultural	79,783	59,801	1,160,919	969,838
Yellow Maize (YMAZ)	Agricultural	15,439	11,949	249,691	228,709
WEAT	Agricultural	24,356	18,758	186,942	200,663
SUNS	Agricultural	3,508	2,989	61,055	56,285
SOYA	Agricultural	109	69	536	3,054
All Share Index	Equity	1,086,767	1,092,112	8,521,365	9,289,443
Industrial Index	Equity	2,934	3,717	79,270	37,117
Gold Mining Index (GLDX)	Equity	6		1,072	9
Financial Index (FINI)	Equity	12,080	240	41,198	15,931
Financial Industrial Index (FNDI)	Equity		1,400		4,892
Government Bond Index (GOVI)	Equity			344	3,103
FTSE/JSE Capped Top 40 Index (CTOP)	Equity		34,938		34,938
FTSE/JSE Shareholder Weighted Top 40 Index (DTOP)	Equity		37,595		37,596
JBAR	Equity			2	951
RESI	Equity	37	368	12,053	2,004
Kruger Rand (KGRD)	Foreign	1,371	13,350	36,323	15,798
R150	Interest			1,794	
R153	Interest	119	45	5,844	8,332
R157	Interest		1	1,340	1,942
R194	Interest		42	1,856	3,872
All Futures on Individual Equities	Indiv. Equity	1,005,763	1,886,347	4,585,919	8,897,187
Futures Total		**2,232,272**	**3,163,721**	**14,947,523**	**19,811,664**
White Maize (WMAZ)	Agric. Opt.	34,294	32,699	535,408	333,285
Yellow Maize (YMAZ)	Agric. Opt.	3,482	1,529	82,062	33,385
WEAT	Agric. Opt.	803	605	22,306	62,434
SUNS	Agric. Opt.	784	241	7,224	5,089
SOYA	Agric. Opt.			80	52
All Share Index	Equity Opt.	1,088,052	839,301	10,501,861	11,267,046
Industrial Index	Equity Opt.	2,934		4,108	
Financial Index (FINI)	Equity Opt.			2,132	
Financial Industrial Index (FNDI)	Equity Opt.		1,717		1,717
RESI	Equity Opt.				
R150	Interest Opt.			590	
R153	Interest Opt.	260	32	16,785	3,349

International Exchanges Futures, Options, and Options on Equities Volume *(Continued)*

	Commodity Group	Dec. 2003	Dec. 2004	Jan.–Dec. 2003	Jan.–Dec. 2004
R157	Interest Opt.	108	15	2,430	2,227
R194	Interest Opt.			1,980	80
All Options on Individual Equities	Ind. Equity Opt.	574,298	136,861	6,877,254	6,827,533
Options Total		**1,705,015**	**1,013,000**	**18,054,220**	**18,536,197**
SAFEX Total		**3,937,287**	**4,176,721**	**33,001,743**	**38,347,861**
TAIWAN FUTURES EXCHANGE					
TAIEX Futures	Equity	575,639	587,627	6,514,691	8,861,278
Mini TAIEX Futures	Equity	99,003	131,080	1,316,712	1,943,269
Taiwan Stock Exchange Electronic Sector Index Futures	Equity	79,187	79,891	990,752	1,568,391
Taiwan Stock Exchange Bank & Insurance Sector Index Fut	Equity	148,941	111,550	1,126,895	2,255,478
Taiwan 50 Futures Index	Equity	229	379	4,068	6,157
Ten-Year Government Bond Futures	Interest		835		67,705
30-Day Commercial Paper Interest Rate Futures	Interest		161		209,561
Futures Total		**902,999**	**911,523**	**9,953,118**	**14,911,839**
TAIEX Options	Equity Opt.	2,836,840	3,783,383	21,720,083	43,824,511
All Options on Individual Equities	Ind. Equity Opt.	3,468	82,919	201,733	410,026
Options Total		**2,840,308**	**3,866,302**	**21,921,816**	**44,234,537**
Taiwan Futures Exchange Total		**3,743,307**	**4,777,825**	**31,874,934**	**59,146,376**
SYDNEY FUTURES EXCHANGE					
SPI 200	Equity	610,359	667,962	4,288,848	4,622,139
Australian Dollar Futures	Foreign	4,929	8,071	25,566	41,862
30-Day Interbank Cash Rate	Interest	11,276	63,270	53,141	659,926
Bank Bills 90-Day	Interest	873,605	982,746	11,435,471	14,213,188
Three-Year Treasury Bonds	Interest	2,003,945	2,374,256	19,246,934	22,805,279
Three-Year Interest Rate Swaps	Interest			401	12,000
Ten-Year Treasury Bonds	Interest	776,196	1,135,960	6,705,904	8,557,437
Ten-Year Interest Rate Swaps	Interest			200	
d-cypha SFE NSW Base Load Electricity	Energy	245		2,730	3,700
d-cypha SFE VIC Base Load Electricity	Energy	205	20	2,766	2,693
d-cypha SFE QLD Base Load Electricity	Energy	85	108	1,335	1,378
d-cypha SFE SA Base Load Electricity	Energy	50	80	1,420	1,630
d-cypha SFE NSW Peak Period Electricity	Energy	155	2	1,927	1,142
d-cypha SFE VIC Peak Period Electricity	Energy	310	85	1,762	1,466
d-cypha SFE QLD Peak Period Electricity	Energy	45	81	660	994
d-cypha SFE SA Peak Period Electricity	Energy	70	60	235	358
d-cypha SFE VIC Base $300 CAP	Energy				10
Fine Wool	Agricultural	151	110	2,467	2,013
Broad Wool	Agricultural	72	33	2,003	826
Greasy Wool	Agricultural	318	568	9,095	9,520

(continues)

International Exchanges Futures, Options, and Options on Equities Volume *(Continued)*

	Commodity Group	Dec. 2003	Dec. 2004	Jan.–Dec. 2003	Jan.–Dec. 2004
MLA/SFE Cattle	Agricultural	119	74	1,175	1,354
All Futures on Individual Equities	Indiv. Equity	3,435	2,379	47,822	29,986
Futures Total		**4,285,570**	**5,235,865**	**41,831,862**	**50,968,901**
SPI 200	Equity Opt.	50,073	43,745	585,620	518,511
SPI 200 Intra Day Cash Settled	Equity Opt.		2,300		4,917
90-Day Bank Bill Options	Interest Opt.	11,955	6,711	250,876	175,286
Three-Year Treasury Bond Options	Interest Opt.	35,555	12,295	220,382	369,708
Overnight Three-Year Treasury Bond Options	Interest Opt.	76,310	72,424	1,151,097	1,262,942
Three-Year Bonds Intra-Day	Interest Opt.	36,172	12,530	583,719	534,302
Ten-Year Treasury Bond Options	Interest Opt.	45	1,985	38,972	60,619
Ten-Year Bonds Intra-Day	Interest Opt.			6,307	1,845
Overnight 10-Year Treasury Bond Options	Interest Opt.	7,228	2,005	86,313	71,140
d-cypha SFE SA Peak Period Electricity	Energy Opt.	10		10	50
d-cypha SFE VIC Peak Period Electricity	Energy Opt.	5		5	65
Greasy Wool	Agric. Opt.	1	97	177	1,159
Options Total		**217,354**	**154,092**	**2,923,478**	**3,000,544**
Sydney Futures Exchange Total		**4,502,924**	**5,389,957**	**44,755,340**	**53,969,445**
TEL-AVIV STOCK EXCHANGE					
TA-25 Index	Equity		5,688	10,210	8,291
Shekel-Dollar Rate	Foreign			85	44
Futures Total		**0**	**5,688**	**10,295**	**8,335**
TA-25 Index Options	Equity Opt.	2,857,723	4,941,761	29,352,985	36,921,511
TA-Banks Index Options	Equity Opt.			610	596
Shekel-Dollar Rate Options	Foreign Opt.	637,268	435,558	8,343,368	5,847,295
Shekel-Euro Rate Options	Foreign Opt.	35,810	54,011	391,221	598,206
Options Total		**3,530,801**	**5,431,330**	**38,088,184**	**43,367,608**
Tel-Aviv Stock Exchange Total		**3,530,801**	**5,437,018**	**38,098,479**	**43,375,943**
WIENER BORSE					
ATX Index	Equity	6,338	6,837	49,441	50,743
ATF	Equity		4,661		25,607
CeCe (5 Eastern European Indexes)	Equity	7,254	13,270	63,439	40,108
All Futures on Individual Equities	Indiv. Equity		2,240		7,862
Futures Total		**13,592**	**27,008**	**112,880**	**124,320**
ATX Index Options	Equity Opt.	1,351	3,434	27,608	36,738
ATF	Equity Opt.		172		4,097
All Options on Individual Equities	Ind. Equity Opt.	144,526	117,955	1,252,041	2,077,320
Options Total		**145,877**	**121,561**	**1,279,649**	**2,118,155**
Wiener Borse Total		**159,469**	**148,569**	**1,392,529**	**2,242,475**
WINNIPEG COMMODITY EXCHANGE					
Wheat	Agricultural	4,231	5,359	59,194	87,758
Flax Seed	Agricultural	25	15	4,438	90

International Exchanges Futures, Options, and Options on Equities Volume *(Continued)*

	Commodity Group	Dec. 2003	Dec. 2004	Jan.–Dec. 2003	Jan.–Dec. 2004
Canola	Agricultural	153,269	196,094	1,547,283	1,737,972
Western Barley	Agricultural	10,977	8,478	200,701	204,635
Futures Total		**168,502**	**209,946**	**1,811,616**	**2,030,455**
Wheat Options	Agric. Opt.	2		4	
Flax Options	Agric. Opt.			10	
Western Barley Options	Agric. Opt.	110		2,778	3,273
Canola Options	Agric. Opt.	3,681	116	28,368	20,568
Options Total		**3,793**	**116**	**31,160**	**23,841**
Winnipeg Commodity Exchange Total		**172,295**	**210,062**	**1,842,776**	**2,054,296**
HONG KONG EXCHANGES AND CLEARING—DERIVATIVES UNIT					
Hang Seng Index	Equity	578,909	778,252	6,800,360	8,601,559
Mini Hang Seng Index	Equity	94,738	128,698	1,248,295	1,457,681
H-Shares Index	Equity	47,941	121,146	47,941	1,743,700
MSCI China Free Index	Equity			190	
Dow Jones Industrial Average	Equity	468	161	9,091	2,673
One-Month HIBOR	Interest	70	5	310	733
Three-Month HIBOR	Interest	3,735	1,907	47,799	58,307
Three-Year Exchange Fund Note	Interest	400		2,012	2,225
All Futures on Individual Equities	Indiv. Equity	1,756	1,564	18,654	17,274
Futures Total		**728,017**	**1,031,733**	**8,174,652**	**11,884,152**
Hang Seng Index	Equity Opt.	115,908	146,362	2,118,792	2,029,068
Mini Hang Seng Index	Equity Opt.	1,845	2,201	32,131	26,882
H-Shares Index	Equity Opt.		10,133		77,758
All Options on Individual Equities	Ind. Equity Opt.	523,359	500,752	4,220,638	5,611,832
Options Total		**641,112**	**659,448**	**6,371,561**	**7,745,540**
HKFE & HKSE Total		**1,369,129**	**1,691,181**	**14,546,213**	**19,629,692**
FUKUOKA FUTURES EXCHANGE, JAPAN					
Red Beans	Agricultural	732	469	40,675	8,297
Imported Soybeans	Agricultural	4,735	635	28,938	31,310
Non-GMO Soybeans	Agricultural	53,388	8,372	499,526	308,943
Refined Sugar	Agricultural	110	110	1,421	1,427
Corn	Agricultural	183,912	145,478	1,881,771	2,406,808
Broiler	Agricultural	6,545	10,085	44,376	92,022
Soybean Meal	Agricultural	24,606	3,172	242,676	187,926
Fukuoka Futures Exchange Total		**274,028**	**168,321**	**2,739,383**	**3,036,733**
KANSAI COMMODITIES EXCHANGE, JAPAN					
Red Beans	Agricultural	717	1,158	12,080	12,851
U.S. Soybeans	Agricultural	2,399		41,126	6,305
Non-GMO Soybeans	Agricultural	47,642	6,661	622,337	276,396
Refined Sugar	Agricultural	220	220	2,842	2,860
Raw Sugar	Agricultural	1,481	2,242	18,956	36,822
Raw Silk	Agricultural	452	673	8,009	6,665
Frozen Shrimp	Agricultural	76,898	247,589	1,144,264	1,385,143

(continues)

International Exchanges Futures, Options, and Options on Equities Volume *(Continued)*

	Commodity Group	Dec. 2003	Dec. 2004	Jan.–Dec. 2003	Jan.–Dec. 2004
Corn 75 Index	Agricultural	37,100	16,209	317,561	350,029
Coffee Index	Agricultural	43,943	59,448	1,274,190	726,741
Futures Total		**210,852**	**334,200**	**3,441,365**	**2,803,812**
Raw Sugar Options	Agric. Opt.	228	228	2,931	2,928
Options Total		**228**	**228**	**2,931**	**2,928**
Kansai Commodities Exchange Total		**211,080**	**334,428**	**3,444,296**	**2,806,740**
CENTRAL JAPAN COMMODITY EXCHANGE					
Red Beans	Agricultural	442		30,100	1,439
Imported Soybeans	Agricultural			409	
Non-GMO Soybeans	Agricultural	9,173		418,476	12,398
Shell Egg	Agricultural	57,200	27,692	399,167	798,308
Gasoline	Energy	781,442	1,134,600	16,705,638	15,869,951
Gas Oil	Energy		29,720		1,056,257
Kerosene	Energy	1,288,489	1,474,655	13,984,740	15,454,906
Central Japan Commodity Exchange Total		**2,136,746**	**2,666,667**	**31,538,530**	**33,193,259**
OSAKA SECURITIES EXCHANGE					
Nikkei 225 Futures	Equity	1,300,109	1,514,244	13,058,425	14,415,884
Nikkei 300 Futures	Equity	40,154	27,202	172,862	167,399
Futures Total		**1,340,263**	**1,541,446**	**13,231,287**	**14,583,283**
Nikkei 225 Options	Equity Opt.	997,910	1,316,784	14,958,100	16,560,874
Nikkei 300 Options	Equity Opt.	117	124	234	491
All Options on Individual Equities	Ind. Equity Opt.	17,263	72,147	45,412	1,481,415
Options Total		**1,015,290**	**1,389,055**	**15,003,746**	**18,042,780**
Osaka Securities Exchange Total		**2,355,553**	**2,930,501**	**28,235,033**	**32,626,063**
OSAKA MERCANTILE EXCHANGE					
Cotton Yarn (20S)	Agricultural			11,681	
Cotton Yarn (40S)	Agricultural			7,687	
Rubber (RSS3)	Agricultural	113,799	50,088	1,550,423	756,411
Rubber (TSR20)	Agricultural	175,176	58,317	1,985,225	826,045
Rubber Index	Agricultural	133,650	46,632	1,423,491	814,328
Aluminum	Nonprecious	68,134	75,988	963,464	1,101,198
Nickel	Nonprecious	35,542	8,054	220,618	344,571
Osaka Mercantile Exchange Total		**526,301**	**239,079**	**6,162,589**	**3,842,553**
TOKYO COMMODITY EXCHANGE					
Gold	Precious	1,302,849	969,974	26,637,897	17,385,766
Silver	Precious	95,670	87,300	1,160,565	1,473,370
Platinum	Precious	1,350,743	881,178	14,211,824	13,890,300
Palladium	Precious	20,810	25,471	275,322	438,934
Aluminum	Nonprecious	28,464	14,042	329,565	321,131
Gasoline	Energy	1,499,984	1,362,013	25,677,079	23,648,587
Kerosene	Energy	1,347,488	831,682	13,208,350	13,036,277
Crude Oil	Energy	148,132	156,568	1,809,711	2,284,572

International Exchanges Futures, Options, and Options on Equities Volume *(Continued)*

	Commodity Group	Dec. 2003	Dec. 2004	Jan.–Dec. 2003	Jan.–Dec. 2004
Gas Oil	Energy	27,089	2,986	372,977	235,844
Rubber	Agricultural	272,070	126,381	3,568,929	1,732,645
Futures Total		**6,093,299**	**4,457,595**	**87,252,219**	**74,447,426**
Gold Options	Precious Opt.		3,834		64,308
Options Total			**3,834**		**64,308**
Tokyo Commodity Exchange Total		**6,093,299**	**4,461,429**	**87,252,219**	**74,511,734**
TOKYO GRAIN EXCHANGE					
U.S. Soybeans	Agricultural	254,026	152,050	1,745,697	2,125,458
Non-GMO Soybeans	Agricultural	1,164,216	710,314	6,735,421	9,971,499
Soybean Meal	Agricultural	5,712	996	52,039	43,553
Arabica Coffee	Agricultural	253,482	443,677	5,019,572	4,293,422
Azuki (Red Beans)	Agricultural	64,104	33,389	555,190	363,328
Corn	Agricultural	699,644	441,767	5,984,743	8,122,448
Refined Sugar	Agricultural	220	220	2,842	2,854
Robusta Coffee	Agricultural	26,501	38,784	617,327	427,466
Raw Sugar	Agricultural	28,825	19,028	371,896	355,659
Futures Total		**2,496,730**	**1,840,225**	**21,084,727**	**25,705,687**
U.S. Soybeans Option	Agric. Opt.	1,249	1,570	17,548	17,758
Corn Options	Agric. Opt.	2,590	528	12,214	16,072
Raw Sugar Options	Agric. Opt.	309	540	5,979	5,405
Options Total		**4,148**	**2,638**	**35,741**	**39,235**
Tokyo Grain Exchange Total		**2,500,878**	**1,842,863**	**21,120,468**	**25,744,922**
TOKYO INTERNATIONAL FINANCIAL FUTURES EXCHANGE					
Three-Month Euroyen	Interest	299,116	507,892	4,155,800	7,259,779
Three-Month Euroyen LIBOR	Interest			3,000	3,000
Five-Year Yen Swapnote	Interest	58,384	10,350	205,092	245,049
Ten-Year Yen Swapnote	Interest	33,460	10,680	408,025	147,482
U.S. Dollar-Japanese Yen	Foreign		200		200
Futures Total		**390,960**	**529,122**	**4,771,917**	**7,655,510**
Options on Three-Month Euroyen	Interest Opt.				2,000
Options Total			**0**		**2,000**
Tokyo International Financial Futures Exchange Total		**390,960**	**529,122**	**4,771,917**	**7,657,510**
TOKYO STOCK EXCHANGE					
Ten-Year Yen Gov't Bond	Interest	533,470	819,392	6,465,073	8,025,268
TOPIX Stock Index	Equity	1,187,790	1,380,132	9,359,047	10,305,318
Electric Applicance Index	Equity			724	741
Bank Index	Equity			140,331	601
Futures Total		**1,721,260**	**2,199,524**	**15,965,175**	**18,331,928**
TOPIX Options	Equity Opt.	1,030	2,880	98,137	17,643
Yen Gov't Bond (10-Year) Options	Interest Opt.	64,991	104,270	972,518	1,262,994
Options Total		**66,021**	**107,150**	**1,070,655**	**1,280,637**
Tokyo Stock Exchange Total		**1,787,281**	**2,306,674**	**17,035,830**	**19,612,565**

(continues)

International Exchanges Futures, Options, and Options on Equities Volume *(Continued)*

	Commodity Group	Dec. 2003	Dec. 2004	Jan.–Dec. 2003	Jan.–Dec. 2004
YOKOHAMA COMMODITY EXCHANGE					
Japan Raw Silk	Agricultural	55,878	16,932	919,049	239,446
International Raw Silk	Agricultural	853	711	11,581	8,470
Dried Cocoon	Agricultural	67		27,368	91
Potato	Agricultural	55,955	51,127	894,160	869,589
Vegetables	Agricultural		47,215		47,215
Yokohama Commodity Exchange Total		**112,753**	**115,985**	**1,852,158**	**1,164,811**
TOTAL FUTURES		**151,733,082**	**169,208,795**	**1,927,572,093**	**2,139,293,501**
Percent Change			**11.52%**		**10.98%**
TOTAL OPTIONS		**315,073,006**	**263,574,697**	**4,012,631,132**	**3,901,937,421**
Percent Change			**–16.34%**		**–2.76%**
GRAND TOTAL		**466,806,088**	**432,783,492**	**5,940,203,225**	**6,041,230,922**
Percent Change			**–7.29%**		**1.70%**
INTERNATIONAL COMMODITY GROUPS					
Futures					
Interest Rate		73,724,063	88,286,642	1,069,762,500	1,206,747,668
Equity Indexes		34,413,838	36,346,385	391,339,615	417,390,392
Agricultural Commodities		14,076,974	11,361,603	152,144,551	148,819,727
Energy Products		7,430,453	7,725,175	105,081,463	109,926,014
Foreign Currency/Index		2,495,994	4,059,787	29,043,842	40,367,088
Precious Metals		2,785,338	1,968,580	42,441,475	33,249,705
Nonprecious Metals		8,095,431	8,190,148	83,405,587	97,016,742
Other		0	0	780	0
Futures on Individual Equities		8,710,991	11,270,475	54,352,280	85,774,165
Total		**151,733,082**	**169,208,795**	**1,927,572,093**	**2,139,291,501**
OPTIONS					
Interest Rate		7,203,169	7,302,066	133,206,408	136,737,718
Equity Indexes		253,806,552	199,182,545	3,147,284,017	2,871,452,916
Agricultural Commodities		79,953	91,325	1,185,515	1,166,129
Energy Products		3,032	7,270	82,874	74,107
Foreign Currency/Index		1,056,793	987,930	12,699,401	11,145,690
Precious Metals		6,110	50,462	255,870	362,744
Nonprecious Metals		388,804	377,241	3,738,173	4,734,928
Other					
Options on Individual Equities		52,528,593	55,575,858	714,178,874	876,265,189
Total		**315,073,006**	**263,574,697**	**4,012,631,132**	**3,901,939,421**
GRAND TOTAL		**466,806,088**	**432,783,492**	**5,940,203,225**	**6,041,230,922**

Source: Futures Industry Association. Information provided by exchanges at FIA's request.

Futures Contract Specifications

The exchanges where these products trade determine what the contract specifications are and have the ability to change them based on exchange rules and market conditions.

These "specs" are for the products traded as of December 2004. The best way to ensure that you have the most current and accurate information is to visit the web site of the exchange where the contract you're interested in is traded.

Explanations of the acronyms used for the exchanges, special codes and symbols, and the letters that represent each contract's delivery months follow.

Exchanges

CBOT	Chicago Board of Trade		**ME**	Montreal Exchange
CME	Chicago Mercantile Exchange		**MEFF**	Mercados Financieros
COMEX	COMEX Division of NYMEX		**MPLS**	Minneapolis Grain Exchange
EUREX	Eurex		**NQLX**	Nasdaq Liffe Markets
EUS	Eurex US		**NYBOT**	New York Board of Trade
HKE	Hong Kong Exchanges		**NYFE**	New York Futures Exchange
IDEM	Italian Derivatives Market		**NYMEX**	New York Mercantile Exchange
IPE	International Petroleum Exchange		**OCX**	OneChicago
KCBT	Kansas City Board of Trade		**SFE**	Sydney Futures Exchange
LIFFE	Euronext.liffe		**SGX**	Singapore Exchange
MATIF	Euronext Paris		**WCE**	Winnipeg Commodity Exchange

Codes

❋ Can be mutually offset at CME and SGX.
✖ GLOBEX only.
✦ e-cbot only.
◆ No limit last trading day.
✱ When the "primary" futures contract is limit bid or limit offer (at its daily price limit), trading in options will be suspended.

▶ Available for ¹/₂ tick trading at prices of less than five ticks.
▲ Circuit breakers.
▼ No limits last 30 minutes daily; adjustable intraday limits.
✚ Trading halted when underlying is halted.

Delivery Months

F	January	H	March	K	May	N	July	U	September	X	November
G	February	J	April	M	June	Q	August	V	October	Z	December

U.S. Futures

Contract	Exchange	Trading Hours (Central Time)	Months	Delivery Size	Contract Quoted in	Price Point Value	Minimum Price Fluctuation	Price Limit
Australian Dollar	CME	7:20 am–2:00 pm 7:20 am–9:16 am LTD spot GLOBEX: Mon–Thurs: 5:00 pm–4:00 pm, Sun & holidays: 5:30 pm–4:00 pm	H,M,U,Z	100,000 AD	¢/AD	1pt=$10.00	1pt=$10.00	None
British Pound	CME	7:20 am–2:00 pm 7:20 am–9:16 am LTD spot GLOBEX: Mon–Thurs: 4:30 pm–4:00 pm, Sun & holidays: 5:30 pm– 4:00 pm	H,M,U,Z	62,500 BP	¢/£	1pt=$6.25	1pt=$6.25	None
Canadian Dollar	CME	7:20 am–2:00 pm 7:20 am–9:16 am LTD spot GLOBEX: Mon–Thurs: 5:00 pm–4:00 pm, Sun & holidays: 5:30 pm–4:00 pm	H,M,U,Z	100,000 CD	¢/CD	1pt=$10.00	1pt=$10.00	None
Cattle, Feeder	CME	9:05–1:00 pm GLOBEX: 9:05 am– 12:00 pm LTD	F,H,J,K,Q,U,V,X	50,000 lbs	$/cwt	1pt=$5.00	2½pts=$12.50	3¢ expandable =300 pts
Cattle, Live	CME	9:05 am–1:00 pm GLOBEX: 9:05 am– 12:00 pm LTD of expiring contracts	G,J,M,Q,V,Z	40,000 lbs	$/cwt	1pt=$4.00	2½pts=$10.00	3¢ expandable =300 pts
Cocoa (Metric)	NYBOT	7:00 am–10:50 am	H,K,N,U,Z	10M ton	$/M ton	1pt=$10.00	1pt=$10.00	None
Coffee "C"	NYBOT	8:15 am–11:30 am	H,K,N,U,Z	37,500 lbs	¢/lb	1pt=$3.75	5pts=$18.75	None
Coffee "C," Mini	NYBOT	8:15 am–11:30 am	G,J,M,Q,X	12,500 lbs	¢/lb	1pt=$1.25	5pts=$6.25	None

Copper, High Grade	COMEX	7:10 am–12:00 pm ACCESS: Sun: 6:00 pm–7:00 am, Mon–Thurs: 2:15 pm–7:00 am	All Months	25,000 lbs	¢/lb	1pt=$2.50	5pts=$12.50	20¢ ▲
Corn	CBOT	9:30 am–1:15 pm e-cbot: Sun–Fri 7:30 pm–6:00 am	F,H,K,N,U,X,Z	5,000 bu	¢/bu	1¢=$50.00	¼¢=$12.50	20¢=$1,000 No limit during +2 days prior
Corn, Mini	CBOT	9:30 am–1:45 pm 9:30 am–12:15 pm LTD	F,H,K,N,U,X,Z	1,000 bu	¢/bu	1¢=$10.00	⅛¢=$1.25	20¢=$200
Cotton	NYBOT	9:30 am–1:15 pm	H,K,N,V,Z	50,000 lbs	¢/lb	1pt=$5.00	1pt=$5.00	3¢=$1,500 =300 pts Variable depending on price
CRB Index	NYBOT	9:00 am–1:30 pm	F,G,J,M,Q,X	500 × CRB Index	100ths/pt	1pt=$5.00	5pts=$25.00	None
Crude Oil	NYMEX	9:00 am–1:30 pm ACCESS: Sun: 6:00 pm–8:30 am, Mon–Thurs: 2:15 pm–8:30 am	All Months	1,000 barrels	$/barrel	1pt=$10.00	1pt=$10.00	Expandable
Dow Jones Average	CBOT	7:20 am–3:15 pm e-cbot: Sun–Fri: 7:15 pm–7:00 am	H,M,U,Z	$10 × DJIA Index	pts	1pt=$10.00	1pt=$10.00	▲
Dow Jones Average, Mini ◆	e-cbot	7:15 pm to 4:00 pm Sun–Fri, 7:15 pm to 3:15 pm LTD	H,M,U,Z	$5 × DJIA Index	pts	1pt=$5.00	1pt=$5.00	▲
Eurodollar ✳	CME	7:20 am–2:00 pm GLOBEX: Mon–Thurs: 5:00 pm–4:00 pm, Sun & holidays: 5:30 pm–4:00 pm	H,M,U,X	$1,000,000	Basis pts	1pt=$25.00	½pt=$12.50 ¼pt nearest month	None
Euroyen ✳	CME	7:20 am–2:00 pm	H,M,U,Z	100 Million Yen	Basis pts	1pt=2500 Yen	½pt=1250 Yen	None

(continues)

U.S. Futures *(Continued)*

Contract	Exchange	Trading Hours (Central Time)	Months	Delivery Size	Contract Quoted in	Price Point Value	Minimum Price Fluctuation	Price Limit
EuroFX	CME	7:20 am–2:00 pm 7:20 am–9:16 am LTD GLOBEX: Mon–Thurs: 5:00 pm–4:00 pm, Sun & holidays: 5:30 pm–4:00 pm	H,M,U,Z	125,000 Euro	US$ per Euro	1pt=$12.50	1pt=$12.50	None
E-Mini EuroFX ✖	CME	5:00 pm–4:00 pm M–Th GLOBEX only: 5:30 pm–4:00 pm Sun & holidays	H,M,U,Z	62,500 Euro	US$ per Euro	1pt=$6.25	1pt=$6.25	None
30-Day Federal Funds	CBOT	7:20 am–2:00 pm e-cbot: Sun–Fri: 7:01 pm–4:00 pm	H,M,U,Z	$5,000,000	pts	1/2pt=20.835	1/2pt=20.835	None
GSCI	CME	8:45 am–1:40 pm	All Months	$250 × GSCI	pts	.05=$12.50	1/2pt=$12.50	None
Gasoline, Unleaded	NYMEX	9:05 am–1:30 pm ACCESS: Sun: 6:00 pm–8:30 am, Mon–Thurs: 2:15 pm–8:30 am	All Months	42,000 gal	¢/gal	1pt=$4.20	1pt=$4.20	None
Gold	COMEX	7:20 am–12:30 pm ACCESS: Sun: 6:00 pm–7:00 am, Mon–Thurs: 1:00 pm–7:00 am	G,J,M,Q,V,Z	100 troy oz	$/oz	1¢=$1.00	10¢=$10.00	$75.00 ▲
Heating Oil	NYMEX	9:05 am–1:30 pm ACCESS: Sun: 6:00 pm–8:30 am, Mon–Thurs: 2:15pm–8:30 am	All Months	42,000 gal	¢/gal	1pt=$4.20	1pt=$4.20	Expandable
Hogs, Lean	CME	9:10 am–1:00 pm GLOBEX: 9:10 am–12:00 pm LTD	G,J,K,M,N, Q,V,Z	40,000 lbs	$/cwt	1pt=$4.00	2½pts=$10.00	2¢=$800= 200 pts (no limits—last 2 spot month)

Commodity	Exchange	Trading Hours	Months	Contract Size	Unit	Min Tick	Tick Value	Limit
Japanese Yen	CME	7:20 am–2:00 pm / 7:20 am–9:16 am LTD / GLOBEX: Mon–Thurs: 5:00 pm–4:00 pm, Sun & holidays: 5:30 pm–4:00 pm	H,M,U,Z	12,500,000 JY	¢/JY	1 pt=$12.50	1 pt=$12.50	None
E-Mini Japanese Yen ✷	CME	5:00 pm– 4:00 pm M-Th / 5:30 pm–4:00 pm Sun & holidays	H,M,U,Z	6,250,000 JY	¢/JY	1 pt=$6.25	1 pt=$6.25	None
Lumber	CME	9:00 am–1:05 pm / 9:00 am–12:05 pm LTD	F,H,K,N,U,X	110,000 bd ft	$/m/bd ft	1 pt=$1.10	10 pts=$11.00	$10=$1,100= 1,000 pts
Mexican Peso	CME	7:20 am–2:00 pm / GLOBEX: Mon–Thurs: 5:00 pm–4:00 pm, Sun & holidays: 5:30 pm–4:00 pm	H,M,U,Z	500,000 NMP	$/NMP	1 pt=$5.00	$2\frac{1}{2}$ pts=$12.50	None
Municipal Bonds	CBOT	7:20 am–2:00 pm / e-cbot: Sun–Fri: 7:04 pm–4:00 pm	H,M,U,Z	$1,000 × Index	32nds/pt	$\frac{1}{32}$=$31.25	$\frac{1}{32}$=$31.25	None
Nasdaq-100 Index	CME	8:30 am–3:15 pm / GLOBEX: Mon–Thurs: 3:30 pm–8:15 am, Sun & holidays: 5:30 pm–8:15 am	H,M,U,Z	$100 × Index	100ths/pt	1 pt=$1.00	5 pt=$5	▲
E-Mini Nasdaq-100 ✷	CME	3:30 pm–3:15 pm M-Th / 5:30 pm–3:15 pm Sun & holidays	H,M,U,Z	$20 × Nasdaq-100 Index	100ths/pt	1 pt=$.20	50 pt=$10	▲
Natural Gas	NYMEX	9:00 am–1:30 pm / ACCESS: Sun: 6:00 pm–8:30 am, Mon–Thurs: 2:15 pm–8:30 am	All Months	10,000 MMBtu	$/MMBtu	1 pt=$10.00	1 pt=$10.00	1,000 pts=$10,000 Initial limit all months expandable

(continues)

U.S. Futures *(Continued)*

Contract	Exchange	Trading Hours (Central Time)	Months	Delivery Size	Contract Quoted in	Price Point Value	Minimum Price Fluctuation	Price Limit
New Zealand Dollar	CME	7:20 am–2:00 pm GLOBEX: Mon–Thurs: 5:00 pm–4:00 pm Sun & holidays: 5:30 pm–4:00 pm; 9:16 pm LTD	H,M,U,Z	100,000 New Zealand Dollar	¢/NE	.0001=$10	.0001=$10.00	None
Nikkei 225 Stock Index	CME	8:00 am–3:15 pm GLOBEX: 3:30 pm–4:30 pm; 2:00 am–3:15 pm Mon–Fri	H,M,U,Z	$5.00 × Index	100ths/pt	1 pt=$5.00	5pts=$25.00	◆ Varies according to index level
Nikkei 225 Stock Index ✖ Eligible for MOS with SGX	CME	5:00 am–3:15 pm (CST) 3:30 pm–4:30 pm (CST), 6:00 am–3:15 pm, 3:30 pm–4:30 pm, 5 pm–6 pm (CDT)	H,K,U,Z + 3 serials	¥500 × Index	100ths/pt	5pts=¥2,500	5pts=¥2,500	1,000–2,000 pts lead-month set
NYSE Composite Index Reg.	NYBOT	8:30 am–3:15 pm	H,M,U,Z	500 × NYFE Composite Index	100ths/pt	1 pt=$5.00	5pts=$25.00	▲
Oats	CBOT	9:30 am–1:15 pm e-cbot: Sun–Fri: 7:33 pm–6:00 am	H,K,N,U,Z	5,000 bu	¢/bu	1¢=$50.00	¹⁄₄¢=$12.50	20¢=$1,000 No limit spot +2 days prior
One-Month LIBOR	CME	7:20 am–2:00 pm 7:20 am–5:00 am LTD GLOBEX: Mon–Thurs: 5:00 pm–4:00 pm, Sun & holidays: 5:30 pm–4:00 pm	All Months	$3,000,000	Basis pts	¹⁄₂pt=$12.50	¹⁄₂pt=$12.50	None
Orange Juice	NYBOT	9:00 am–12:30 pm	F,H,K,N,U,X	15,000 lbs	¢/lb	1 pt=$1.50	5pts=$7.50	500 pts; Spot+ second mo. after FND, 1,000 pts

Commodity	Exchange	Trading Hours	Months	Contract Size	Units			
Palladium	NYMEX	7:30 am–12:00 pm ACCESS: Sun: 6:00 pm–7:00 am, Mon–Thurs: 2:15 pm–7:00 am	H,M,U,Z	100 troy oz	$/oz	1pt=$1.00	5pts=$5.00	None
Platinum	NYMEX	7:20 am–12:05 pm ACCESS: Sun: 6:00 pm–7:00 am, Mon–Thurs: 2:15 pm–7:00 am	F,J,N,V	50 troy oz	$/oz	1pt=$.50	10pts=$5.00	$50=$2,500 No limit nearest cycle month
Pork Bellies	CME	9:10 am–1:00 pm GLOBEX: 9:10 am–12:00 pm LTD of expiring contracts	G,H,K,N,Q	40,000 lbs	¢/lb	1pt=$4.00	2½pts=$10.00	3¢=$1,200 =300 pts
Rough Rice	CBOT	9:15 am–1:30 pm 9:15 am–12:00 pm LTD of expiring contracts e-cbot: Sun–Fri: 7:33 pm–6:00 am	F,H,K,N,U,X	2,000 cwt	¢/cwt	1pt=$20	.5pts=$10.00	50¢=$1,000 No limit spot +2 days prior
Russell 2000	CME	8:30 am–3:15 pm GLOBEX: Mon–Thurs: 3:30 pm–8:15 am, Sun & holidays: 5:30 pm–3:15 pm	All Months	$500 × Index	pts	.01=$5.00	.05=$25.00	▲
E-Mini Russell 2000 ✱	CME	Mon–Thurs: 3:30 pm–3:15, pm Sun & holidays: 5:30 pm–3:15 pm, 3:30 pm–8:30 am LTD	All Months	$100 × Index	pts	.01=$1.00	.1=$10.00	▲
Silver	COMEX	7:25 am–12:25 pm ACCESS: Sun: 6:00 pm–7:00 am, Mon–Thurs: 1:00 pm–7:00 am	H,K,N,U,Z	5,000 troy oz	¢/oz	1pt=$.50	50pts=$25.00	$1.50 ▲
Soybean Meal	CBOT	9:30 am–1:15 pm e-cbot: Sun–Fri: 7:31 pm–6:00 am	F,H,K,N,Q,U,V,Z	100 tons	$/ton	1pt=$1.00	10pts=$10.00	$20=$2,000 No limit spot +2 days prior

(continues)

U.S. Futures (Continued)

Contract	Exchange	Trading Hours (Central Time)	Months	Delivery Size	Contract Quoted in	Price Point Value	Minimum Price Fluctuation	Price Limit
Soybean Oil	CBOT	9:30 am–1:15 pm e-cbot: Sun–Fri: 7:31 pm–6:00 am	F,H,K,N,Q, U,V,Z	60,000 lbs	¢/lb	1pt=$6.00	1pt=$6.00	2¢=$1,200 No limit spot +2 days prior
Soybeans	CBOT	9:30 am–1:15 pm e-cbot: Sun–Fri: 7:31 pm–6:00 am	F,H,K,N,Q,U,X	5,000 bu	¢/bu	1pt=$50.00	¼¢=$12.50	50¢=$2,500 No limit spot +2 days prior
Soybeans, Mini	CBOT	9:30 am–1:45 pm 9:30 am–1:15 pm LTD	F,H,K,N,Q,U,X	1,000 bu	¢/bu	1pt=$10.00	⅛¢=$1.25	50¢=$500 No limit spot +2 days prior
S&P 500 Index ·	CME	8:30 am–3:15 pm GLOBEX: Mon–Thurs: 3:30 pm–8:15 am, Sun & holidays: 5:30 pm–8:15 am	H,M,U,Z	250 × S&P 500 Index	100ths/pt	1pt=$2.50	10pts=$25.00	▲
E-Mini S&P 500 ✖	CME	Mon–Thurs: 3:30 pm–3:15 pm, Sun & holidays: 5:30 pm–3:15 pm, 3:30 am LTD	H,M,U,Z	$50 × S&P 500 Index	100ths/pt	1pt=$.50	25pt=$12.50	▲
S&P MidCap 400 Index	CME	8:30 am–3:15 pm GLOBEX: Mon–Thurs: 3:30 pm–8:15 am, Sun & holidays: 5:30 pm–8:15 am	H,M,U,Z	500 × S&P MidCap 400 Index	100ths/pt	1pt=$5.00	5pts=$25.00	▲
E-Mini S&P MidCap 400 ✖	CME	Mon–Thurs: 3:30 pm–3:15 pm, Sun & holidays: 5:30 pm–3:15 pm	All Months	$100 × S&P MidCap 400 Index	pts	.01=$1.00	10pt=$10.00	▲

Product	Exchange	Trading Hours	Months	Size	Quote			Limit
Sugar #11	NYBOT	8:00 am–11:00 am	F,H,K,N,V	112,000 lbs	¢/lb			None
Swiss Franc	CME	7:20 am–2:00 pm 7:20 am–9:16 am LTD GLOBEX: Mon–Thurs: 5:00 pm–4:00 pm, Sun & holidays: 5:30 pm– 4:00 pm	H,M,U,Z	125,000 SF	¢/SF	1pt=$12.50	1pt=$12.50	None
Treasury Bonds	CBOT	7:20 am–2:00 pm 7:20 pm–12:00 pm LTD e-cbot: Sun–Fri: 7:00 pm–4:00 pm 7:00 pm–4:00 pm 12:00pm LTD	H,M,U,Z	$100,000	32nds/pt	$\frac{1}{32}$=$31.25	$\frac{1}{32}$=$31.25	None
	EUS	7:00 pm–4:00 pm 7:00 pm–4:00 pm 12:00pm LTD	H,M,U,Z	$100,000	32nds/pt	$\frac{1}{2}$ of $\frac{1}{32}$	$15.625	None
Treasury Notes, 10-Year	CBOT	7:20 am–2:00 pm 7:20 pm–12:00 pm LTD e-cbot: Sun–Fri: 7:00 pm–4:00 pm 7:00 pm–4:00 pm 12:00pm LTD	H,M,U,Z	$100,000	32nds/pt	$\frac{1}{32}$=$31.25	$\frac{1}{2}$ of $\frac{1}{32}$= $15.625	None
	EUS	7:00 pm–4:00 pm 7:00 pm–4:00 pm 12:00pm LTD	H,M,U,Z	$100,000	32nds/pt	$\frac{1}{2}$ of $\frac{1}{32}$	$15.625	None
Treasury Notes, 5-Year	CBOT	7:20 am–2:00 pm 7:20 pm–12:00 pm LTD e-cbot: Sun–Fri: 7:01 pm–4:00 pm 7:00 pm–4:00 pm 12:00 pm LTD	H,M,U,Z	$100,000	32nds/pt	$\frac{1}{2}$ of $\frac{1}{32}$= $15.63	$\frac{1}{2}$ of $\frac{1}{32}$= $15.63	None
	EUS	7:01 pm–4:00 pm 7:00 pm–4:00 pm 12:00 pm LTD	H,M,U,Z	$100,000	32nds/pt	$\frac{1}{2}$ of $\frac{1}{32}$	$15.625	None
Treasury Notes, 2-Year	CBOT	7:20 am–2:00 pm 7:20 pm–12:00 pm LTD e-cbot: Sun–Fri: 7:00 pm–4:00 pm 7:00 pm–4:00 pm 12:00 pm LTD	H,M,U,Z	$200,000	32nds/pt	$\frac{1}{4}$ of $\frac{1}{32}$= $15.63	$\frac{1}{4}$ of $\frac{1}{32}$= $15.63	None
	EUS	7:00 pm–4:00 pm 12:00 pm LTD	H,M,U,Z	$200,000	32nds/pt	$\frac{1}{4}$ of $\frac{1}{32}$	$15.625	None

(continues)

U.S. Futures (Continued)

Contract	Exchange	Trading Hours (Central Time)	Months	Delivery Size	Contract Quoted in	Price Point Value	Minimum Price Fluctuation	Price Limit
U.S. Dollar Index	NYBOT NYBOT	6:00 pm–9:00 pm Dublin: Sun–Fri: 2:00 am–7:05 am 7:05 am–2:00 pm— Expiring contractts close at 9:00 am on LTD	H,M,U,Z	1,000 × U.S. Dollar Index	100ths/pt	1pt=$10.00	1pt=$10.00	200 pts ▼ ◆
Value Line	KCBT	8:30 am–3:15 pm	H,M,U,Z	100 × Value Line Index	100ths/pt	1pt=$1.00	5pts=$5.00	▲
Wheat	CBOT	9:30 am–1:15 pm 9:30 pm–12:00 pm LTD e-cbot: Sun–Fri: 7:32 pm–6:00 am	H,K,N,U,Z	5,000 bu	¢/bu	1¢=$50.00	$1/4$¢=$12.50	30¢=$1,500 No limit spot +2 days prior
Wheat	KCBT	9:30 am–1:15 pm	H,K,N,U,Z	5,000 bu	¢/bu	1¢=$50.00	$1/4$¢=$12.50	30¢=$1,500
Wheat	MPLS	9:30 am–1:15 pm	H,K,N,U,Z	5,000 bu	¢/bu	1¢=$50.00	$1/4$¢=$12.50	30¢=$1,500
Wheat, Mini	CBOT	9:30 am–1:45 pm 9:30 am–12:15 pm LTD	H,K,N,U,Z	1,000 bu	¢/bu	1¢=$10.00	$1/8$¢=$1.25	30¢=$300 No limit spot +2 days prior

Source of data: Futures and options exchanges. This information is believed to be reliable. Lind-Waldock cannot be held responsible for either its accuracy or its completeness.

Options on U.S. Futures

Contract	Exchange	Trading Hours (Central Time)	Contract Size	Minimum Price Fluctuation	Price Limit
Australian Dollar ◗	CME	7:20 am–2:00 pm	100,000 AD	1pt=$10	None
British Pound ◗	CME	7:20 am–2:00 pm GLOBEX: Mon–Fri: 2:30 pm–7:05 am, Sun & holidays: 5:30 pm–7:05 am	62,500	.01¢/£ ($6.25)	None
CRB Index	NYFE	9:00 am–1:30 pm	500 × CRB Index	5pt=$25.00 OK at 1pt if <5pts	None
Canadian Dollar ◗	CME	7:20 am–2:00 pm GLOBEX: Mon–Fri: 2:30 pm–7:05 am, Sun & holidays: 5:30 pm–7:05 am	100,000 CD	1pt=$10	None
Cattle, Feeder	CME	9:05 am–1:02 pm	50,000 lbs	2½¢ per cwt. ($12.50)	None
Cattle, Live	CME	9:05 am–1:02 pm	40,000 lbs	2½¢ per cwt. ($10.00)	None
Cocoa	NYBOT	7:00 am–10:50 am	10 metric tons	1pt=$10	None
Coffee "C"	NYBOT	8:15 am–11:30 pm	37,500 lbs	$.0001 per lb ($3.75)	None
Copper, High Grade	COMEX	7:10 am–12:00 pm	25,000 lbs	5pts=$12.50	None
Corn	CBOT	9:30 am–1:15 pm e-cbot: Sun–Fri: 7:32 pm–6:00 am	5,000 bu	⅛¢ per bu ($6.25)	20¢ per bu
Cotton	NYBOT	9:30 am–1:15 pm	50,000 lbs	1¢ per cwt. ($5.00)	300pt= $1,500 None; spot month after first notice day
Crude Oil	NYMEX	9:00 am–1:30 pm	1,000 barrels	1pt=$10	None
Dow Jones	CBOT	7:20 am–3:15 pm e-cbot: Sun–Fri: 7:17 pm–7:00 am	$10 × DJIA Index	½pt=$5.00	*
E-Mini S&P 500 ✖	CME	Mon–Thur: 3:30 pm–3:15 pm; Sun: 5:30 pm– 3:15 pm	$50 ≠ S&P 500 Index	25pts=$12.50	*
EuroFX ◗	CME	7:20 am–2:00 pm GLOBEX: Mon–Fri: 5:00 pm–4:00 pm, Sun & holidays: 5:30 pm–4:00 pm	Euro 125,000	$.0001/Euro=$12.50/ contract	None

(continues)

Options on U.S. Futures *(Continued)*

Contract	Exchange	Trading Hours (Central Time)	Contract Size	Minimum Price Fluctuation	Price Limit
Eurodollar	CME	7:20 am–2:00 pm GLOBEX: Mon–Fri: 2:10 pm–7:05 am, Sun & holidays: 5:30 pm–7:05 am	$1,000,000	½pt=$12.50	None
Euroyen	CME	7:20 am–2:00 pm	100 million yen	.01=1.250 yen	None
Gasoline, Unleaded	NYMEX	9:05 am–1:30 pm	42,000 gallons	1pt=$4.20	None
Gold	COMEX	7:20 am–12:30 pm	100 oz	10¢/oz=$10.00	None
GSCI	CME	8:15 am–2:15 pm	$250 × GSCI	.05=$12.50	None
Heating Oil	NYMEX	9:05 am–1:30 pm	42,000 gallons	1pt=$4.20	None
Hogs, Lean	CME	9:10 am–1:02 pm	40,000 lbs	2½¢ per cwt. ($10.00)	None
Japanese Yen ▶	CME	7:20 am–2:00 pm GLOBEX: Mon–Thur: 2:30 pm–7:05 am, Sun & holidays: 5:30 pm–7:05 am	12,500,000	1pt=$12.50	None
Lumber	CME	9:00 am–1:07 pm	110,000 bd. ft.	10pts=$11.00	None
Mexican Peso ▶	CME	7:20 am–2 pm GLOBEX: Mon–Thur: 2:30 pm–7:05 am, Sun & holidays: 5:30 pm–7:05 am	500,000 NMP	2½pts=$12.50	None
Nasdaq-100	CME	8:30 am–3:15 pm GLOBEX: Mon–Thur. 3:30 pm–8:15 am, Sun & holidays: 5:30 pm–8:15 am	$100 × Nasdaq-100 Index	5pts=$5.00	None
Natural Gas	NYMEX	9:00 am–1:30 pm	10,000 MMBtu	1pt=$10.00	None
Nikkei 225 Stock Index	CME	8:00 am–3:15 pm	$5.00 × Index	5pts=$25.00	None
NYSE Composite Index	NYFE	8:30 am–3:15 pm	500 × NYSE Index	5pts=$25.00	None
Oats	CBOT	9:30 am–1:15 pm e-cbot: Sun–Fri: 7:35 pm–6:00 am	5,000 bu	⅛¢ per bu ($6.25)	20¢ per bu No limit LTD

Options on U.S. Futures *(Continued)*

Contract	Exchange	Trading Hours (Central Time)	Contract Size	Minimum Price Fluctuation	Price Limit
One-Month LIBOR	CME	7:20 am–2:00 pm	3,000,000	.5=$12.50	None
Orange Juice	NYBOT	9:00 am–12:30 pm	15,000 lbs	5pts=$7.50	None
Platinum	NYMEX	7:20 am–12:05 pm	50 oz	$.10=$5.00	None
Pork Bellies	CME	9:10 am–1:02 pm	40,000 lbs	2½¢ per cwt. ($10.00)	None
Rough Rice	CBOT	9:15 am–1:30 pm e-cbot: Sun–Fri: 7:35 pm–6:00 am	2,000 cwt	¼¢ per cwt ($5.00)	50¢ per cwt No limit LTD ♦
Russell 2000	CME	8:30 am–3:15 pm	$500 × Russell 2000 Index	.05=$25.00	None
S&P 500 Index	CME	8:30 am–3:15 pm GLOBEX: Mon–Fri: 3:30 pm–8:15 am, Sun & holidays: 5:30 pm–8:15 am	$250 × S&P 500 Index	10pts=$25.00	*
S&P MidCap 400 Index	CME	8:30 am–3:15 pm GLOBEX: Mon–Fri: 3:30 pm–8:15 am, Sun & holidays: 5:30 pm–8:15 am	$500 × MidCap Index	5pts=$15.00	*
Silver	COMEX	7:25 am–12:25 pm	5,000 oz	⅒¢/oz=$5.00	None
Soybeans	CBOT	9:30 am–1:15 pm e-cbot: Sun–Fri: 7:33 pm–6:00 am	5,000 bu	⅛¢ per bu ($6.25)	50¢ per bu= $2,500 ♦
Soybean Meal	CBOT	9:30 am–1:15 pm e-cbot: Sun–Fri: 7:33 pm–6:00 am	100 tons	5¢ per ton ($5.00)	$20.00= $2,000 ♦
Soybean Oil	CBOT	9:30 am–1:15 pm e-cbot: Sun–Fri: 7:33 pm–6:00 am	60,000 lbs	½ of 1pt ($3.00)	2¢= $1,200 ♦
Sugar #11	NYBOT	8:00 am–11:00 am	112,000 lbs	.01¢/lb=$11.20	None
Swiss Franc ▶	CME	7:20 am–2:00 pm GLOBEX: Mon–Fri: 2:30 pm–7:05 am, Sun & holidays: 5:30 pm–7:05 am	125,000 SF	.01¢/SF=($12.50)	None
Treasury Bond	CBOT	7:20 am–2:00 pm e-cbot: Sun–Fri: 7:02 pm–4:00 pm	$100,000	¹⁄₆₄pt=$15.63	None

(continues)

Options on U.S. Futures *(Continued)*

Contract	Exchange	Trading Hours (Central Time)	Contract Size	Minimum Price Fluctuation	Price Limit
T-Note (10-Year)	CBOT	7:20 am–2:00 pm e-cbot: Sun–Fri: 7:02 pm–4:00 pm	$100,000	$1/_{64}$pt=$15.63	None
T-Note (5-Year)	CBOT	7:20 am–2:00 pm e-cbot: Sun–Fri: 7:02 pm–4:00 pm	$100,000	$1/_{64}$pt=$15.63	None
T-Note (2-Year)	CBOT	7:20 am–2:00 pm e-cbot: Sun–Fri: 7:02 pm–4:00 pm	$200,000	$1/_2$ of $1/_{64}$pt=$15.63	None
US $ Index	NYBOT	7:05 am–2:00 pm 6:00 pm–9:00 pm Dublin: 2:00 am–7:05 am	1,000 × US $ Index	1pt=$10.00	None
Value Line	KCBT	8:30 am–3:15 pm	100 × Value Line Index	5pts=$5.00	▲
Wheat	CBOT	9:30 am–1:15 pm e-cbot: Sun–Fri: 7:34 pm–6:00 am	5,000 bu	$1/_8$¢ per bu ($6.25)	30¢ per bu=$1,500
Wheat	KCBT	9:30 am–1:25 pm	5,000 bu	$1/_8$¢ per bu ($6.25)	30¢ per bu=$1,500
Wheat	MPLS	9:30 am–1:30 pm	5,000 bu	$1/_8$¢ per bu ($6.25)	30¢ per bu=$1,500

Source of data: Futures and options exchanges. This information is believed to be reliable. Lind-Waldock cannot be held responsible for either its accuracy or its completeness.

Security Futures

	Contract			
	Single Stocks	**Single Stocks**	**ETF Futures**	**ETF Futures (100 Shares)**
Exchange	NQLX	OCX	OCX	NQLX
Trading Hours (Central Time)	8:30 am–3:00 pm	8:30 am–3:00 pm	8:30 am–3:15 pm	8:30 am–3:15 pm
Months	2 serial + HMUZ	2 serial + HMUZ	2 serial + HMUZ	2 serial + HMUZ
Delivery Size	100 shares	100 shares	100 shares	100 shares
Contract Quoted In	$/share	$/share	$/share	$/share
Price Point Value	.01 = $1.00	.01 = $1.00	.01 = $1.00	.01 = $1.00
Minimum Price Fluctuation	$0.01	$0.01	$0.01	$0.01
Price Limit	None ✦	None ✦	None ✦	None ✦

Source of data: Futures and options exchanges. This information is believed to be reliable. Lind-Waldock cannot be held responsible for either its accuracy or its completeness.

Non-U.S. Markets

Contract	Exchange	Trading Hours (Central Time)	Delivery Months	Contract Size	Price Quoted In	Minimum Price Fluctuation	Price Limit
Cocoa #7	LIFFE	3:30 am–10:50 am	H,K,N,U,Z	10 tons	£ per ton	£1 per ton (£10)	
Euribor	LIFFE	1:00 am–12:00 Noon	H,M,U,Z	1,000,000 Euro	Basis pts	.5pt=12.50 Euro	None
Euro Swiss	LIFFE	1:30 am–12:00 Noon	H,M,U,Z	SF 1,000,000	Basis pts	1pt=25 SF	None
FTSE 100	LIFFE	2:00 am–11:30 am	H,M,U,Z	£10 × Index	100th/pt	0.5pt=£5	None
Gilt	LIFFE	2:00 am–12:00 Noon	H,M,U,Z	£100,000	100th/pt	1pt=£10	None
Robusta Coffee	LIFFE	3:40 am–10:55 am	F,H,K,M,N,U,X	5 tons	$ per ton	$1.00 per ton ($5.00)	None
Short Sterling	LIFFE	1:30 am–12:00 Noon	H,M,U,Z	500,000 Sterling	100th/pt	1pt=12.5 Sterling	None
White Sugar	LIFFE	3:45 am–11:30 am	H,K,Q,V,Z	50 tons	¢ per ton	10¢ per ton ($5.00)	None
Conf Bond (Swiss 10-yr)	Eurex	1:30 am–10:00 am	H,M,U,Z	CHF 100,000	Basis pts	1pt=10 CHF	None
DAX	Eurex	1:50 am–1:00 pm	H,M,U,V,Z	25 Euro × Index	Basis pts	.5pt=12.5 Euro	None
Dow Jones Euro STOXX 50	Eurex	1:50 am–1:00 pm	H,M,U,Z	10 Euro × Index	Basis pts	1pt=10 Euro	None
Euribor (3-month)	Eurex	1:30 am–12:00 Noon	H,M,U,Z	1,000,000 Euro	Basis pts	.5pt=12.5 Euro	None
Euro-Bund	Eurex	1:00 am–12:00 Noon	H,M,U,Z	100,000 Euro	Basis pts	1pt=10 Euro	None
Euro-Bobl	Eurex	1:00 am–12:00 Noon	H,M,U,Z	100,000 Euro	Basis pts	1pt=10 Euro	None
Euro-Schatz	Eurex	1:00 am–12:00 Noon	H,M,U,Z	100,000 Euro	Basis pts	1pt=10 Euro	None
MIB 30 Index	IDEM	2:00 am–10:40 am	H,M,U,Z	5 Euro × Index	Basis pts	5pt=25 Euro	None
Brent Crude Oil	IPE	Open Outcry: 4:02 am–1:30 pm Electronic: Sun–Wed: 8:00 pm–4:00 pm, Thurs: 8:00 pm–2:30 pm	All months	1,000 barrels	¢ per barrel	1¢ per barrel ($10.00)	None

Product	Exchange	Trading Hours	Months	Contract Size	Quote	Tick Value	Limit
Gas Oil	IPE	Open Outcry: 3:15 am–11:27 am Electronic: Sun–Wed: 8:00 pm–4:00 pm, Thurs. 8:00 pm–2:30 pm	All months	100 metric tons	¢ per ton	25¢ per ton ($25.00)	None
3-month Banker Acceptance	ME	7:00 am–2:00 pm	H,M,U,Z	C$1,000,000	Basis pts	.005pt=C$12.50	None
10-yr Canadian Bond	ME	7:20 am–2:00 pm	H,M,U,Z	C$1,000,000	Basis pts	.01pt=C$10.00	3 pts
S&P Canada 60	ME	8:30 am–3:15 pm	H,M,U,Z	C$200 × Index	Basis pts	.10pt=C$20.00	▲
Eurodollar ✳	SGX	5:45 pm–5:00 am	H,M,U,Z	$1,000,000	Basis pts ½pt, first 4 cycles	0.25=$6.25 spot month 0.50=$12.50 back months	None
Euroyen ✳	SGX	5:43 pm–5:05 am 5:40 pm–5:05 am electronic	H,M,U,Z	¥100,000,000	Basis pts	0.5pt=¥1,250	None
JGB, Mini	SGX	5:45 pm–3:15 am	H,M,U,Z	¥10,000,000	Basis pts	1pt=¥1,000	None
MSCI Taiwan	SGX	6:45 pm–11:45 pm 6:45 am–12:45 am electronic 2:00 am–5:00 am electronic (T+1)	All months	US$100 × Index	Basis pts	0.1 pt=US$10.00	7–15% ◆
NIKKEI	SGX	5:55 pm–8:15 pm 9:15 pm–12:25 am (1:30 am–5:00 am ETH = T+1)	H,M,U,Z	¥500 × Nikkei 225 Index	Basis pts	5pt=¥2,500	7.50% Expandable
Hang Seng	HKE	7:45 pm–10:30 pm 12:30 am–2:15 am	All months	HK$50 × Hang Seng Index	Basis pts	1pt=HK$50.00	None
10-yr Bond*	SFE	3:30 pm–11:30 pm 12:10 am–2:00 pm	H,M,U,Z	AD$100,000	Basis pts	0.5pt=AD$40.00	None
3-yr Bond*	SFE	3:30 pm–11:30 pm 12:10 am–2:00 pm	H,M,U,Z	AD$100,000	Basis pts	1pt=AD$28.00	None

(continues)

Non-U.S. Markets (*Continued*)

Contract	Exchange	Trading Hours (Central Time)	Delivery Months	Contract Size	Price Quoted In	Minimum Price Fluctuation	Price Limit
90-Day Bank Bills*	SFE	3:30 pm–11:30 pm 12:10 am–2:00 pm	H,M,U,Z	AD$1,000,000	Basis pts	1pt=AD$24.00	None
SPI*	SFE	12:10 am–2:00 pm 4:50 pm–11:30 pm	H,M,U,Z	Share Price Index × 25 AD	Basis pts	1pt=AD$25.00	None
Canola	WCE	9:30 am–1:15 pm	F,H,K,N,U,X	20 metric tons	CD$/tonne	CD10¢ per tonne	CD $30/ton
CAC 40	MATIF	1:00 am–10:30 am 10:30 am–1:00 pm	All months	10 Euro × CAC40 Index	Index with 1 decimal	.5pt=5 Euro	250 pts
10-yr Spanish Bond	MEFF	1:00 am–10:15 am	H,M,U,Z	100,000 Euro	Basis pts	1pt=10 Euro	None
IBEX-35	MEFF	2:00 am–10:35 am	H,M,U,Z	10 Euro × IBEX-35 Index	100th/pt	1pt=10 Euro	None

*Trading times vary with U.S. daylight saving time.

Source of data: Futures and options exchanges. This information is believed to be reliable. Lind-Waldock cannot be held responsible for either its accuracy or its completeness.

Speculative Margins

These are the original/initial and maintenance margin requirements for futures contracts traded on U.S. and foreign exchanges. Margin requirements may change within a trading day, so the best way to be certain that you have the most current information is to check with your brokerage firm.

U.S. Markets

	Exchange	Original	Maintenance
Currencies			
Euro FX	IMM	2700	2000
British Pound	IMM	1890	1400
Japanese Yen	IMM	2430	1800
Swiss Franc	IMM	1958	1450
Australian Dollar	IMM	1688	1250
Canadian Dollar	IMM	1215	900
Mexican Peso	IMM	1875	1500
US $ Index	NYBOT	1330	1000
Yen E-mini	IMM	1215	900
Euro E-mini	IMM	1350	1000
Financial Instruments			
Eurodollar	IMM	945	700
Treasury Bonds	CBOT	1755	1300
Treasury Bonds, Mini	CBOT	878	650
Treasury Notes, 10-yr	CBOT	1178	850
Treasury Notes, Mini	CBOT	574	425
Treasury Notes 5-yr	CBOT	810	600
Treasury Notes 2-yr	CBOT	743	550
Muni Bonds	CBOT	1215	900
Treasury Bonds	Eurex US	2015	1550
Treasury Notes 10-yr	Eurex US	1365	1050
Treasury Notes 5-yr	Eurex US	975	750
Stock Index			
Dow Jones Average $10	CBOT	5000	4000
Dow Jones Average $5	CBOT	2500	2000
S&P 500 Index	IOM	20000	16000
S&P 500 E-mini	IOM	4000	3200
Nasdaq 100 Index	IOM	18750	15000
Nasdaq 100 E-mini	IOM	3750	3000
Nikkei 225	IOM	4063	3250
Value Line 100	KCBT	4500	3600
Mid Cap	IOM	17500	14000
Russell 2000	IOM	17500	14000
Other Indexes			
CRB Index	NYFE	2400	2400
Metals			
Copper, High Grade	COMEX	2700	2000
Gold	COMEX	2025	1500
Silver	COMEX	2700	2000
Platinum	NYMEX	2700	2000
Palladium	NYMEX	2700	2000

U.S. Markets *(Continued)*

	Exchange	Original	Maintenance
Energy			
Crude Oil	NYMEX	4725	3500
e-miNY Crude Oil	NYMEX	2363	1750
Gasoline, unleaded	NYMEX	4725	3500
Heating Oil	NYMEX	5,063	3750
Natural Gas	NYMEX	10125	7500
e-miNY Natural Gas	NYMEX	5063	3750
Grains and Fiber			
Corn	CBOT	338	250
Mini Corn	CBOT	68	50
Wheat	CBOT	675	500
Wheat	KCBT	625	500
Wheat	MPLS	650	500
Soybeans	CBOT	1620	1200
Mini Soybeans	CBOT	324	240
Soybean Meal	CBOT	743	550
Soybean Oil	CBOT	878	650
Oats	CBOT	405	300
Cotton	NYBOT	1680	1200
Livestock & Meats			
Cattle, Live	CME	1418	1050
Cattle, Feeder	CME	1958	1450
Frozen Bellies	CME	1620	1200
Hogs, Lean	CME	1080	800
Foods			
Sugar	NYBOT	700	500
Coffee "C"	NYBOT	2625	1875
Cocoa (Metric)	NYBOT	1680	1200
Orange Juice	NYBOT	1050	750
Forest Products			
Lumber	CME	1650	1100

Security Futures

Security futures margins are 20% of the contract value, based on the previous day's settlement price; some contracts may be higher.

Source of data: Futures and options exchanges. This information is believed to be reliable. Lind-Waldock cannot be held responsible for either its accuracy or its completeness.

Foreign Markets

	Exchange	Original	Maintenance
Short Sterling	LIFFE	£270	£270
Euribor EI	LIFFE	€540	€540
Long Gilt	LIFFE	£1270	£1270
Euro-Bund	Eurex	€1400	€1400
DAX	Eurex	€7700	€7700
FT-SE 100 Index	LIFFE	£1300	£1300
Brent Crude Oil	IPE	$3370	$3370
CAC40 IX	MATIF	€2250	€2250
Australian Bond 10-yr AK	Sydney	AD2000	AD2000
Australian T-Bill AF	Sydney	AD600	AD600
Nikkei Index	SGX	¥262500	¥210000
Mini JGB	SGX	¥108000	¥80000
Hang Seng	HKFE	HK$40750	HK$40750

Source of data: Futures and options exchanges. This information is believed to be reliable. Lind-Waldock cannot be held responsible for either its accuracy or its completeness.

Glossary

This glossary is a compilation of industry terms derived from a number of sources. The definitions are not meant to state or suggest the correct legal significance or meaning of any word or phrase. The terms and definitions were collected to help enhance your understanding of the futures and options language used in this book.

arbitrage The simultaneous purchase and sale of identical or equivalent financial instruments or commodity futures in order to benefit from a discrepancy in their price relationship.

arbitration The procedure of settling disputes between members, or between members and customers.

assignment To make an option seller perform his or her obligation to assume a short futures position (as a seller of a call option) or a long futures position (as a seller of a put option).

associated person (AP) An individual who solicits orders, customers, or customer funds (or who supervises persons performing such duties) on behalf of a futures commission merchant, an introducing broker, a commodity trading advisor, or a commodity pool operator.

at-the-money option An option with a strike price that is equal, or approximately equal, to the current market price of the underlying futures contract.

back months The futures or options on futures months being traded that are furthest from expiration.

bar chart   A chart that graphs the high, low, and settlement prices for a specific trading session over a given period of time.

basis   The difference between the current cash price and the futures price of the same commodity. Unless otherwise specified, the price of the nearby futures contract month is generally used to calculate the basis.

bear   One who believes prices will move lower.

bear market   A market in which prices are declining.

bear spread   In most commodities and financial instruments, the term refers to selling the nearby contract month and buying the deferred contract, to profit from a change in the price relationship.

bid   Indicates a willingness to buy a futures or options contract at a specified price. Opposite of **offer**.

broker   A company or individual that executes futures and options orders on behalf of financial and commercial institutions and/or the general public.

bull   One who expects prices to rise.

bull market   A market in which prices are rising.

bull spread   In most commodities and financial instruments, the term refers to buying the nearby month and selling the deferred month, to profit from the change in the price relationship.

butterfly spread   The placing of two interdelivery spreads in opposite directions with the center delivery month common to both spreads.

buy (buy order)   A transaction type that indicates you wish to make a purchase or to go long. The opposite of selling or going short.

buy on close   To buy at the end of a trading session at a price within the closing range.

buy on opening   To buy at the beginning of a trading session at a price within the opening range.

call   An option to buy a commodity, security, or futures contract at a specific price at any time between now and the expiration of the option contract.

call option   An option that gives the option buyer the right, but not the obligation, to purchase (go long) the underlying futures contract at the strike price on or before the expiration date.

cancel order   An order that removes a customer's previous order from the market.

carrying charge (cost of carry)   For physical commodities such as grains and metals, the cost of storage space, insurance, and finance charges incurred by holding a physical commodity. In interest rate futures markets, it refers to the differential between the yield on a cash instrument and the cost necessary to buy the instrument.

carryover Grain and oilseed commodities not consumed during the marketing year and remaining in storage at year's end. These stocks are carried over into the next marketing year and added to the stocks produced during that crop year.

cash commodity An actual physical commodity someone is buying or selling, such as soybeans, corn, gold, or Treasury bonds. Also referred to as actuals.

cash contract A sales agreement for either immediate or future delivery of the actual product.

cash market A place where people buy and sell the actual commodities, such as a grain elevator or bank. See **forward contract**; **spot**.

cash settlement Transactions generally involving index-based futures contracts that are settled in cash based on the actual value of the index on the last trading day. Cash settlement is in contrast to those contracts that specify the delivery of a commodity or financial instrument.

charting The use of charts to analyze market behavior and anticipate future price movements. Those who use charting as a trading method plot such factors as high, low, and settlement prices, average price movements, volume, and open interest. Two basic price charts are bar charts and point-and-figure charts. See **technical analysis**.

clear The process by which a clearinghouse maintains records of all trades and settles margin flow on a daily mark-to-market basis for its clearing members.

clearinghouse An agency or separate corporation of a futures exchange that is responsible for settling trading accounts, clearing trades, collecting and maintaining margin monies, regulating delivery, and reporting trading data. Clearinghouses act as third parties to all futures and options contracts, acting as a buyer to every clearing member seller and a seller to every clearing member buyer.

clearing member A member of a clearinghouse. Memberships in clearing organizations are usually held by companies. Clearing members are responsible for the financial commitments of customers that clear through their firm.

close The period at the end of the trading session. Sometimes used to refer to the closing range. See **opening**.

closing range A range of prices at which transactions took place at the closing of the market; buy and sell orders during the closing period may have been filled at any point within such a range.

commission fee A fee charged by a broker for executing a transaction.

commodity An article of commerce or a product that can be used for commerce. In a narrow sense, products traded on an authorized commodity exchange.

The types of commodities include agricultural products, metals, petroleum, foreign currencies, and financial instruments and indexes, to name a few.

Commodity Futures Trading Commission (CFTC) A federal regulatory agency established under the Commodity Futures Trading Commission Act, as amended in 1974, that oversees futures trading in the United States.

commodity pool An enterprise in which funds contributed by a number of persons are combined for the purpose of trading futures contracts or commodity options.

commodity pool operator (CPO) An individual or organization that operates or solicits funds for a commodity pool.

commodity trading advisor (CTA) A person who, for compensation or profit, directly or indirectly advises others as to the value or the advisability of buying or selling futures contracts or commodity options. Advising indirectly includes exercising trading authority over a customer's account as well as providing recommendations through written publications or other media.

contract Unit of trading for a financial or commodity future. Also, actual bilateral agreement between the parties (buyer and seller) of a futures or options on futures transaction as defined by an exchange.

contract month The specified month in which futures contracts may be satisfied by making or accepting delivery. See **delivery month**.

convergence A term referring to cash and futures prices tending to come together (i.e., the basis approaches zero) as the futures contract nears expiration.

conversion factor A factor used to equate the price of Treasury bond and Treasury note futures contracts with the various cash Treasury bonds and Treasury notes eligible for delivery.

coupon The interest rate on a debt instrument expressed in terms of a percent on an annualized basis that the issuer guarantees to pay the holder until maturity.

crop (marketing) year The time span from harvest to harvest for agricultural commodities. The crop marketing year varies slightly with each agricultural commodity, but it tends to begin at harvest and end before the next year's harvest. For example, the marketing year for soybeans begins September 1 and ends August 31. The futures contract month of November represents the first major new-crop marketing month, and the contract month of July represents the last major old-crop marketing month for soybeans.

crop reports Reports compiled by the U.S. Department of Agriculture on various agricultural commodities that are released throughout the year. Information in the reports includes estimates on planted acreage, yield, and expected production, as well as a comparison of production from previous years.

cross-hedging Hedging a cash commodity using a different but related futures contract when there is no futures contract for the cash commodity being hedged and the cash and futures markets follow similar price trends—for example, using soybean meal futures to hedge fish meal.

current yield   The ratio of the coupon to the current market price of the debt instrument.

customer margin   Within the futures industry, financial guarantees required of both buyers and sellers of futures contracts and sellers of options contracts to ensure fulfillment of contract obligations. Futures commission merchants are responsible for overseeing customer margin accounts.

daily trading limit   The maximum price range set by the exchange each day for a contract.

day order   An order that is placed for execution during only one trading session. If the order cannot be executed during that session, it is automatically canceled.

day trade   The purchase and sale of a futures or an options contract in the same day session, thus ending the day with no established position in the market (i.e., being flat).

deferred delivery month   The more distant month(s) in which futures trading is taking place, as distinguished from the nearby delivery month.

deliverable grades   The standard grades of commodities or instruments listed in the rules of the exchanges that must be met when delivering cash commodities against futures contracts. Grades are often accompanied by a schedule of discounts and premiums allowable for delivery of commodities of lesser or greater quality than the standard called for by the exchange.

delivery   The transfer of the cash commodity from the seller of a futures contract to the buyer of a futures contract. Each futures exchanges has specific procedures for delivery of a cash commodity. Some futures contracts, such as stock index contracts, are cash-settled.

delivery month   A specific month in which delivery may take place under the terms of a futures contract. Also referred to as **contract month**.

delivery points   The locations and facilities designated by a futures exchange where stocks of a commodity may be delivered in fulfillment of a futures contract, under procedures established by the exchange.

delta   A measure of how much an option premium changes, given a unit change in the underlying futures price.

differentials   Price differences between classes, grades, and delivery locations of various stocks of the same commodity.

disclosure document   A statement that must be provided to prospective customers that describes trading performance, strategy, fees, performance, and so on.

discount method   A method of paying interest by issuing a security at less than par and repaying par value at maturity. The difference between the higher par value and the lower purchase price is the interest.

discretionary account   An arrangement by which the holder of the account gives written power of attorney to another person, often his or her broker, to make trading decisions. Also known as a controlled or managed account.

Eurodollars   U.S. dollars on deposit with a bank outside of the United States and, consequently, outside the jurisdiction of the United States. The bank could be either a foreign bank or a subsidiary of a U.S. bank.

European terms   A method of quoting exchange rates that measures the amount of foreign currency needed to buy one U.S. dollar (i.e., foreign currency unit per dollar).

exchange of futures for physicals (EFP)   A transaction generally used by two hedgers who want to exchange futures for cash positions. Also referred to as "against actuals" or "versus cash."

exercise   The action taken by the holder of a call option who wishes to purchase the underlying futures contract or by the holder of a put option who wishes to sell the underlying futures contract.

exercise price   The price at which the futures contract underlying a call or put option can be purchased (if a call) or sold (if a put). Also referred to as **strike price**.

expiration date   The last day that an option may be exercised into the underlying futures contract. Also, the last day of trading for a futures contract.

extrinsic value   See **time value**.

Federal Reserve System   A central banking system in the United States, created by the Federal Reserve Act in 1913, designed to assist the nation in attaining its economic and financial goals. The structure of the Federal Reserve System includes a Board of Governors, the Federal Open Market Committee, and 12 regional Federal Reserve Banks.

fill-or-kill (FOK)   A customer order that is a price limit order that must be filled immediately or canceled.

financial instrument   There are two basic types: (1) a debt instrument, which is a loan with an agreement to pay back funds with interest; (2) an equity security, which is a share of stock in a company.

first notice day   The first day on which a notice of intent to deliver a commodity in fulfillment of a given month's futures contract can be made by the clearinghouse to a buyer. The clearinghouse also informs the seller who they have been matched up with.

floor broker An individual on an exchange trading floor who executes orders for the purchase or sale of any commodity futures or options contract on any contract market for any other person. A floor broker executing orders must be licensed by the CFTC.

floor trader An exchange member who generally trades only for his/her own account or for an account controlled by him/her. Also referred to as a local.

forex market An over-the-counter market where buyers and sellers conduct foreign exchange business by telephone and other means of communication. Also referred to as foreign exchange market.

forward contract A cash contract in which a seller agrees to deliver a specific cash commodity to a buyer sometime in the future. Forward contracts, in contrast to futures contracts, are privately negotiated and are not standardized.

fundamental analysis A method of anticipating future price movement using supply and demand information.

futures A term used to designate all contracts covering the purchase and sale of financial instruments or physical commodities for future delivery on a commodity futures exchange.

futures commission merchant (FCM) A firm or person engaged in soliciting or accepting and handling orders for the purchase or sale of futures contracts, subject to the rules of a futures exchange, who, in connection with solicitation or acceptance of orders, accepts any money or securities to margin any resulting trades or contracts.

futures contract A legally binding agreement, made on a futures exchange, to buy or sell a commodity or financial instrument sometime in the future. Futures contracts are standardized according to the quality, quantity, and delivery time and location.

futures exchange A central marketplace with established rules and regulations where buyers and sellers meet to trade futures and options on futures contracts.

gamma A measurement of how fast delta changes, given a unit change in the underlying futures price.

good till canceled (GTC) An order worked by a broker until it can be filled or until canceled. Same as **open order**.

grantor A person who sells an option and assumes either the obligation to sell (in the case of a call) or to buy (in the case of a put) the underlying futures contract at the exercise price. Also referred to as an **option seller** or a **writer**.

gross domestic product (GDP) The value of all final goods and services produced by an economy over a particular time period, normally a year.

gross national product (GNP)   Gross domestic product plus the income accruing to domestic residents as a result of investments abroad less income earned in domestic markets accruing to foreigners abroad.

gross processing margin (GPM)   The difference between the cost of soybeans and the combined sales income of the processed soybean oil and meal.

hedge   The purchase or sale of a futures contract as a temporary substitute for a cash market transaction to be made at a later date. Usually it involves opposite positions in the cash market and futures market at the same time. See **long hedge**; **short hedge**.

hedger   An individual or company owning or planning to own a cash commodity—such as corn, soybeans, wheat stocks, or U.S. Treasury bonds, notes, or bills—and concerned that the cost of the commodity may change before either buying or selling it in the cash market. A hedger achieves protection against changing cash prices by purchasing (or selling) futures contracts of the same or similar commodity and later offsetting that position by selling (or purchasing) futures contracts of the same quantity and type as the initial transaction.

hedging   The practice of offsetting the price risk inherent in any cash market position by taking an equal but opposite position in the futures market. Hedgers use the futures markets to protect their businesses from adverse price changes. See **long hedge**; **purchasing hedge**; **selling hedge**; **short hedge**.

high   The highest price for a particular futures contract over a specified time period.

holder   One who purchases an option.

horizontal spread   The purchase of either a call option or a put option and the simultaneous sale of the same type of option with typically the same strike price but with a different expiration month. Also referred to as a calendar spread.

initial margin   The minimum value on deposit in your account to establish a new futures or options position, or to add to an existing position. Initial margin amount levels differ by contract. A brokerage firm sets the level of initial margin required, based on exchange-set minimums, and may change it at any time. Increases or decreases in initial margin levels reflect anticipated or actual changes in market volatility.

intercommodity spread   The purchase of a given delivery month of one futures market and the simultaneous sale of the same delivery month of a different, but related, futures market.

interdelivery spread   The purchase of one delivery month of a given futures contract and simultaneous sale of another delivery month of the same commodity on the same exchange. Also referred to as an intramarket or calendar spread.

intermarket spread   The sale of a given delivery month of a futures contract on one exchange and the simultaneous purchase of the same delivery month and futures contract on another exchange.

in-the-money option   An option with intrinsic value. A call option is in-the-money if its strike price is below the current price of the underlying futures contract. A put option is in-the-money if its strike price is above the current price of the underlying futures contract. See **intrinsic value**.

intrinsic value   The amount by which an option is in-the-money.

introducing broker (IB)   A person or organization that solicits or accepts orders to buy or sell futures contracts or commodity options but does not accept money or other assets from customers to support such orders.

inverted market   A futures market in which the relationship between two delivery months of the same commodity is abnormal.

last trading day   The final day when trading may occur in a given futures or options contract month. Futures contracts outstanding at the end of the last trading day must be settled by delivery of the underlying commodity or securities or by agreement for monetary settlement, in some cases by exchanges of futures for physicals (EFPs).

leverage   The ability to control large dollar amounts of a commodity with a comparatively small amount of capital.

limit order   An order given for an options or futures trade specifying a certain maximum (or minimum) price, beyond which the order (buy or sell) is not to be executed.

limit price   See **maximum price fluctuation**.

linkage   The ability to buy (or sell) contracts on one exchange, such as the Chicago Mercantile Exchange, and later sell (or buy) them on another exchange, such as the Singapore Exchange.

liquid   A characteristic of a security or commodity market with enough units outstanding to allow large transactions without a substantial change in price. Institutional investors are inclined to seek out liquid investments so that their trading activity will not influence the market price.

liquidate   To sell (or purchase) futures contracts of the same delivery month purchased (or sold) during an earlier transaction or to make (or take) delivery of the cash commodity represented by the futures contract. See **offset**.

long   One who has bought a futures or options on futures contract to establish a market position through an offsetting sale. The opposite of **short**.

long hedge   The purchase of a futures contract in anticipation of an actual purchase in the cash market. Used by processors or exporters as protection against an advance in the cash price. See **hedge; short hedge**.

low   The lowest price of a specified time period for a particular futures contract.

maintenance margin   The minimum value required in an account in order to continue to hold a position. The maintenance margin is typically less than the initial margin, and also differs by contract. If your account falls below the maintenance margin requirement, you will receive a margin call. If you wish to continue to hold the position, you will be required to restore your account to the full initial margin level (not to the maintenance margin level).

managed futures   Represents an industry comprised of professional money managers known as commodity trading advisors, who manage client assets using global futures markets as an investment medium.

margin   See **performance bond**.

margin call   A call from a clearinghouse to a clearing member, or from a brokerage firm to a customer, to bring margin deposits up to a required minimum level.

market if touched (MIT)   A price order that automatically becomes a market order if the price is reached.

market on close (MOC)   An order to buy or sell at the end of the trading session at a price within the closing range of prices.

market order (MKT)   An order to buy or sell a specified commodity, including quantity and delivery month, at the best possible price available, as soon as possible.

mark-to-market   The daily adjustment of margin accounts to reflect profits and losses based on that day's price changes in each market.

maximum price fluctuation   The maximum amount the contract price can change, up or down, during one trading session, as stipulated by exchange rules. Also known as the daily price limit or **limit price**.

minimum price fluctuation   The smallest increment of price movement possible in trading a given contract, often referred to as a **tick**.

moving average charts   A statistical price analysis method of recognizing different price trends. A moving average is calculated by adding the closing prices for a predetermined number of days and then dividing by the number of days.

National Futures Association (NFA)   An industrywide, self-regulatory organization for futures and options markets. The primary responsibilities of the NFA are to enforce ethical standards and customer protection rules, screen futures professionals for membership, audit and monitor professionals for financial and general compliance rules, and provide for arbitration of futures-related disputes.

nearby   The nearest active trading month of a futures or options on futures contract. Also referred to as the lead month.

net liquidation value   Total trade equity plus net options value, on a marked-to-market basis. It is the value of your account if you were to liquidate all positions in your account. This information appears on your account statement.

net options value   The credit or debit value of all option positions combined, marked to market.

notice day   The second day of the three-day delivery process when the clearing corporation matches the buyer with the oldest reported long position to the delivering seller and notifies both parties. See **first notice day**.

offer   Indicates a willingness to sell a futures or options contract at a specified price. Opposite of **bid**.

offset   To take a second futures or options position opposite to the initial or opening position. This means selling, if one has bought, or buying, if one has sold, a futures or option on a futures contract. See **liquidate**.

open interest   Total number of futures or options on futures contracts that have not yet been offset or fulfilled by delivery. An indicator of the depth or liquidity of a market (the ability to buy or sell at or near a given price) and of the use of a market for risk and/or asset management.

open order   An order to a broker that is good until it is canceled or executed. Same as **good till canceled (GTC)**.

open outcry   Method of public auction for making verbal bids and offers in the trading pits or rings of futures exchanges.

open trade equity   The difference between the initial trade price and the last tick of the market. It is marked to market. It is the value of the positions you are holding, if you were to close the position at the last tick.

opening   The period at the beginning of the trading session during which all transactions are considered made or first transactions were completed.

opening range   The range of prices at which the first bids and offers were made or first transactions were completed.

option   A contract giving the holder the right, but not the obligation (hence, "option"), to buy (call option) or sell (put option) a futures contract in a given market at a specified price at any time between now and the expiration of the option contract.

option buyer   The purchaser of either a call or a put option. Option buyers receive the right, but not the obligation, to assume a futures position at the option's strike price. Also referred to as the **holder**.

option premium   The price of an option. The sum of money that the option buyer pays and the option seller receives for the rights granted by the option.

option seller   The person who sells an option in return for a premium and is obligated to perform when the holder exercises his or her right under the option contract. Also referred to as the **grantor** or **writer**.

option spread The simultaneous purchase and sale of one or more options contracts, futures, and/or cash positions.

or better (OB) A variation of a limit order in which the market is at or better than the limit specified.

out-of-the-money option An option with no intrinsic value (i.e., a call whose strike price is above the current futures price or a put whose strike price is below the current futures price). Its value is solely time related.

overbought When the market has risen too steeply and too fast in relation to underlying fundamental factors.

oversold When the market has fallen too steeply and too fast in relation to underlying fundamental factors.

over-the-counter (OTC) market A market where a product such as stocks, foreign currencies, and other cash items are bought and sold by telephone and other means of communication.

par The face value of a security. For example, a bond selling at par is worth the same dollar amount when it was issued, or the price at which it will be redeemed at maturity.

performance bond Funds that must be deposited by a customer with a broker, by a broker with a clearing member, or by a clearing member with the clearinghouse to initiate or maintain a market position. The performance bond helps to ensure the financial integrity of brokers, clearing members, and the exchange. Also known as **margin**.

pit The area on an exchange trading floor where futures and options on futures contracts are bought and sold. Pits are usually raised octagonal platforms with steps descending on the inside that permit buyers and sellers of contracts to see each other.

point-and-figure charts Charts that show price changes of a minimum amount regardless of the time period involved.

position A market commitment. A buyer of a futures contract is said to have a long position and, conversely, a seller of futures contracts is said to have a short position.

position limit The maximum number of speculative futures contracts one can hold as determined by the Commodity Futures Trading Commission and/or the exchange upon which the contract is traded. Also referred to as trading limit.

position trader An approach to trading in which the trader either buys or sells contracts and holds the long or short position for an extended period of time.

premium The excess of one futures contract price over that of another, or over the cash market price. Also, the amount agreed upon between the purchaser and seller for the purchase or sale of a futures option—the purchaser pays the premium and the seller receives the premium.

price discovery   The generation of information about future cash market prices through the futures markets.

price limit   The maximum advance or decline from the previous day's settlement price permitted for a contract in one trading session by the rules of the exchange. See also **maximum price fluctuation; variable limit**.

primary dealer   A designation given by the Federal Reserve to commercial banks or broker/dealers who meet specific criteria. Among the criteria are capital requirements and meaningful participation in the Treasury auctions.

primary market   Market of new issues of securities.

purchase and sale (P&S) statement   A statement sent by a commission house to a customer, showing the number of contracts bought or sold, the prices at which the contracts were bought or sold, the gross profit or loss, the commission charges, and the net profit or loss on the transactions.

purchasing hedge   Buying futures contracts to protect against a possible price increase of cash commodities that will be purchased in the future. At the time the cash commodities are bought, the open futures position is closed by selling an equal number and type of futures. Same as **long hedge**.

purchasing power   Total trade equity minus initial margin. Your purchasing power represents funds available to you to establish new positions. Your purchasing power changes throughout the day as your total trade equity and margins change. If you have options positions, margin amounts are based on a calculation of total portfolio risk.

put   An option to sell a commodity, security, or futures contract at a specified price at any time between now and the expiration of the option contract.

put option   An option that gives the option buyer the right, but not the obligation, to sell (go short) the underlying futures contract at the strike price on or before the expiration date.

rally   An upward movement of prices following a decline; the opposite of a reaction.

reaction   A decline in prices following an advance; the opposite of rally.

registered representative   A person employed by, and soliciting business for, a commission house or a futures commission merchant.

resistance   A level above which prices have had difficulty penetrating.

round turn   Procedure by which a long or short position is offset by an opposite transaction or by accepting or making delivery of the actual financial instrument or physical commodity.

scalp   To trade for small gains. Scalping normally involves establishing and liqui-dating a position quickly, often within just a few minutes.

self-regulatory organization   A membership organization that enforces mini-mum financial and sales practice requirements on its members.

sell (sell order)   An offer. This transaction type indicates you wish to sell or to go short. The opposite of buying or going long.

selling hedge   Selling futures contracts to protect against possible declining prices of commodities that will be sold in the future. At the time the cash com-modities are sold, the open futures position is closed by purchasing an equal num-ber and type of futures contracts as those that were initially sold. Same as **short hedge**.

settlement price   The last price paid for a commodity on any trading day. The exchange clearinghouse determines a firm's net gains or losses, margin require-ments, and the next day's price limits, based on each futures and options contract settlement price. If there is a closing range of prices, the settlement price is deter-mined by averaging those prices. Also referred to as settle or closing price.

short   One who has sold futures contracts or plans to purchase a cash commod-ity. Selling futures contracts or initiating a cash forward contract sale without off-setting a particular market position. The opposite of **long**.

short hedge   The sale of a futures contract in anticipation of a later cash market sale. Used to eliminate or lessen the possible decline in value of ownership of an approximately equal amount of the cash financial instrument or physical commod-ity. See **hedge**; **long hedge**.

short options value   The total cost of purchasing back all short options on a marked-to-market basis.

simulated trading   The process of buying and selling without actually entering the market or risking any real funds.

speculator   One who attempts to anticipate price changes and, through buying and selling futures contracts, aims to make profits. A speculator does not use the futures market in connection with the production, processing, marketing, or han-dling of a product.

spot   Usually refers to a cash market price for a physical commodity that is avail-able for immediate delivery. Also can refer to the contract delivery month of a fu-tures contract that is the same as the current calendar month.

spread   The price difference between two related markets or commodities.

spreading   The simultaneous buying and selling of two related markets in the expectation that a profit will be made when the position is offset. Examples in-clude: buying one futures contract and selling another futures contract of the same commodity but different delivery month; buying and selling the same delivery month of the same commodity on different futures exchanges; buying a given delivery month of one futures market and selling the same delivery month of a different, but related, futures market.

stock index   An indicator used to measure and report value changes in a selected group of stocks. How a particular stock index tracks the market depends on its composition, the sampling of stocks, the weighting of individual stocks, and the method of averaging used to establish an index.

stop order   An order to buy or sell when the market reaches a specified point. A stop order to buy becomes a market order when the futures contract trades (or is bid) at or above the stop price. A stop order to sell becomes a market order when the futures contract trades (or is offered) at or below the stop price. An order to buy or sell at the market when and if a specified price is reached.

stop with limit   A variation of a stop order. A stop with limit order to buy becomes a limit order when the futures contract trades (or is bid) at or above the stop price. A stop order to sell becomes a limit order when the futures contract trades (or is offered) at or below the stop price.

straight cancel   An order that signals that a customer does not want to fill an order that is currently working.

strike price   The price at which the holder (buyer) may purchase or sell the underlying futures contract upon the exercise of an option.

support   The place on a chart where the buying of futures contracts is sufficient to halt a price decline.

technical analysis   A method of anticipating future price movement using historical prices, trading volume, open interest, and other trading data to study price patterns.

tick   The smallest allowable increment of price movement for a contract. Also referred to as **minimum price fluctuation**.

time and sales   The registered times of prices traded and bids and offers on a given market.

time-stamped   Part of the order-routing process in which the time of day is stamped on an order either manually or electronically.

time value   The amount of money option buyers are willing to pay, above the intrinsic value, for an option in the anticipation that, over time, a change in the underlying futures price will cause the option to increase in value. In general, an option premium is the sum of time value and intrinsic value. Any amount by which an option premium exceeds the option's intrinsic value can be considered time value. Also referred to as extrinsic value.

trend   The general direction of the market.

underlying futures contract   The specific futures contract that is bought or sold by exercising an option.

variable limit   An expanded allowable price range set during volatile markets.

variation margin   During periods of great market volatility, or in the case of high-risk accounts, additional margin deposited by a clearing member firm to an exchange clearinghouse.

vertical spread   Buying and selling puts or calls of the same expiration month but different strike prices.

volatility   A measurement of the change in price over a given time period. It is often expressed as a percentage and computed as the annualized standard deviation of percentage change in daily price.

volume   The number of transactions in a futures or options on futures contract made during a specified period of time.

warehouse receipt   A document guaranteeing the existence and availability of a given quantity and quality of a commodity in storage; commonly used as the instrument of transfer of ownership in both cash and futures transactions.

writer   An individual who sells an option. See **grantor**; **option seller**.

yield   A measure of the annual return on an investment.

yield curve   A chart in which the yield level is plotted on the vertical axis and the term to maturity of debt instruments of similar creditworthiness is plotted on the horizontal axis. The yield curve is positive when long-term rates are higher than short-term rates.

yield to maturity   The rate of return an investor receives if a fixed-income security is held to maturity.

Index